1/5/98 AAT 2847 48.00

Critical Essays on
SHAKESPEARE'S
Romeo and Juliet

CRITICAL ESSAYS
ON
BRITISH LITERATURE

Zack Bowen, General Editor
University of Miami

Critical Essays on
SHAKESPEARE'S
Romeo and Juliet

edited by

JOSEPH A. PORTER

G. K. Hall & Co.
An Imprint of Simon & Schuster Macmillan
New York

Prentice Hall International
London   Mexico City   New Delhi   Singapore   Sydney   Toronto

·   G. K. Hall & Co.
An Imprint of Simon & Schuster Macmillan
1633 Broadway
New York, NY 10019

Library of Congress Cataloging-in-Publication Data

Critical essays on Shakespeare's Romeo and Juliet / edited by Joseph A.
    Porter.
        p.   cm. — (Critical essays on British literature)
    Includes bibliographical references and index.
    ISBN 0-7838-0016-9 (alk. paper)
    1. Shakespeare, William, 1564–1616.   Romeo and Juliet.
2. Shakespeare, William, 1564–1616—Characters—Mercutio.
3. Mercutio (Fictitious character)   4. Tragedy.   I. Porter, Joseph
Ashby, 1942–   .   II. Series.
PR2831.C75   1997   96-53884
822.3'3—dc21   CIP

The paper used in this publication meets the minimum requirements of
American National Standard for Information Sciences—Permanence of Paper
for Printed Library Materials. ANSI Z3948-1984. ∞™

10 9 8 7 6 5 4 3 2 1

Printed in the United States of America

For that gallant spirit,
Yves Orvoën

Contents

General Editor's Note

◆

The Critical Essays on British Literature series provides a variety of approaches to both classical and contemporary writers of Britain and Ireland. The formats of the volumes in the series vary with the thematic designs of individual editors, and with the amount and nature of existing reviews and criticism, augmented, where appropriate, by original essays by recognized authorities. It is hoped that each volume will be unique in developing a new overall perspective on its particular subject.

Joseph Porter's general introduction and prefatory notes to each section augment a selection of essays at the very core of current Shakespearean critical debate. The essays are divided into three sections: the first on Mercutio as a key to the shifting issues and scholarly attention, the second dealing with the sexual aspects of the text, and the third with the new focus on the meaning of Shakespeare's revisions and variations as the key to his composition process.

The book concludes with Donald Foster's new and groundbreaking computer-assisted analysis of the text(s). The essay, written especially for this volume, dates Shakespeare's acquisition of verbal constructions and signifiers, producing convincing cases regarding influences and the chronology of their adaptions in the play, and certifying his comparisons to sources both for the original texts and subsequent revisions.

ZACK BOWEN
University of Miami

Publisher's Note

◆

Producing a volume that contains both newly commissioned and reprinted material presents the publisher with the challenge of balancing the desire to achieve stylistic consistency with the need to preserve the integrity of works first published elsewhere. In the Critical Essays series, essays commissioned especially for a particular volume are edited to be consistent with G. K. Hall's house style; reprinted essays appear in the style in which they were first published, with only typographical errors corrected. Consequently, shifts in style from one essay to another are the result of our efforts to be faithful to each text as it was originally published.

Introduction

JOSEPH A. PORTER

These essays continue a discourse extending from "earliest times" into the foreseeable future, about conflicts between individual experience and the social web of group claims of gender, family, class, and state, claims codified in the institution of European bourgeois marriage, as focused in and on an epochal love tragedy written four centuries ago by a youngish recent transplant to London who had begun to shift allegiance from narrative and lyric verse to verse drama, and who may even then have had inklings of how decisively this play would intervene in hearts and minds.

The play concerns matters of the most enduring timeliness, which in 1590s England grow especially urgent, in part because of the new prominence and flux of the institution in question. Today in Western (and above all U.S.) culture, that institution, where increasingly adversarial forces of the secular and the religious square off, finds itself under unprecedented pressure, outside the law to maintain its value and status, inside the law to rationalize its privileges, and, whether within or without the law, either to justify or end its exclusion of all but female-male pairings. And similarly with another major concern of the play, which has been variously termed the modern Western subject, or individuality, or consciousness of self: arguably nascent in 1590s England, it finds itself under many sorts of siege throughout the West at the end of the twentieth century.

However, despite the enduring and now acute importance of matters this play engages, and despite the play's steady popularity, judicious observers have nearly all placed it below the first rank of Shakespeare's plays. Even those who most love and admire *Romeo and Juliet* typically feel obliged to excuse such perceived deficiencies as a certain thinness in the main plot, or an intermittently uncertain control of tone. In fact, with no other Shakespeare play is there so great an apparent disproportion between the work's intrinsic excellence or worth and its importance.

Few other Shakespeare plays besides *Hamlet* have so wide (if sometimes shallow) a currency in the general public mind, where "To be or not to be" may be rivaled in familiarity by Shakespeare's most misquoted and misunderstood line, "Oh Romeo, Romeo, wherefore art thou Romeo." The play's prominence in the public consciousness stems in part of course from its regularly being set as the introductory taste of Shakespeare for U.S. secondary schoolers, who may be assumed to thrill especially to a tale of young passion. But the warmth of audience response to *Romeo and Juliet,* from the 1590s to the present, has finally to do with the importance of the play's subject, with what the play addresses, with its remarkable reach and the unsettling conclusions it suggests, for all its deficiencies.

As has been said in the past, here in *Romeo and Juliet* Shakespeare first outdistances his early rival Christopher Marlowe. The nature of that outdistancing, which entails declining the Marlovian trajectory and marking out directions untried by Marlowe, is currently much in view in Shakespeare study, in part because of upheaval and revision in the understanding of Marlowe, catalyzed by widespread acknowledgment of his sexuality. The traditional assessment of this particular facet of *Romeo and Juliet*—that Shakespeare here bypasses Marlowe in giving rein to his own distinctive sympathy for the naïve, the doomed, the idiosyncratic—while true, only begins, we now believe, to tell the story that several of the present essays advance.

Furthermore (as again these essays unfold in new ways), Shakespeare in *Romeo and Juliet* decisively breaks free (with the occasional later relapse) from a hold that nondramatic verse has on him heretofore. Shakespeare here throws off the shackles of the hierarchy that ranked Petrarchan and other lyric verse above verse drama. Concerning these matters, the relation of *Romeo and Juliet* to the sonnet tradition and to Shakespeare's own sonnets has traditionally been seen as important. Now that the accepted date for the bulk of Shakespeare's sonnets has moved forward, *Romeo and Juliet* may be seen to figure differently. Indeed we may now see the sonnets more clearly as capitalizing on advances made in *Romeo and Juliet,* to surpass Petrarch, Sidney, and others, not by continuing in mapped directions but by turning aside and breaking through into the vexed subjectivity that comes to be called modern, perhaps first broached in the young lovers' soliloquies, and with it the vexed modern sensitivity to otherness that may have its uncanny birth in Romeo's wondering recollection of the apothecary in act 5, scene 1.

Yet even though the play's importance may outweigh its intrinsic merit, that importance entails considerable merit. And certainly despite certain deficiencies—of youth, really, and of the last vestiges of apprenticeship—all the world knows that *Romeo and Juliet* is mostly very fine indeed, and sometimes breathtaking.

The earliest of the essays collected here is from 1976, and all the others are from the past decade, so that the collection participates in and exemplifies the rich diversity of current Shakespeare study. Several particular critical discourses evident in current ways of coming to terms with *Romeo and Juliet* are variously manifest here. The older of these, Foucauldian, Derridean, new historicist, and cultural materialist discourses, now somewhat taken for granted as features of the critical landscape, variously contribute to these essays.

More prominently, perhaps, these essays address two topics that have recently heated up. One of these is Shakespeare's practice of composition, specifically his revisions, and also his witting or unwitting recycling of his own and others' words. Shakespearean revision has been on a front burner since the early eighties, when Stephen Urkowitz, Gary Taylor, Michael Warren, and others demonstrated that there are two authoritative texts of *King Lear*.[1]

Several of the following essays are germane to the question of Shakespeare's revision or reworking of *Romeo and Juliet*. Perhaps the most remarkable discoveries are those Donald W. Foster makes with Shaxicon, his electronic Shakespeare database. Illuminating Shakespeare's recycling of his own and others' language, Foster's discoveries are changing the very landscape of the subject of revision.[2]

The other front-burner topic (in Shakespeare study generally, and particularly with recent study of *Romeo and Juliet*) addressed by a number of these essays is that of sexuality and gender. Of course with the passion of Romeo and Juliet, and with the bawdiness of the Nurse and Mercutio, the subject has generally stayed in view in commentary. Still, the past decade or so has seen an unprecedented amalgam of psychoanalytic, cultural, feminist, and queer studies empowering discussion of the play.[3]

By virtue of the developments in both these currently very lively arenas, the textual and the sexual, it has very quickly—suddenly, even—come to seem possible to know the mind of William Shakespeare very much better than might have been suspected even as recently as 25 years ago.

The character Mercutio, as it happens, has some special prominence in both arenas, the textual because his Queen Mab speech seems to have been added after the play's first performances, and the sexual for reasons elaborated on by several of the essays to follow. Leech grants Mercutio still another kind of prominence. Indeed one distinguishing mark of *Romeo and Juliet* commentary of the past two decades is the unprecedented amount of attention given to Mercutio.

In selecting these essays (other than my own, which the General Editor suggested I include), I have been guided by timeliness and intrinsic merit, and also by variety of procedure. For instance, while some of the commentators maintain a tight focus (Riess and Williams, and Pearlman), others (Porter, and Belsey) in ranging more widely register the present importance of *Romeo and Juliet*. Another selection criterion has been the colloquy that collocation can foreground. All but one of these essays are separately accessible, and yet their present gathering provides access to what otherwise might, at least for the nonspecialist, remain practically inaccessible: the lively statement and response, agreement and disagreement in recent scholarly discourse, and even the occasional unexpected silence and failure of response.

Given how variously the essays overlap, and in some cases specifically address each other, a number of sequences might have made sense for this collection. The sequence chosen proceeds chronologically, but for a small switchback, from the earliest essay to the most recent. At the same time the essays make up three topical groups, with reevaluations under the aegis of Mercutio (Leech and Porter), followed by probes into newly accessible depths of textual sexuality (Whittier, Belsey, and Goldberg), and they by fresh vantage into the working of Shakespeare's mind (Riess and Williams, Pearlman, and Foster). None has been previously reprinted, and one (Foster) appears here for the first time.[4]

Notes

1. See Urkowitz, *Shakespeare's Revision of "King Lear"* (Princeton: Princeton University, 1980; and Taylor and Warren, eds., *The Division of the Kingdoms: Shakespeare's Two Versions of "King Lear"* (Oxford: Clarendon, 1983; reprint, Oxford: Clarendon, 1986). Since then, Grace Ioppolo, *Revising Shakespeare* (Cambridge, Mass.: Harvard, 1991) surveys current evidence for revision in other Shakespeare plays, including *Romeo and Juliet*. In the spirit of the "new revisionism," as it has been called, John Jones, *Shakespeare at Work,* carries out minute scrutiny of numerous cases of apparent revision, including *Romeo and Juliet*. E. A. J. Honigman, *The Texts of "Othello" and Shakespearean Revision* (London: Routledge, 1996), argues that, with the two texts of *Othello* (and perhaps with other multitext plays), what in the present climate may seem instances of revision may in fact have other explanations.

2. Several complete editions of Shakespeare are now available in electronic form. The forthcoming Oxford *Romeo and Juliet,* ed. Jill L. Levenson, is to have a complementary database on a World Wide Web site with information about cuts and staging in more than 170 extant promptbooks examined by Levenson. Foster, later in this volume, describes his powerful electronic Shaxicon, and the use he makes of the electronic *Oxford English Dictionary,* the Vassar English Text Archive, and the Chadwyck-Healey Full-Text Databases of English Poetry, English Verse Drama, and English Prose Drama.

3. An additional currently prominent critical discourse may seem somewhat slighted in this collection, namely, what has been called "performance criticism," which Harry Berger has called the new histrionicism. Nevertheless, performance is a concern in most of the commentary here gathered.

4. Electronic archives obviate compiling a traditional bibliography of commentary on *Romeo and Juliet.* Furthermore the essays collected here engage much other significant study of the play, and textual citations are indexed. However, it is worth mentioning three recent collections of essays on the play: *"Romeo and Juliet": Critical Essays,* ed. John F. Andrews (New York: Garland, 1993), *"Roméo et Juliette": Nouvelles Perspectives Critiques,* ed. Jean-Marie Maguin and Charles Whitworth (Montpellier: Publications de l'Université Paul-Valéry, 1993), and *Shakespeare's "Romeo and Juliet": Texts, Contexts, and Interpretation,* ed. Jay Halio (Newark: University of Delaware Press, 1995).

MERCUTIO REVENANT

◆

Shakespeare's most substantial alteration of the tale he adapts from Arthur Brooke, *The Tragical History of Romeus and Juliet,* is his conversion of a story of love into a story of conflict between love and friendship, by dint of his radical development of the role of Mercutio. While the character has generally been a favorite, of audiences and players alike, his fortunes have varied more than those of other characters in the play. His bawdiness subjects him to extremes of censorship, cutting, and other sorts of denial through the nineteenth and early twentieth centuries, and our present, more tolerant climate is allowing him to come into his own again. Other deeper cultural shifts may also be felt in Mercutio's recent ascendancy, as witness the first three essays gathered here, along with portions of those that follow.

We now can better see, in the light of Mercutio's ascendancy, how Shakespeare in *Romeo and Juliet* begins his decisive engagement of the mysteries of character and of death, and how here he frees himself from the specter of Christopher Marlow. And, to be sure, Mercutio in his ascendancy is changing how the titular characters (and all the other dramatis personae) now look, and how they affect and serve us.

Clifford Leech, "The Moral Tragedy of *Romeo and Juliet,*" situates the play in contexts of preceding English attempts at tragedy, particularly love-tragedy, and of early modern doctrines of love, and also in the context of Shakespeare's own later more fully realized tragedies. Leech argues that overall the play falls short of the full tragic effect because of its insistence that the deaths of the young lovers support a moral lesson. There is, however, according to Leech, "a small achieved tragedy embodied within this play" in the death of Mercutio.

The excerpts from my *Shakespeare's Mercutio: His History and Drama* constitute the ways into and out of a consideration of how Mercutio figures in the play's web of cultural negotiations. In "Mercutio's Brother," considering the "ghost character" of Valentine, I trace some characterological shifts that occur as Shakespeare adapts the plot of Brooke's poem to his own uses. In "Mercutio's Shakespeare" I address Mercutio's instrumentality in new roles Shakespeare now plays for us.

Clifford Leech (1909–1977), professor and administrator at universities including Durham and Ontario, author of many books on Shakespeare and other early modern drama, edited the New American Library *Two Noble Kinsmen* and the Arden *Two Gentleman of Verona* and served as General Editor (with T. W. Craik) of The Revels History of Drama in English series, 1958–1970.

In books and articles I, Joseph A. Porter, Professor of English at Duke University, have concerned myself with Shakespearean characterology and pragmatics.

The Moral Tragedy of *Romeo and Juliet*

Clifford Leech

How adventurous Shakespeare was in writing *Romeo and Juliet* in 1594 or 1595 we do not always realize. First, there had been few tragedies written for the public theaters before then, and none in the first rank except Marlowe's. Shakespeare himself had doubtless already written *Titus Andronicus,* an exercise after Seneca and with many memories of Ovid. Kyd too had popularized Seneca in *The Spanish Tragedy.* Marlowe had had his imitators: Greene's *Alphonsus King of Aragon* had echoed the enthusiasm for the aspiring mind, but with none of the ambivalence that was deep in Marlowe. *Selimus,* which may also be Greene's, presented the other side of the picture—an Asian king who tyrannized and manifestly deserved to be destroyed. Marlowe's plays continued as a prominent part of the repertory, but only Shakespeare gives evidence of responding to their complexity.[1] Moreover, few tragedies before *Romeo and Juliet* had taken love as a central theme. It is true that *Dido Queen of Carthage,* attributed to Marlowe and Nashe on its title page of 1594 (where it was also declared to have been acted by the Children of the Queen's Chapel), was a play about love. But it is dubious whether we can accept this as a love-tragedy: "ironic comedy" would seem to fit it better.[2] It did indeed end with three deaths, and we must recognize that the idea of love leading to disaster was an occasional concern of the private stage in these years. *Gismond of Salerne* was acted at the Inner Temple in 1566 or 1568: it is a Senecan play, and the lovers never appear on the stage together. The lost *Quintus Fabius* of 1574, acted by the Windsor Boys at court, apparently had for its subject Xerxes' violent passion for the daughter of his sister-in-law.[3] Richard Edwardes's lost play *Palamon and Arcite* was acted at Christ Church, Oxford, before Elizabeth in 1566: coming from Chaucer's *The Knight's Tale,* its ending must have included destruction for one of the lovers. All these, however, clearly belong to the private stages. Arthur Brooke in the address to the reader prefixed to his poem *Romeus and Juliet* (1562) refers to having "lately" seen the story on the stage—there is no indication whether the stage referred

Clifford Leech, "The Moral Tragedy of *Romeo and Juliet,*" *English Renaissance Drama: Essays in Honor of Madeleine Doran and Mark Eccles,* ed. Standish Henning, Robert Kimbrough, and Richard Knowles. Copyright © 1976 by Southern Illinois University Press. Reprinted with permission of SIU Press.

to was public or private. Until Shakespeare wrote *Romeo and Juliet,* love on the public stage appears to have been solely an element either in comedy or in those romantic plays which Sidney mocked in his *Apology for Poetry* and which are vestigially preserved for us in *Sir Clyamon and Clamydes* (ca. 1570) and *Common Conditions* (ca. 1576).

Shakespeare, however, in the early years of his career showed a readiness to try every mode of playwriting. He had contributed to, and perhaps even invented,[4] the history play based on the English chronicles; he had written various types of comedy: a derivative from Plautus in *The Comedy of Errors,* a romantic wandering play in *The Two Gentlemen of Verona,* an Italianate intrigue affair in *The Taming of the Shrew;* now he wanted to try tragedy again—though he was to neglect that kind for some years afterward—and chose to make a play out of Arthur Brooke's thirty-year-old poem. It was a fascinating tale that had come from Italy, dramatized also in Spain by Lope de Vega in *Castelvines y Monteses* (though we have no reason to believe that either dramatist knew the other's work), and Shakespeare took over from his own comedies much that seemed to fit his new purpose.

But if he was to write a tragedy about love, what attitude should he take up to it? His inheritance was complex. From Galen in the second century A.D. there came the idea that love was a form of "melancholy," an idea that continued to be held fast in the late sixteenth- and seventeenth-century mind. The frontispiece to the original edition of Burton's *Anatomy of Melancholy* shows "Inamorato" as a chief "melancholy" type. Nevertheless, Aristotle had declared that melancholy was a privileged state which enabled men to see more clearly into things than a normal man could.[5] Moreover, there was Plato, with his notion of a ladder leading from the simplest sensual love to love of the highest. The Neoplatonists, exemplified splendidly in Castiglione's *The Courtier,* seemed to demand a kicking away of the lower rungs of the ladder as one ascended higher (which surely Plato never demanded), but nevertheless they saw love as an ultimate, a mode of experiencing the ideas of Goodness and Beauty. There was, too, the legacy from Courtly Love, which Spenser responded to, but which was perhaps now growing rather thin. And there was the attitude of churchmen, varying from a total contempt for women to a more discreet insistence on the need for man not to put any woman in the place that God alone should occupy. A Courtly Love poet customarily ended with a palinode, rejecting the devotion that he had before exhibited, and in *The Romance of the Rose* Jean de Meun's satiric presentation of the love-condition followed on Guillaume de Lorris's much briefer account of the lover's devotion. An Elizabethan sonneteer could see his love as his way to an apprehension of the godlike, or he might, as Shakespeare does, find submission to his mistress "Th' expense of spirit in a waste of shame." In addition we must not forget the surely ever-recurrent view of the lover, or of the husband, as an essentially comic figure. In *The Second Shepherds' Play* in the Wakefield cycle, one of the shepherds makes the common medieval joke about his wife's shrewishness and warns the young men in the audience not to let falling in love lead them into marriage. In the early sixteenth century the lover's comical extravagances are at the center of Udall's *Ralph Roister Doister.* To write a play about love and to disregard this common view of it would be to exclude a major part of human experience in relation to the play's subject. Thus a playwright choosing to make love central in a tragedy had little warrant for presenting the condition as simply ennobling: other views of it were exerting a good deal of pressure in Elizabethan times.[6]

Romeo and Juliet has proved a problem for Shakespeare critics. Franklin M. Dickey has seen it as exhibiting a simple moral lesson: to be taken up wholly by one's passion for another human being would, he argues, be seen by an Elizabethan as a moral imperfection, as likely to induce a general disregard of the moral law: so Shakespeare's play, despite its sympathy with the lovers, must be seen in relation to the contemporary idea of moral responsibility.[7] But to argue in this way is to take *Romeo and Juliet* as Roy Battenhouse has taken Marlowe's *Tamburlaine:*[8] Battenhouse tries to disregard the grandeur that goes along with the evil in Marlowe's hero; Dickey misses the sense of an enhanced degree of life which Shakespeare's lovers experience along with the danger they freely encounter. Nicholas Brooke is aware of the problem that faced Shakespeare: he suggests that the love of Romeo and Juliet is tested against the presentation of the normal current of life, which is indeed strong in the play, and that this love just—and only just—makes itself acceptable as an achieved good.[9] Indeed, when we remember the likely date of Shakespeare's play, we shall not be surprised at this. In *Love's Labour's Lost* he had made fun of the devotion that the King of Navarre and his three lords had manifested to the Princess of France and her three ladies: the men are made to endure a year-long penance, and Berowne's required sojourn in a hospital is, Berowne himself recognizes, almost an impossible demand. Can love outlast the waiting-time? Can it be related to the agony of the sick and the dying? In any event it must, the ending of the play suggests, be put into a total context, not being capable of replacing that context. In *The Two Gentlemen of Verona* love is juxtaposed with the idea of friendship, which, being as it was alleged purely altruistic, had a high standing indeed in the Renaissance, and love was there mocked through the figures of Launce and Speed, who took a more commonplace view of relations between the sexes. At the end it is the sympathetically opportunistic Julia who gets things straightened out. If the heroic lover and friend Valentine had been solely in charge of the play's termination, only disaster would have been possible. In writing a play in which the love of a young man and a young woman was to be considered a proper motive for tragedy, Shakespeare was bound to draw on his earlier treatments of love in comedy, but he would need to make a major departure too.

Certainly there is plenty of comedy here. Were it not for the declaration of the Prologue, with its references to "star-cross'd lovers" and to the ending of the feud through their deaths, we might well take the first two acts as moving toward a fortunate issue for the young people. The atmosphere is here generally one of pleasurable excitement, although Shakespeare has given Juliet a moment of premonition in the first balcony scene:

> Although I joy in thee,
> I have no joy in this contract to-night.
> It is too rash, too unadvis'd, too sudden;
> Too like the lightning, which doth cease to be
> Ere one can say 'It lightens.'
>
> (II.ii.116–20)

More of such premonitions will be noted later. But, until the moment when Mercutio is killed, the threat is not anywhere heavy. When Romeo and Juliet declare their love, there are moments of pure comedy. Thus Romeo compares himself to a schoolboy, reluctant to go to his books as Romeo is reluctant to leave Juliet: "Love goes toward love as schoolboys from their books; / But love from love, toward school with heavy looks" (II.ii.157–58). And there is a touch of absurdity, which we shall applaud when we remember what we all have done in distantly comparable circumstances, when Juliet says she has forgotten why she called him back, and he says he is ready to stay till she remembers:

> I have forgot why I did call thee back.
> *Rom.* Let me stand here till thou remember it.
> *Jul.* I shall forget, to have thee still stand there,
> Rememb'ring how I love thy company.
> *Rom.* And I'll still stay, to have thee still forget,
> Forgetting any other home but this.
>
> (II.ii.172–77)

We may remember too that Romeo has wished to be the glove on Juliet's hand, a mildly ludicrous idea, and that both lovers would like Romeo to be Juliet's pet bird:

> *Jul.* 'Tis almost morning. I would have thee gone—
> And yet no farther than a wanton's bird,
> That lets it hop a little from her hand,
> Like a poor prisoner in his twisted gyves,
> And with a silk thread plucks it back again,
> So loving-jealous of his liberty.
> *Rom.* I would I were thy bird.
> *Jul.* Sweet, so would I.
> Yet I should kill thee with much cherishing.
>
> (II.ii.178–85)

They will speak differently in the second balcony scene, but even there they will only dimly apprehend the world that threatens them.

Before this, of course, Romeo had been almost totally a figure of fun when he was giving voice to his love for Rosaline, and after meeting Juliet he is in a situation of some embarrassment when he goes to tell the Friar of his new love and of his wish for a secret marriage. When he admits that he has not been in his bed during the night that has just passed, he has to hear the Friar exclaim "God pardon sin! Wast thou with Rosaline?" (II.iii.144), and there is a particularly ludicrous touch when the Friar claims to see on Romeo's cheek a tear shed for Rosaline's love and not yet washed off. Even so, Shakespeare makes it plain that the new love is a thing of true moment. This is made evident not only in the authority of language that the lovers are sometimes allowed, during their interchange of words at their first meeting in the Capulet house and in the first balcony scene, but also in Romeo's premonition of disaster when he is on his way to the first meeting:

> my mind misgives
> Some consequence, yet hanging in the stars,
> Shall bitterly begin his fearful date
> With this night's revels and expire the term
> Of a despised life, clos'd in my breast,
> By some vile forfeit of untimely death.
> But he that hath the steerage of my course
> Direct my sail! On, lusty gentlemen!
>
> (I.iv.106–13)

Because we have hints enough that disaster lies ahead, we cannot see the love merely in terms of comedy.

Moreover, Romeo's behavior when he meets Mercutio and Benvolio again after he has talked with the Friar shows him as a young man ready to cope with danger for his love's sake and also ready, as now an adult lover, to give over affectation and to feel able to parry Mercutio's jests. Then, after the marriage, he has dignity both in his first refusal to fight with Tybalt, his new kinsman, and in his entering into the fray because he has by ill luck been responsible for Mercutio's death. At least, it may at first seem like ill luck, but we are made to see that Romeo's refusal to fight, Mercutio's indignation, and Romeo's revenge for his friend's death all arise, by necessity or at least probability, out of the nature of the characters and their situation in Verona. "O, I am fortune's fool!"—Romeo's cry after Tybalt's death—is comment enough on his inability to cope with the situation engendered by the feud, which previously he had been overconfident about. How precarious is his hold on his new adult status is underlined in the scene in the Friar's cell, where his love is expressed again in ludicrous terms:

> More validity,
> More honourable state, more courtship lives
> In carrion flies than Romeo. They may seize
> On the white wonder of dear Juliet's hand
> And steal immortal blessing from her lips,
> Who, even in pure and vestal modesty,
> Still blush, as thinking their own kisses sin;
> But Romeo may not—he is banished.
> This may flies do, when I from this must fly;
> They are free men, but I am banished.
>
> (III.iii.33–42)

The poor girl, with those flies on her hand and lips; those lips, so beautifully red because they are kissing each other; that shocking pun of "flies" and "fly": Romeo had uttered no more immature lines when the thought of Rosaline was on him. His extravagance here is similar to that of Valentine in *The Two Gentlemen of Verona,* who was similarly banished from the town where Silvia lived. And the mocker or rebuker is present with both: Launce the clown makes fun of Valentine; Romeo is described by the Friar as "with his own tears made drunk." He will recover dignity before the play's end, but he has lost hold of it here.

Juliet, on the other hand, has not Romeo's initial disadvantage of a previous, and ludicrous, love-attachment. We see her first as the dutiful daughter, ready to prepare herself to fall in love with Paris, as her parents would like her to. But Romeo is her first true commitment, and if she expresses herself comically at times in the first balcony scene, that is only a reminder of her extreme youth. And she is much more practical than he is: it is she who suggests how the wedding shall be arranged. Shakespeare has, moreover, given two almost parallel scenes in which she is the central figure: II.v, when she awaits the Nurse's return from her mission to Romeo, and III.ii, when she is looking forward to the coming wedding night. In both instances we have first a soliloquy from Juliet, expressing impatience that time goes for her so slowly, then the Nurse entering and delaying the news she has to give, and finally the Nurse's assurance that things after all will be well. But the differences between the scenes are remarkable. The news that the Nurse withholds is good in the first instance: everything is in order for the secret wedding. In the second instance it is bad news: Tybalt is dead and Romeo banished. The Nurse's delay, moreover, is a matter of teasing in the first scene, the result of incoherent grief in the second. And, although at the end of the second scene the Nurse promises to find Romeo and bring him to comfort Juliet, there is now true darkness here. Act II, scene v ended with Juliet's cry "Hie to high fortune! Honest nurse, farewell." The pun is evidence of pure excitement, and we can imagine Juliet giving the Nurse a quick and affectionate embrace as she goes off to her wedding. The second scene ends also with words from the girl: "O, find him! give this ring to my true knight / And bid him come to take his last farewell" (III.ii.142–43). The echo of Courtly Love in "true knight" has something forced and pathetic in it, and "last farewell" will prove to be a fact. Now, too, it is the Nurse who goes. Juliet must wait.

Yet in both scenes Juliet's youth is most poignantly brought out. Her impatience in II.v is of course amusing: for the moment we forget the omens, and know that the Nurse will truly impart her good news. And III.ii opens with one of the most famous speeches in the play, Juliet's soliloquy beginning "Gallop apace, you fiery-footed steeds / Towards Phoebus' lodging!" Here we find Juliet trying out image after image to give appropriate expression to her love, her desire to be wholly at one with Romeo. There is an overelaborateness in her invocation of Phoebus and Phaeton, of the "sober-suited matron," "civil night" ("civil" because she gives privacy to her citizens), who will teach Juliet "how to lose a winning match, / Play'd for a pair of stainless maidenhoods"; there is a playing with the idea of contrast when she sees Romeo as lying "upon the wings of night / Whiter than new snow upon a raven's back"; and she reaches a grotesque extravagance in the famous lines:

> Give me my Romeo; and, when he shall die,
> Take him and cut him out in little stars,
> And he will make the face of heaven so fine
> That all the world will be in love with night
> And pay no worship to the garish sun.
>
> (III.ii.21–25)

The extravagance is, of course, understandable: we do not have to forgive it. Juliet has seen Romeo only at night: she will never see him by daylight, except for the brief moment of their wedding and that half-light of dawn in the second balcony scene. So she can reject the "garish sun" that has never shone on them out of doors. Something more mature immediately follows: "O, I have bought the mansion of a love, / But not possess'd it; and though I am sold, / Not yet enjoy'd" (III.ii.26–28). R. W. Bond noted how the words of Valentine in *The Two Gentlemen of Verona* provided an earlier use of the same image: "O thou that dost inhabit in my breast, / Leave not the mansion so long tenantless, / Lest growing ruinous, the building fall / And leave no memory of what it was![10] The change of sex is interesting here: Juliet knows that the man is possessed by the woman while he merely penetrates her. Yet we still feel that this inexperienced girl is straining after an appropriate image, trying to be more "grown-up" than she really is. Suddenly the speech ends with an image wholly fitting this character who so recently was herself a child:

> So tedious is this day
> As is the night before some festival
> To an impatient child that hath new robes
> And may not wear them.
>
> (III.ii.28–31)

She is no longer a child, but her childhood memory is here linked with the new experience. Because the memory is now only a memory (yet a vivid one), because Romeo's body will be so startlingly her new clothes (Donne said: "What needst thou have more covering than a man," Elegy XIX), she in using this image from childhood grows suddenly mature as we hear her speak. It will take a good deal longer for Romeo to produce any comparable utterance. Doubtless Shakespeare realized that he had gone further with the girl than with the boy: it was convenient therefore to give the whole of act IV to her concerns, Romeo leaving for Mantua before act III is over and not entering the play again till act V begins.[11]

In giving us these two related scenes in *Romeo and Juliet,* II.v and III.ii, Shakespeare was repeating a device he had twice used in *Richard III.* There he had two wooing scenes and two "lamentation scenes" (to use A. P. Rossiter's term),[12] both pairs being marked by resemblance and difference. Richard wooed Anne successfully against all the odds, and then he wooed his brother's widow Elizabeth for the hand of her daughter: there is an obvious difference between wooing a potential bride and wooing a potential mother-in-law. Moreover, the second of these scenes is left open-ended, and only later are we told that Elizabeth has agreed that her daughter shall marry Richmond, the future Henry VII. Both scenes leave Richard confident. He thinks he has won, and in his second apparent triumph expresses contempt for Elizabeth as he had earlier done for Anne. But the later use of the earlier kind of approach suggests in certain lines both obstinacy and fatigue. The two "lamentation scenes" are also differentiated in that at first Margaret is the adversary, the denunciator of the house of York, and then in the second scene she joins with the women of York in expressing their grief and their horror at the evil that Richard for them represents. Indeed, parallel with variation was one of Shakespeare's special devices in these early plays, as in those scenes of *The Two Gentlemen of Verona* where Launce echoes or indirectly comments on the love-preoccupations of Proteus and Valentine.

In act V of *Romeo and Juliet* Romeo at once shows signs of a new status. His response to the false news of Juliet's death has a directness very different from his behavior in the Friar's cell when he was lamenting his banishment: "Is it e'en so? Then I defy you stars!" And he at once gives directions to Balthasar on the journey he plans to Verona and Juliet's tomb. Of course, he could have explored the matter more fully. It occurs to him to ask if no letters from the Friar have come with Balthasar, but when he receives a negative answer his "No matter. Get thee gone / And hire those horses" shows the rashness we have seen in him throughout. Left alone, with the desire for poison in his mind, he turns his attention to the apothecary's shop and to the situation of poor men. This is psychologically true, for in a moment of anguish we naturally tend to take refuge in a thought of something other than a demand that is immediately on us. After that, Romeo's recognition that the gold he gives is a worse poison than the one he buys is largely a Renaissance commonplace, but the eloquence with which he expresses it gives him an authority he has previously lacked:

> There is thy gold—worse poison to men's souls,
> Doing more murther in this loathsome world,
> Than these poor compounds that thou mayst not sell.
> I sell thee poison; thou hast sold me none.
> Farewell. Buy food and get thyself in flesh.
>
> (V.i.80–84)

Earlier Romeo had to face the distinction between "loving" and "doting" that the Friar insisted on: the young man "doted" on Rosaline, which the Friar could not approve, and he must love Juliet "moderately." Yet of course he did not follow the Friar's advice, though he thought that his love for Juliet was something the Friar could understand. Shakespeare suggests another distinction between love and love: the kind you simply like to maunder over, the kind that ultimately commits you. We do not, as Romeo does, usually kill ourselves for love, but we remember to the end a girl that truly mattered. The utterances from the sympathetic Friar, who thinks the Capulet-Montague feud may come to peace through the marriage, are an echo of the church's view of love in the Middle Ages. The total commitment to another person is, we have seen, in that view a dangerous thing if not kept properly subordinate to one's love of God. Romeo cannot follow the Friar in this: he is so totally committed to Juliet that he will kill himself in her tomb. There is indeed a threefold presentation of love here, not a dichotomy: there is the affected, superficial concern with Rosaline, there is the fatal commitment to Juliet, and there is the "moderation" counseled by the Friar and illustrated in the play's older married couples. Shakespeare gives utterance to the church's counsel, neither endorsing nor rejecting it. If the play's lovers could have lived, some different things would have conditioned their relations to each other: perhaps they were lucky to avoid it. We may be reminded of the ultimate return to Lisa in James Branch Cabell's *Jurgen*.

When Romeo and Juliet commit suicide rather than live without each other, their last words have a special eloquence. Suicide, we must remember, was a mortal sin, yet many men of the Renaissance took a dissident view of it. In particular, Montaigne saw it as man's last available card to play.[13] The classical precedents, moreover, were numerous and powerful.[14] Nowhere in this play is it suggested that damnation lies in wait for the lovers. The audience were likely to feel that Romeo and Juliet had dared greatly: they could not be, in the absence of any comment from the chorus or from the characters who survived them, likely to have in their minds the idea of damnation.

There is, after all, a kind of "happy ending." The feud will be ended, the lovers will be remembered. We may be reminded of the commonplace utterance that we have two deaths: the moment of actual ceasing to be, and the moment when the last person who remembers us dies. These lovers have their being enshrined in a famous play. So they are remembered in perpetuity, and their lives, according to the play itself, will be recorded in their statues.[15] Certainly this is a sad affair, like that of Paolo and Francesca in *The Divine Comedy*. But we may ask, is it tragic?

Tragedy seems to demand a figure or figures that represent us in our ultimate recognition of evil. We need to feel that such figures are our kin, privileged to be chosen for the representative role and coming to the destruction that we necessarily anticipate for ourselves. The boy and girl figures in *Romeo and Juliet* are perhaps acceptable as appropriate representatives for humankind: after all, they do grow up. What worries us more, I think, in trying to see this play as fully achieved "tragedy," is the speech of the Duke at the end, which suggests that some atonement will be made through the reconciliation of the Montague and Capulet families. We are bound to ask "Is this enough?" It appears to be offered as such, but we remember that the finest among Verona's people are dead.

Shakespearean tragedy commonly ends with a suggestion of a return to normality, to peace. Fortinbras will rule in Denmark, Malcolm in Scotland, Iago will be put out of the way. But these later tragedies leave us with a doubt whether the peace is other than a second-best, whether indeed it is in man's power ever to put things right. In *Romeo and Juliet* the ending of the feud is laboriously spelled out.

But there is also the matter of Fate and Chance. Romeo kills Paris: at first glance that was a quite fortuitous happening. Paris was a good man, devoted to Juliet, who unfortunately got in the way of Romeo's approach to Juliet's tomb. At this point Romeo's doom is sealed: he might kill Tybalt and get away with it; he could not get away with killing an innocent Paris, who was moreover the Prince's kinsman. Now it is inevitable that he will die, whatever the moment of Juliet's awakening. There is indeed a "star-cross'd" pattern for the lovers, there is no way out for Romeo once he has come back to Verona. But perhaps Paris's important function in the last scene is not sufficiently brought out: the spectator may feel that there is simple chance operating in Romeo's arrival before Juliet wakes, in his killing himself a moment too early, in the Friar's belated arrival. Later I must return to the matter of the play's references to the "stars": for the moment I merely want to refer to the fact that tragedy can hardly be dependent on "bad luck."

Even so, though simple chance will not do, we may say that tragedy properly exists only when its events defy reason. The Friar thought the marriage of the young lovers might bring the feud to an end, and that was a reasonable assumption. Ironically, it did end the feud but at the expense of Romeo's and Juliet's lives, at the expense too of Mercutio's, Tybalt's, and Lady Montague's lives. The element of *non sequitur* in the train of events common to tragedy—despite the fact that, with one part of our minds, we see the operation of "probability or necessity," as Aristotle has it—is well described by Laurens van der Post in his novel *The Hunter and the Whale:*

> I was too young at the time to realise that tragedy is not tragedy if one finds reason or meaning in it. It becomes then, I was yet to learn, a darker form of this infinitely mysterious matter of luck. It is sheer tragedy only if it is without discernible sense or motivation.[16]

We may balk at "luck," as I have already suggested, but "mysterious" is right indeed (as Bradley splendidly urged on us in the First Lecture of *Shakespearean Tragedy*), for what "sense" or "motivation" does there seem to be in tragedy's gods? The sense of mystery is not, however, firmly posited in *Romeo and Juliet*. Rather, it is laboriously suggested that the Montagues and the Capulets have been taught a lesson in a particularly hard way.

Thus we have several reasons to query the play's achievement in the tragic kind. Do the lovers take on themselves the status of major figures in a celebration of a general human woe? Is the ending, with its promise of reconciliation, appropriate to tragic writing? We have seen that the lovers grow up, and they give us the impression of justifying human life, in their best moments, more than most people do. But the suggestion that their deaths will atone, will bring peace back, seems nugatory: no man's death brings peace, not even Christ's—or the Unknown Soldier's. The play could still end tragically if we were left with the impression that the survivors were merely doing what they could to go on living in an impoverished world: we have that in *Hamlet* and the later tragedies too. Here the laboriousness with which Shakespeare recapitulates all the events known to us, in the Friar's long speech, is surely an indication of an ultimate withdrawal from the tragic: the speech is too much like a preacher's résumé of the events on which a moral lesson will be based. We can accept Edgar's long account of Gloucester's death in *King Lear*, because we need a moment of recession before the tragedy's last phase, where we shall see Lear and Cordelia dead, and because no moral lesson is drawn from Gloucester's death; but at the end of this earlier play, when Romeo and Juliet have already eloquently died, we are with difficulty responsive to the long reiteration of all we have long known through the play's action.

Shakespeare has not here achieved the sense of an ultimate confrontation with evil, or the sense that the tragic figure ultimately and fully recognizes what his situation is. Romeo and Juliet die, more or less content with death as a second best to living together. Montague and Capulet shake hands, and do what is possible to atone. The lovers have the illusion of continuing to be together—an illusion to some extent imposed on the audience. The old men feel a personal guilt, not a realization of a general sickness in man's estate. But perhaps only Lear and Macbeth and Timon came to that realization.

We can understand why Shakespeare abandoned tragedy for some years after this play. It had proved possible for him to touch on the tragic idea in his English histories, making them approach, but only approach, the idea of humanity's representative being given over to destruction, as with the faulty Richard II, the saintly Henry VI, the deeply guilty yet none the less sharply human Richard III. He had given his theater a flawed yet impressive Titus Andronicus and in the same play an Aaron given almost wholly to evil but obstinately alive. But in these plays the main drive is not tragic. The histories rely on the sixteenth-century chronicles, *Titus* on that tradition of grotesque legend that came from both Seneca and Ovid. The past was to be relived and celebrated in the histories; *Titus* was more of a literary exercise in antique horror than a play embodying a direct reference to the general human condition. In *Romeo and Juliet* Shakespeare for the first time essayed tragedy proper—that is, by wanting to bring the play's events into relation to things as they truly are—and he used a tale often told but belonging to recent times and concerned with people whom the spectators were to feel as very much their own kin. He may well have been particularly attracted to the story he found in Brooke's poem for the very reason that its figures and events did not have the authority of history and belonged to the comparatively small world of Verona. No major change in the political order can result from what happens in this play's action. No individual figure presented here is truly given over to evil. Without any precedents to guide him, he aimed at writing about eloquent but otherwise ordinary young people in love and about their equally ordinary friends and families. Only Mercutio has something daemonic in him, in the sense that his quality of life transcends the normal level of being.

We have seen that, if Shakespeare had no useful dramatic precedents in this task, he had a manifold heritage of ideas about the nature of love; and many parts of that heritage show themselves in the play. The immoderateness and rashness that the Friar rebukes seem, on the one hand, to lead—in the fashion of a moral play—to the lovers' destruction. On the other hand, not only is our sympathy aroused but we are made to feel that what Romeo and Juliet achieve may be a finer thing than is otherwise to be found in Verona. Both views are strongly conveyed, and either of them might effectively dominate the play. Of course, they could coexist and interpenetrate—as they were to do much later in *Antony and Cleopatra*—but here they seem to alternate, and to be finally both pushed into the background in the long insistence that the feud will end because of the lovers' deaths. The "moral" is thus finally inverted: the lovers' sequence of errors has culminated in the error of suicide, but now we are made to turn to their parents' error and to the consolation that Romeo and Juliet will be remembered through their golden statues. And it is difficult for us to get interested in these statues, or to take much joy in the feud's ending.

Yet the deepest cause of uneasiness in our response to the play is, I believe, to be found in the relation of the story to the idea of the universe that is posited. We are told in the Prologue of "star-cross'd lovers," and there are after that many references to the "stars." So there is a sense of "doom" here, but we are never fully told what is implied. Many coincidences operate: Romeo meets Tybalt just at the wrong moment; the Friar's message to Romeo about Juliet's alleged death goes astray; Romeo arrives at the tomb just before Juliet awakens; the Friar comes too late. I have already drawn attention to Shakespeare's device by which Romeo has to kill Paris, so that, even if he had arrived at the right time, there would have been no way out for him. We may feel that a similar sequence of chances operates in *Hamlet:* if Hamlet had not killed Polonius in a scared moment, if he had not had his father's seal with him on the voyage to England, if he had not managed to escape on the hospitable pirates' ship, if the foils had not been exchanged in the fencing bout with Laertes, if Gertrude had not drunk from the poisoned cup, things might indeed not have been disposed so as to lead him to Claudius's killing at the moment when it actually occurred. Even so, we can feel that, after all, the end would have been much as it is. Hamlet was a man in love with death, far more in love with death than with killing: we may say that only in the moment of death's imminence was he fully alive, freed from inhibition, able to kill Claudius: somehow or other, whatever the chances, this play demanded a final confrontation between the uncle-father and nephew-son. In *Romeo and Juliet,* on the other hand, we could imagine things working out better: the lovers are doomed only by the words of the Prologue, not by anything inherent in their situation. It is not, as it is in Hardy's novels, that we have a sense of a fully adverse "President of the immortals": there is rather an insufficient consideration of what is implied by the "stars." Of course, in *King Lear,* in all later Shakespearean tragedy, there is a sense of an ultimate mystery in the universe: "Is there any cause in nature that makes these hard hearts?" Lear asks in his condition of most extreme distress. Bradley recognized that this mystery was inherent in the idea of tragedy,[17] as is implied too in the passage from Laurens van der Post I have already quoted. But in *Romeo and Juliet* there is no sense of the mystery being confronted: rather it is merely posited in a facile way, so that we have to accept the lovers' deaths as the mere result of the will of the "stars" (the astrological implication is just too easy), and then we are exhorted to see this as leading to a reconciliation between the families.

The final "moral" of the play, as we have seen, is applied only to Old Montague and Old Capulet: they have done evil in allowing the feud to go on, and have paid for it in the deaths of their children and of Lady Montague. But, largely because Romeo and Juliet are never blamed, the children themselves stand outside the framework of moral drama. They have, albeit imperfectly, grown up into the world of tragedy, where the moral law is not a thing of great moment. They have been sacrificed on the altar of man's guilt, have become the victims of our own outrageousness, have given us some relief because they have died and we still for a time continue living. I have argued elsewhere[18] that we can hardly forgive ourselves for accepting such a sacrifice, can hardly accept a frame of things which seems to demand such a sacrifice. To that extent, *Romeo and Juliet* is "tragic" in a way we can fully recognize. But its long-drawn-out ending, after the lovers are dead, with the pressing home of the moral that their deaths will bring peace, runs contrary to the notion of tragedy. There is a sanguineness about the end of it, a suggestion that after all "All shall be well, and / All manner of thing shall be well," as Eliot quotes from Julian of Norwich in *Little Gidding,* and we can hardly tolerate the complacency of the statement.

So in *Romeo and Juliet,* understandably in view of its early date, we cannot find that tragedy has fully emerged from the moral drama and the romantic comedy that dominated in the public theaters of Shakespeare's earliest time. Here he attempted an amalgam of romantic comedy and the tragic idea, along with the assertion of a moral lesson which is given the final emphasis—although the force of that lesson is switched from the lovers to their parents. But tragedy is necessarily at odds with the moral: it is concerned with a permanent anguishing situation, not with one that can either be put right or be instrumental in teaching the survivors to do better. When Shakespeare wrote "love-tragedy" again, in *Othello* and in *Antony and Cleopatra,* he showed that love may be a positive good but that it was simultaneously destructive and that its dramatic presentation gave no manumission from error to those who contemplated the destruction and continued to live. Nowhere, I think, does he suggest that love is other than a condition for wonder, however much he makes fun of it. But in his mature years he sees it as not only a destructive force but as in no way affording a means of reform. That *Romeo and Juliet* is a "moral tragedy"—which, I have strenuously urged, is a contradiction in terms—is evident enough. It is above all the casualness of the play's cosmology that prevents us from seeing it as tragedy fully achieved: we have seen the need for a fuller appreciation of the mystery. As with *Titus Andronicus,* the nearest play to *Romeo and Juliet* overtly assuming a tragic guise in the chronology of Shakespeare's works, the march toward disaster is too manifestly a literary device. At this stage in his career Shakespeare had not worked as free from the sixteenth-century moral play as Marlowe had done in *Tamburlaine, Faustus,* and *Edward II.*

Even so, there is a small achieved tragedy embodied within this play. I have described Mercutio as "daemonic," and that is an adjective we can appropriately apply to every tragic hero: he has fire within him—whether he is Oedipus, Orestes, Hamlet, Macbeth, Racine's Phèdre, Ibsen's Brand, or any of the men and women who occupy the center of Lorca's stage—and the fire ultimately consumes. We can call this "hubris," but the rashness implied in that word is not a matter for moral comment. Mercutio has no Friar to counsel "moderation" to him: even if he had, we cannot imagine him as paying more attention than Giovanni did in Ford's 'Tis Pity She's a Whore. Certainly Benvolio urges him not to stay in the sun when the Capulets are abroad, but this friend speaks as one man to another, hoping to save his friend from physical danger, not as concerned with his moral health. Mercutio, careless of what may come (as Hamlet was to be), draws his sword and goes to his death. His last words are ironic and resentful. The wound was so small, yet fatal. The quarrel between the "houses" was no concern of his. Yet the wound is "enough," the feud has finished him. No lesson is drawn from this destruction; there is no suggestion that good may come out of it. It has simply happened, to the world's impoverishment.

We cannot certainly know whether Shakespeare had already planned Mercutio's death when he gave him the "Queen Mab" speech. What we do know is that the character is virtually Shakespeare's own invention, hardly a trace of it being in Brooke's poem. But we can guess that the speech prefigures the death and that Shakespeare knew, as early as the first act of the play, that its speaker was soon to die. That does not excuse the crassness of some recent directors who have made the actor of Mercutio's part show a trepidation of his own when, near the end of the speech, he refers to a soldier's dream: our anguish at his death is all the more poignant if he does not show fear or anticipation. All sorts of reasons have been given for the insertion of the speech in the play: it makes Mercutio prominent in our minds, as he needs to be because he will play a crucial role in the plot; it hints at a fantastic dreamworld which will make us aware of a mystery not sufficiently explicit, as we have seen, within the play as a whole; it provides a choric commentary on the loves, for Rosaline and then for Juliet, that Romeo experiences; it mocks indeed not only at sex-relationships but at all men's dreams—and Romeo, just before Mercutio enters on his fantasy, has referred to an ominous dream that he has just had. Does Romeo ever have anything more than a dream, though a splendid and entrancing one? But what is perhaps most important is that the speech puts Mercutio outside the general Christian framework of the play. He is surely a pure pagan: his last call is for a surgeon, not a priest. There is an angriness in him that is a link with Hamlet, Othello, Lear, Macbeth: these characters are by no means all unbelievers, but their final acts are those of men standing alone, without help from the general current of thought in their world, with a full realization too of their loneliness. They take the Protestantism of Shakespeare's time to a desperate limit. Here, not in the oblivious Liebestod of the lovers, for all its pre-Wagnerian eloquence, we find the true germ of Shakespeare's later development. One may suspect that Mercutio haunted this playwright, that the character and his death provided a foundation on which the later tragedies could be securely built.

Notes

1. See Nicholas Brooke, "Marlowe as Provocative Agent in Shakespeare's Early Plays," *ShS,* 14 (1961), 34–44.

2. See my "Marlowe's Humor," in *Essays on Shakespeare and Elizabethan Drama in Honor of Hardin Craig,* ed. Richard Hosley (Columbia, 1962), pp. 69–81. For a contrary view see J. B. Steane, *Marlowe: A Critical Study* (Cambridge, 1964), ch. II.

3. See F. P. Wilson, *The English Drama 1485–1585* (Oxford, 1969), pp. 146–47.

4. See F. P. Wilson, *Marlowe and the Early Shakespeare* (Oxford, 1953), p. 108.

5. See *The Poetics,* ch. XVII: "Poetry demands a man with a special gift for it, or else one with a touch of madness in him; the former can easily assume the required mood, and the latter may be naturally beside himself with emotion" (Bywater's translation). In his note on this passage Bywater refers to relevant comments in Aristotle's other writings. See *Aristotle on the Art of Poetry* (Oxford, 1909), pp. 244–45.

6. For a major scholarly discussion of love-melancholy, see Lawrence Babb, *The Elizabethan Malady* (East Lansing, 1951).

7. *Not Wisely but Too Well: Shakespeare's Love Tragedies* (San Marino, 1957), esp. pp. 116–17.

8. *Marlowe's Tamburlaine: A Study in Renaissance Moral Philosophy* (1941; rpt. Nashville, 1964).

9. *Shakespeare's Early Tragedies* (London, 1968), esp. pp. 102–3.

10. *TGV* V.iv.7–10. See my new Arden edition of *TGV* (London, 1969), p. 112.

11. The act-divisions derive of course only from the Folio, but in this play they seem to have high authority.

12. "The Structure of *Richard the Third,*" *DUJ,* 31 (Dec., 1938), 63.

13. *The Essayes of Michael Lord of Montaigne translated by John Florio* (London, 1897), II, 149.

14. On this matter see "Le dénouement par le suicide dans la tragédie élisabethaine et jacobéenne," in *Le Théâtre tragique,* ed. Jean Jacquot (Paris, 1962), pp. 179–89.

15. On the curious ambivalence in the fact that the statues are golden, see my British Academy lecture, *Shakespeare's Tragic Fiction* (London, 1973), p. 7.

16. (London, 1967), p. 135.

17. *Shakespearean Tragedy* (1904; rpt. London, 1951), pp. 38–39.

18. *Tragedy* (London, 1969), pp. 53–54.

Mercutio's Brother

JOSEPH A. PORTER

In *The Most Excellent and Lamentable Tragedy of Romeo and Juliet* 1.2 Romeo obliges Capulet's illiterate servant by reading the guest list for Capulet's feast, whereupon Benvolio remarks that, since "the fair Rosaline, whom thou so loves" (1.2.85)[1] is among the invited, Romeo should attend. Since Capulet has just invited Paris in person on the spur of the moment, we don't expect to find his name in the list. We do find the name of Tybalt, who has skirmished with Benvolio in the first scene, but otherwise the play has not yet identified any of the dozen or so named guests with their unnamed but listed daughters, beauteous sisters, and lovely nieces. In particular, the play has not yet provided any handle for the two guests named in line 68, one of whom soon proves memorable, the other of whom is never again mentioned: "*Mercutio and his brother Valentine*" (1.2.68).

Valentine is a kind of ghost character, one of those "introduced in stage directions or briefly mentioned in dialogue who have no speaking parts and do not otherwise manifest their presence" (Smidt, "Absent Characters," p. 398). If Valentine is ever onstage, it is as a guest at the feast in 1.5. But if so, nothing in the text suggests anything to distinguish him from the other guests—nothing like, for instance, a word with his brother. Mercutio himself, it is true, goes into a kind of suspended animation in 3.1 with Benvolio as Tybalt recognizes and prepares to fight not Benvolio again (as we might expect) but rather Romeo. And it is true that none of the other ghost guests has a speech or stage direction. Still, none of the other ghosts is linked to the main action as firmly as is Valentine by the bond of brotherhood, so that we might reasonably expect him to bear some small part in the action. Unless he is unexplainedly absent from the feast, then, Valentine is as retiring as Rosaline at the same occasion.

Romeo and Juliet, by the way, seems marked by an unusually high degree of corporeal or ontological indeterminateness. Benvolio, pretty constantly onstage until the middle of the play, inexplicably vanishes thereafter. In 3.1

Joseph A. Porter, "Mercutio's Brother," reprinted from *Shakespeare's Mercutio: His History and Drama,* by Joseph A. Porter. Copyright © 1989 by the University of North Carolina Press. Used by permission of the publisher.

Paris may be "certainly . . . present at the feast though he is not mentioned in direction or dialogue" (Newman & Williams, "Paris," p. 16n), or it may be that "not only Rosaline but Count Paris, too, is a defaulter at Capulet's feast" (Smidt, p. 402). In such a world it is perhaps understandable that even as informed a commentator as Brian Gibbons should hallucinate an unquestionably absent character as present when he writes that, in the scene with the guest list, "Romeo, Benvolio *and Mercutio* [emphasis added] learn by accident from Capulet's illiterate servant of the ball" (p. 41). Only Romeo, Benvolio, and the servant appear in the scene.

Valentine, though, is less present in the play than even Rosaline. Absent from Smidt's treatment of absent characters, he is a ghost of a ghost, and he raises interesting questions of ontology. In the responses and memories of the play's audience he is far less real than, say, Queen Mab. On the other hand he may have as good a claim to actual onstage presence at the Capulet feast as do Rosaline and Paris. And this ghostly Valentine's effective momentary presence in Shakespeare's mind raises other sorts of questions as well: what is he doing in the play at all, where does he come from, what are we to make of him? Who is Valentine really? Frivolous though it might seem to pose such questions, attempting to answer them leads quickly into deep waters.

The obvious place to begin a search for answers to these questions is Arthur Brooke's 1562 translation from the Italian of Bandello, *The Tragicall Historye of Romeus and Juliet,*[2] Shakespeare's source and one he followed with unusual faithfulness. Were Valentine in Brooke, his presence in Shakespeare might be attributable to a certain inertia of imagination. But in Brooke there is no Valentine.

Indeed Mercutio himself makes a very brief, though tantalizing, appearance in Brooke, at the Capulet feast where Romeus has adroitly seated himself next to Juliet's chair while she dances:

> Fayre Juliet tourned to her chayre with pleasant cheere
> And glad she was her Romeus approached was so neere.
> At thone side of her chayre, her lover Romeo
> And on the other side there sat one cald Mercutio,
> A courtier that eche where was highly had in pryce,
> For he was coorteous of his speeche, and pleasant of devise
> Even as a Lyon would emong the lambes be bold,
> Such was emong the bashful maydes, Mercutio to behold.
> With friendly gripe he ceasd fayre Juliets snowish hand.
> A gift he had that nature gave him in his swathing band,
> That frosen mountayne yse was never halfe so cold
> As were his handes, though nere so neer the fire he dyd them holde.
> Within his trembling hand her left hath loving Romeus caught
>
> (ll. 251–64)

· ·

[to Romeus, Juliet] sayd with smyling cheere
Mervayle no whit my heartes delight, my only knight and fere,
Mercutio's ysy hande had all to frosen myne
And of thy goodness thou agayne hast warmed it with thine.

(ll. 287–90)

The passage contains hints of Mercutio's characterization and story in Shake-speare, and thereby, indirectly some of Valentine's raison d'être. Here Mercu-tio has the same name, social station, and apparent approximate age as in Shakespeare, and Brooke's characterizing touches of assurance, sensuality, and precipitateness (ll. 257–59, 263) all flower in Shakespeare. But the differ-ences between Brooke and Shakespeare are perhaps more striking than the similarities.

Nothing in Brooke establishes that Mercutio even knows Romeo, much less that they are boon companions. Instead, Mercutio in Brooke is a bested rival or would-be rival for Juliet's attentions. He doesn't stand a chance, as the first two quoted lines make clear, and Juliet's rejection of him provides her with an occasion to open conversation with the more tremulous (l. 264) Romeus. And then there are Mercutio's icy hands (ll. 260–62), that disarm-ing detail few commentators can resist.[3]

Shakespeare resisted incorporating them directly into his play, perhaps because such fabulous iciness would have been inappropriately comical on the stage. But the detail seems too remarkable to have simply disappeared as Mer-cutio came into Shakespeare. The coldness of Mercutio's hands in Brooke may have figured in the early demise Shakespeare gives the character—in Brooke he merely drops from sight. It may also be (and here, as will be seen, Valentine lingers in the wings) that Shakespeare responded to a certain inconsistency between the friendliness of Mercutio's *gripe* (l. 259) and the coldness of his hands. That inconsistency in Brooke's Mercutio, I would argue, gives him an instability that makes him ripe for the development he undergoes as he comes into Shakespeare, a development in which Valentine plays a key part.

Another detail from Brooke that may well have influenced Shakespeare's transformation of Mercutio and creation of his brother is the rhyme of

At thone side of her chayre, her lover Romeo
And on the other side there sat one cald Mercutio.

(ll. 253–54)

While in Painter and in other versions Juliet's lover's name has the form Shakespeare uses (despite Painter's spelling to Holofernes's taste, "Rhomeo"), he is "Romeus" in Brooke everywhere except here. Warned by Shakespeare's play against being too cavalier about what's in a name, we may give some weight to the fact that Romeus becomes Romeo for the sake of a rhyme with Mercutio. "Now for this one pair of lines, and because of me," Mercutio might have said, "now art thou Romeo; now art thou what thou art." He might have added, "Now art thou sociable," too. The association, merely phonetic at this point in Brooke, becomes crucial in Shakespeare, where it characterizes Mercutio far more than Romeo, and where Mercutio's attribution of it to Romeo amounts to a sort of wishful thinking.[4]

Neither in this passage nor elsewhere in Brooke is there any mention of Mercutio's brother Valentine. To find where he comes from, how he is in solution in Brooke, and why he precipitates out in Shakespeare, one must look further. Two questions are at issue. First, why does Mercutio generate a ghost brother in the transition from Brooke into Shakespeare? Second, why is that brother named Valentine, or, where does the name come from? Let me address the second question first.

The name Valentine, a diminutive of the present participle of the Latin *valeo,* was of course familiar to Shakespeare in the form of St. Valentine. Two or three saints seem to have been conflated for the saint on whose February 14 feast day birds traditionally begin to court.[5] And Shakespeare uses the name twice before *Romeo and Juliet* for nonghost characters—for a very minor role in *Titus Andronicus* and for one of the protagonists in *The Two Gentlemen of Verona.* We might expect earlier Elizabethan dramatists to have capitalized on the name's Italianate amorousness (as did the creators of Rudolph Valentino), but in fact Shakespeare seems to be the only English dramatist to have used the name for a character before *Romeo and Juliet.* Therefore his earlier uses of the name have a special relevance.[6]

In *Titus Andronicus* Valentine is a kinsman of Titus with a single nonspeaking appearance. In *The Two Gentlemen of Verona,* however, where Valentine the constant lover is tested by his fickle friend Proteus's temporary rivalry in love, we have Shakespeare's only extensive use of the name. Although the main source for *The Two Gentlemen of Verona* is an English translation (from French) of the Spanish *Diana Enamorada* of Montemayor, the source for several incidents is Brooke's *The Tragicall Historye of Romeus and Juliet.*[7] In those incidents, without exception, the antecedent for the Valentine of *The Two Gentlemen of Verona* turns out to be Brooke's Romeus. Thus Shakespeare's association of the name Valentine with the Brooke version, and in particular with the character of Romeus, dates back at least to the composition of *Two Gentlemen.* Once established, the association lies dormant for a couple of years until Shakespeare uses Brooke again, more extensively and exclusively, for a play about other gentlemen of Verona.[8]

But where then does *Two Gentlemen*'s Valentine come from?—for the name does not appear in the play's sources. Clifford Leech advises that "the name suggests 'lover' " (*Two Gentlemen,* p. 2n) and that the connotations and associations of the saint's name may have figured in Shakespeare's choosing it for the play's constant lover. In addition to "lover," the name could well have suggested "brother" to Shakespeare, specifically "one of two brothers approximately the same age," and this because of two other Valentines perhaps known to Shakespeare.

Valentine and Orson, the English prose romance of the Charlemagne cycle, which was translated by Wynkyn de Worde's apprentice Henry Watson from the French *Valentin et Orson,* appeared in three sixteenth-century editions.[9] Furthermore, in the work's most recent edition, Arthur Dickson (*Valentine,* p. li) observes: "That our romance was well known in sixteenth-century England is indicated by the appearance of Valentine and Orson in the coronation pageant of 1547; Sidney's allusion to Pacolet's horse in the *Apologie for Poetrie;* the use of *Valentine and Orson* in *The Seven Champions of Christendom;* the record of two lost plays; and the account of a boy's reading given by Robert Ashley." Thus Shakespeare might well have had some familiarity with the romance in 1595. Dickson (p. lix) and others also have seen an allusion to the romance in the reference to stories of wolves and bears suckling children in *The Winter's Tale* 2.3.186–88 (a surmise that gains credence from the numerous other resonances between *Romeo* and *Winter's Tale* discussed below passim).

The titular heroes are twins separated at birth when a bear carries Orson off to feed her cubs. She relents and raises Orson as her own (hence his name). Through the course of adventures (involving, for instance, a magician, a dragon, and a green knight) the brothers meet, fight each other, and then join forces; Orson learns to speak and eventually they learn that they are brothers. Valentine is a model of knightly virtues, including constancy in love; Orson falls a bit short of that, and some other virtues, and may be the more interesting thereby.

Memories of the romance may have figured in Shakespeare's choice of the name Valentine for the more constant lover of *The Two Gentlemen of Verona.* Proteus does not especially recall Orson, but in *Romeo and Juliet* one may find a touch of the rough-and-ready Orson in Valentine's brother Mercutio. Indeed an associative resonance might seem the more likely with the latter play inasmuch as the earlier of the two lost plays (both titled *Valentine and Orson*) mentioned above by Dickson is entered in the *Stationers' Register* for 1595, the date customarily given to *Romeo and Juliet.*[10]

The name Valentine may also have suggested to Shakespeare "one of a pair of brothers" because of the brotherhood of Valentinianus, Roman emperor of the West 364–78, and Valens, emperor of the East 364–75. Because of the number of their joint edicts contained in the Theodosian Code and in the many anthologies of legal *sententiae* available by the sixteenth century, their names were customarily coupled.[11] Nor was knowledge of the two emperors confined to the legal profession. For instance, a character in the 1598 *Courtiers Academie* speaks of "another testimoniall of *Valente* and *Valentino.*"[12]

Familiarity with these paired brother emperors would have given the name Valentine a valence suitable for one of the protagonists in *The Two Gentlemen of Verona* and for the character referred to only as Mercutio's brother in *Romeo and Juliet*. Indeed Shakespeare's presumed familiarity with the paired emperors' names probably made Valentine in line 68 of the Capulet guest list call up another ghost three lines later: "*Signor Valentio and his cousin Tybalt*" (1.2.71).

In light of these earlier Valentines—the saint, the bear's foster child's brother, and the emperor—one may begin to see why it is that Mercutio in his passage from Brooke to Shakespeare should generate a brother so named.

Shakespeare's most extensive use of the name Valentine is in *The Two Gentlemen of Verona,* "a play on the *debat*-theme of love versus friendship" (Leech, ed., *Two Gentlemen,* p. lxxv), of the amatory versus the amicable or fraternal. Leech associates the name with "the great mass of friendship-literature that extends through the Middle Ages to the seventeenth century" (*Two Gentlemen,* p. xxxv). His use of Brooke as a source for certain episodes of that play has, I suggest, a similar effect: that use associates Brooke firmly with the tradition of friendship literature. Therefore when the playwright returned to Brooke in 1595 he may well have seen the love-tragedy as if through a filter, with a residual idiosyncratic coloring of the fraternal and amicable.

That coloring is nowhere more notable in *Romeo and Juliet* than in the character of Mercutio, transformed from a bit part as Romeus's rival in love to Romeo's friend, the scoffer at love whose death "is the keystone of the plot's structure" (Hosley, "Children," p. 171). And Valentine, I suggest, figures importantly if briefly in Mercutio's transformation.

Mercutio develops a brother, however ghostly and evanescent, in *Romeo and Juliet* because of the increased brotherliness and decreased amorousness he also develops there. Valentine is thus a symptom or by-product of Mercutio's transformation; he also facilitates that transformation in quite specific ways. At their first mention in Capulet's guest list Valentine serves as an object of what is to be an essential characteristic of Mercutio, his brotherliness: Valentine is there to begin the characterization of Mercutio as fraternal. At the same time, Valentine by his name serves as a sort of lightning rod to draw off and embody whatever residual amorousness Mercutio retains from Brooke. Valentine by his brief appearance, then, initiates the characterization of Mercutio that blossoms in the man's strong brotherly friendship and scorn of love. Valentine's name, because of its amorous and fraternal associations (including its previous uses by Shakespeare) was peculiarly, perhaps even uniquely, suited for its function in *Romeo and Juliet.*

Mercutio's brotherliness manifests itself in his confraternity with Benvolio and Romeo. An easy camaraderie links each with the other two. But as for Benvolio, though he appears in the play before either of the others, and though he is given a few intriguing touches of characterization—such as the troubled mind he says led him out for a predawn walk (1.1)—still a certain blandness in him makes him begin to dissolve into good wishes toward both his friends even before he slips out of the play midway through, not anchored even by his cousinship with Romeo.

The important friendship bond is thus that between Mercutio and Romeo. Mercutio is Romeo's "very friend" (3.1.108). Their friendship leads Mercutio to take Romeo's part against Tybalt, leads Romeo to rush between them and, after Tybalt has thrust under his arm and given Mercutio his deathblow, to fight and kill Tybalt. And the profoundly consequential friendship and fraternal loyalty between these two gentlemen of Verona may shed a bit more light on the ghostly Valentine.

Who is he really? In a sense Valentine is a possibly subliminal double of the play's lover-hero Romeo. By virtue of that ancestry they share—

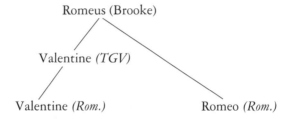

a certain equivalence or deep identity obtains between Valentine and Romeo. I call Valentine a possibly subliminal double because, while Shakespeare would hardly have been unaware of his earlier use of the name in *The Two Gentlemen of Verona,* and while the various associations noted above for the name would have been available to him, nevertheless those associations seem unobtrusive enough to have gone unnoticed in the quick forge and working house of thought. Even the precise bearing of the earlier tale of Verona on the new one may well have been, in rhe phrase of Armstrong (*Imagination,* p. 55); "below the level of full awareness" on Shakespeare's part.

However conscious it was, the evolution that leads to Mercutio's brother Valentine looks something like the following. The potential triangle from Brooke—Mercutio . . . Juliet . . . Romeo—with each young man holding one of Juliet's hands, and with the men perhaps not even acquaintances, undergoes a sea change as it comes into Shakespeare, where, in its new configuration— Mercutio . . . Romeo . . . Juliet—Romeo has traded places with Juliet and taken the center for himself. Brooke's empty Romeo-Mercutio bond is thus filled, with a friendship strong as brotherhood, and simultaneously the Mercutio-Juliet bond is erased. And thus Mercutio's first mention in *Romeo and Juliet* marks him as brotherly rather than amorous, and at the same time, as it were, creates the role Romeo is to fill, that of Mercutio's amorous brother.

The question of Mercutio himself remains. Why, that is, should Shakespeare have found the sketchy portrayal in Brooke worthy of, or necessitating, its huge development—of which the generation of a ghost Valentine is after all a minor component—in the movement into the play? Who really was the Mercutio Shakespeare found, who did he become, and how, and why? Such are the sorts of questions the remainder of this study attempts to answer. And as with Valentine, so the more with Mercutio: throughout, I assume that the answers I propose must be at once provisional and overdetermined, complex and incomplete. Jones (Review, p. 359) expresses a nearly universal assumption when he writes that "Shakespeare's method of composition, much of which was no doubt outside his conscious control, was complexly accretive." The same may be said of the long communal thought process in which a particular god, Mercury, composes himself to become a major constituent of Shakespeare's Mercutio. Similarly with that character's transformation through four centuries. That is, just as with the thresholds Valentine passes to appear for half a line in *Romeo and Juliet,* so too as we turn to Valentine's brother Mercutio: the evolutionary crossings are complex in the extreme, and tracing some parts of them involves considerable shuttling back and forth in the intertextual web.[13]

Notes

1. Gibbons, *Romeo and Juliet,* 1980. Unless otherwise noted, all quotations from *Romeo* are from this edition. Quotations from other Shakespeare works are from Harbage, *Works,* 1977, unless otherwise noted.

2. J. J. Munro, ed., Brooke's *"Romeus and Juliet" Being the Original of Shakespeare's "Romeo and Juliet";* quotation is from this edition.

3. See Bullough, *Sources,* p. 272, and Gibbons, *Romeo,* p. 34. The cold hands come into the story with Bandello's source da Porto.

4. Given *Two Gentlemen*'s casting of Proteus as the less true lover, the phonetic chime Proteus-Romeus may have felt inappropriate to Shakespeare and so figured in his rejection of Brooke's form of the hero's name. The charged Mercutio passage in Brooke is intriguing for its general emphasis on the manual (ll. 259, 260–62, 264, 289–90), which in Shakespeare informs the opening interchanges of Romeo and Juliet (1.5.92–103), and for its careful specification that Mercutio takes Juliet's right, Romeo her left hand. Tilley (*Proverbs*) lists as H84 (1666) "The left hand is the hand of the heart."

5. The two St. Valentines with 14 February as their feast day are (1) a priest of Rome and (2) a bishop of Terni, both third century. According to Attwater the supposed acts of (1) seem to derive from those of two other saints, while (2) is only a doublet of (1). "There is nothing in either Valentine legend to account for the custom of choosing a partner of the opposite sex and sending 'valentines' on 14 February; it apparently arose from the old idea that birds begin to pair on that date, but it may have a more remote pagan origin" (Attwater, *Dictionary of Saints,* p. 334). The "old idea" about birds is referred to by Theseus: "Saint Valentine is past. / Begin these woodbirds but to couple now?" (*MND* 4.1.138–39). See Tilley S66 (1477), "On Saint Valentine's Day all the birds in couples do join." Dent, *Language,* p. 204, calls the idea "more folklore than proverb." Jenkins, in his note to Ophelia's song about St. Valentine's day, says that Valentine means "sweetheart according to the ancient custom which recognized as such the first person of the opposite sex seen on St. Valentine's day" (Jenkins, *Ham.*

4.5.51n). Kelly, *Chaucer,* pp. 120–27, holds that Chaucer commemorates the marriage of Richard II and Anne of Bohemia by associating St. Valentine with lovers.

6.   The lost first *Valentine and Orson* (to which I return below) could have just preceded *Romeo and Juliet* since it was registered in 1595, the generally accepted date for *Romeo and Juliet.* Berger and Bradford, *Index of Characters,* list dramatic uses of the name. Intriguing but beyond the scope of this study are Shakespeare's later uses of the name, especially in *Measure for Measure* ("Valentinus") with its ghostly Juliet.

7.   Noted by Leech, *TGV,* pp. xliii–xliv, Gibbons, *Rom.,* pp. 27–29, and others.

8.   Leech (*TGV,* p. xxxv) concludes that the composition of *Two Gentlemen* extends through several phases from 1592 to late 1593. An additional link in the Brooke-Valentine association, as was noted by Leech (*TGV* 1.2.12n), is the name "Mercatio" mentioned in *Two Gentlemen,* effecting a chime with Mercutio (see below, chap. 5).

9.   See Dickson's Introduction to *Valentine and Orson,* 1937. Probable dates for the three editions are 1503–5, 1548–58, 1565–67.

10.   For Thomas Gosson and Raffe Hancock, 23 May 1595, "Entred for theire Copie an enterlude of Valentyne and Orsson, plaid by hir maiesties Players" (*Register,* 2:298). The second play of the same title, by Hathaway and Munday, is from 1598, listed by Henslowe, *Diary,* 1:90 and 2:195.

11.   Peck, *Dictionary,* pp. 1630–31, surveys the brothers' history. For the Code see Pharr, *Theodosian Code,* and the bibliography for sixteenth-century anthologies of sententiae. John Fletcher's play *Valentinian* is about a different emperor, Valentinian III.

12.   Romei, *Courtiers,* sig. H4 (printed by Valentine [!] Sims, 1598). The speaker Barisano is cited by Henderson, *Family,* pp. 152–67, as an analogue of Mercutio. Since the book, at least in its English version, postdates *Romeo and Juliet,* the names of its author and printer are probably coincidental. (Valentine Sims, or Simmes, printed *R2, 1H4, 2H4, Ado,* and *Ham.* 1597–1604.) Ferguson (*Simmes*) nowhere suggests that the printer would have been on Shakespeare's mind in 1595.

13.   Most of this introduction, in substantially the same form, appeared in *South Atlantic Review* as "Mercutio's Brother."

Mercutio's Shakespeare

JOSEPH A. PORTER

Clifford Leech, "The Moral Tragedy of *Romeo and Juliet,*" p. 73, holds that "moral tragedy" is a contradiction in terms since "tragedy is necessarily at odds with the moral: it is concerned with a permanent anguishing situation, not with one that can either be put right or be instrumental in teaching the survivors to do better." He finds a certain sanguineness about the conclusion of the play that prevents the deaths of the lovers from achieving genuine tragic status. The sanguineness, according to Leech, inheres in the "long-drawn-out ending, after the lovers are dead, with the pressing home of the moral that their deaths will bring peace" (p. 73), which features themselves derive from the tradition of sixteenth-century moral drama, a tradition Shakespeare in *Romeo and Juliet* has not yet "worked as free from . . . as Marlowe had done in *Tamburlaine, Faustus,* and *Edward II*" (p. 73).

It might seem to some that Leech's finding of a however restrained san-guineness grants insufficient weight to the "glooming . . . sorrow . . . sad . . . woe" of the Prince's final speech, but the question is a nice one of emphasis, and it seems likely that most playgoers and readers through most of this century would find themselves in substantial agreement with Leech that the woeful story of Juliet and her Romeo falls short of the tragic idea embodied in *Hamlet, Othello, King Lear,* and *Macbeth.*[1]

What Leech says about Mercutio, however, would seem likely to be a good deal more surprising to most of the play's audience in this century until very recently, and even now it would seem easily the most controversial of his claims about the play. I quote at some length because Leech's observations seem to me to stand as a landmark of the revision of character, play, and author. Even though the titular characters fall short of tragedy, Leech writes,

> Even so, there is a small achieved tragedy embodied within this play. I have described Mercutio as "daemonic," and that is an adjective we can appropri-ately apply to every tragic hero: he has fire within him . . . and the fire ulti-mately consumes. We can call this "hubris," but the rashness implied in that

word is not a matter for moral comment. . . . Mercutio, careless of what may come . . . draws his sword and goes to his death. His last words are ironic and resentful. . . . No lesson is drawn from this destruction; there is no suggestion that good may come out of it. It has simply happened, to the world's impover-ishment. . . . [The Queen Mab speech] puts Mercutio outside the general Christian framework of the play. . . . his last call is for a surgeon, not a priest. There is an angriness in him that is a link with Hamlet, Othello, Lear, Mac-beth: . . . their final acts are those of men standing alone, without help from the general current of thought in their world, with a full realization too of their loneliness. Here . . . we find the true germ of Shakespeare's later development. One may suspect that Mercutio haunted this playwright, that the character and his death provided a foundation on which the later tragedies could be securely built. ("Moral Tragedy," pp. 74–75)

In the context of the previous chapter these remarkable observations, with which the present study is very much in accord, exemplify a further stage in Mercutio's evolution, and reveal some of the ways his transformation, still in progress, figures in the transformations of his play, his author, and his audience. This concluding chapter considers these matters in three somewhat artificially separated ways. First I treat Mercutio as an index of larger cultural and critical changes he participates in, with particular attention to the issue of postfeminist criticism. Then from a different vantage I treat him as a particu-lar kind of poststructuralist and postmodernist entity, the diachronic dramatic character. Finally I treat Mercutio as constitutive or catalytic, as I consider changes currently under way in our understanding of Shakespeare—which is to say, in our understanding.

Although Leech includes Zeffirelli by extension among recent directors whose handling of the Queen Mab speech he disapproves of,[2] in fact Leech's Mercu-tio continues in the same general direction as Zeffirelli's, a direction of recov-ery from the various kinds of reduction, suppression, containment, and mar-ginalization that intervene between 1595 and the recent past, reaching their peak with the peak of Victorianism. But Leech's Mercutio proceeds along that road, or at least one branch of it, well past Zeffirelli's. Indeed in Leech Mercu-tio goes well beyond restoration of his Shakespearean prominence, and he pulls after him the entire play. In Leech Mercutio stands forth as the rightful, if not the actual, titular character of *The Tragedy of. . . .*[3]

It is an extraordinary itinerary that runs from the simultaneously subor-dinated and foregrounded god of boundary and agora, calculation and dream, through Shakespeare's gallant spirit and saucy merchant, and through his decline and marginalization during the seventeenth and eighteenth centuries to his nineteenth-century nadir, followed by his twentieth-century recovery and increasing centrality. As Brown and Burkert show with the earliest portions of that itinerary, so with every succeeding step of the way: it reflects prevail-ing cultural and political constructs of many sorts. The present study, primarily in chapters 4–6, has paid most attention to a single stage of that journey, the moment in 1595 when Brooke's trace Mercutio flowers in Shakespeare's mind. Any other stage of the journey might repay equivalent attention, and one other stage, the present, is inevitably of particular interest. Inevitably too, that stage, whether invoked or not, is more or less legible in everything said above. It seems well, then, here to invoke that stage once more in a consideration of a contradiction apparent in the present critical assessment of Mercutio. For, as will be remembered, current feminist and psychoanalytic assessments run decidedly counter to Leech's. But this current contradiction reveals itself most fruitfully, I believe, when it is set in relief against a particular stage of Mercutio's itinerary.

The Victorian documentation of the previous chapter may have seemed almost superfluous inasmuch as even the most nodding acquaintance with the period and with Mercutio would lead to the conclusion that this must be the nadir of his journey. Of course his bawdiness grows most indecorous then, and much else about him does also. In an age celebrating domesticity and middle-class marriage, Mercutio's ranging liminality and his scorn of love and houses grow exceptionally indecorous. So too does his frank corporeality even when it is not bawdy, and so too his traces of misogyny. The story of male attitudes toward women during Victoria's reign is a long one still being told, but there seems at the moment to be at least something of a consensus suggesting that the obverse of the familiar sentimentalization is a rapacious degradation. By contrast, Mercutio's light intermittent misogyny comes across as a reflex of a fundamental lack of interest in women. While this stance of his, with antecedents in Mercury and in Marlowe, is restrained by the fact that it first takes shape under a female monarch, at the same time the stance is authorized by her own mercurial holding off from marriage—whereas Victoria by her own example stood firmly for marriage and married procreation. Other rationales for the suppression of Mercutio may also be found in Victorian England. An empire the sun never sets on, for instance, might be expected to have peculiarly little use for a liminal figure descended from the god of borders.[4]

Mercutio's recovery from the extremes of Victorian censorship, then, may be read as an index of the supercession of these Victorian verities. Analogously his present status indicates verities of ours. In particular, his present status is a function of changes and hindrances to change in the realm of gender relations. Specifically, Mercutio's current contradictory assessments seem to mark a crisis in the evolution of feminist critical thought.

It can hardly be accidental that, as discussed above in chapter 6, Mercutio's post-Victorian advance in status meets roadblocks in feminist accounts. His advance, especially in its acceleration over the past two or three decades, is most obviously an index of a nearly unprecedented lessening of moralistic censorship combined with a widespread interest in sexual matters, an interest so vigorous as to have been at times obsessive. Mercutio, with his easy bawdy and, perhaps more important, his quick contempt for what may be called the antibawdy, thus finds a more receptive audience in the present than he has found since Shakespeare's time. Similarly, a sophisticated and variously materialist (and anti-idealist) time such as ours naturally finds Mercutio to its taste. But these reasons for Mercutio's advance in status seem not to lie behind the feminist resistance to that advance. True, some of our time's kinds of materialism and interest in sexuality are unquestionably antifeminist and antihumanist, but here, despite feminist sniping at him, I find Mercutio largely innocent. The causes of the sniping seem to lie elsewhere.

The continuing recognition of Mercutio's importance, not only in his play but also in his author's development—Shakespearean tragedy itself, at least in Leech's view, stems from Mercutio—that recognition depends on numerous features of the present moment, including our increasing enfranchisement of the previously marginal, our increasing reluctance to be bound by received interpretations and constructions of "reality," and our increased familiarity with the entirely realistic and unsentimentalized possibility of entire absolute loss. But if this much seems clear, the question remains, why the new reactionary feminist attempts to contain and suppress Mercutio?

A documented answer to the question is obviously beyond the scope of this study, but the preceding consideration of Mercutio may provide the basis for an educated hypothesis. In brief, Mercutio by his phallocentrism, his scorn of heterosexual love, and his own invulnerability to the wounds of heterosexual love, seems subversive to the project of feminist (and psychoanalytic) criticism of a certain sort, that project being the continuing politicization and prescriptivization of gender and affectional orientation, in ways that exclude Mercutio. The contemporary impulse toward a re-reduction of Mercutio then, is an index of an important, and probably inherent, inadequacy in the feminist critical stance. For that stance itself is paradoxical: feminism as a reaction to antifeminism tends to render itself superfluous by its successes, and yet no beachhead as hard won as the feminist is likely to be abandoned easily.[5] It is for some such reason, I believe, that feminist criticism, which is effecting revolutionary change in our understanding of much of Shakespeare, stalls and turns regressive when it comes to Mercutio.

But such need not be the case. Mercutio's light intermittent misogyny does not in the least entail antifeminism. It may well be that Romeo's and even Juliet's stances may come to seem antihumanist and so antifeminist—there is reason to suppose that some such evolution is under way—but as for Mercutio, his stance seems postfeminist rather than antifeminist. What he bodes fair to indicate for criticism at the present moment is whether the gains made by feminism will seem sufficient, and we stall in an equally tyrannical negation of the old sexist tyranny, or whether we will be able to make our way into a genuine postfeminism that subsumes the gains of feminism.

In the preceding pages I have intentionally refrained from any careful acknowledgment at every turn that Mercutio is fictional, and indeed I have at times let myself speak of him as if he were not fictional. In part the procedure grew out of simple curiosity about a fashion so old as no longer even to be démodé. So much time has passed since we concerned ourselves with Lady Macbeth's children, and we are so irreversibly insulated from that sort of naiveté, that we may permit ourselves to slip into the old garment, if only for the sake of gratifying some nostalgic curiosity about how wearing it might have felt, even though we know that that curiosity can only be gratified with a sense of knowledge, and never with knowledge itself.

Then too we have progressed so far in our understanding of the constructedness—indeed the fictionality—of the "true" and the "real" that, even though in a general way we routinely distinguish between personages like Mercutio and persons like Shakespeare, like ourselves, still any careful policing of the border would seem at present to be a waste of troop strength at best.

But the main reason for my letting myself sometimes talk about Mercutio much in the way I talk about Shakespeare has to do with the postmodernist disintegrationist denial of the usefulness, and even the very viability, of the notion of fictional character or personhood, a matter addressed briefly above in "Part Two: Shakespeare's Mercutio" and to which I return for a moment here, to say once more that I find the position untenable. The commonplace about Shakespeare's characters' seeming more real than real people may have worn threadbare as praise, but its psychological basis seems as sound as ever, for surely we all automatically think of all fictional personages as if they were real persons. We make the initial assumption that personages are persons not only because they are so meant—so conceived by their authors—but also because it is otherwise nearly impossible for us to find any mental purchase on a fiction. The "we" here is meant to include all of us who concern ourselves in any way with fictional personages—the student taking care to spell Nausicaa correctly, the machinist amused by Dagwood's morning adventure, the critical polemicist staking a new claim. We think of fictional people as real in part for the same reason we think of real people as real: it is the only way to arrive at any coherence.

Of course at the same time, as noted, we routinely distinguish between fictional and nonfictional people. Among the numerous grounds we employ for the distinction, one seems especially noteworthy here. With luck, Dagwood will continue to solve a new problem every morning of the future, but leaving him aside for the present we may say that a basic difference between Mercutio and Shakespeare is that with Mercutio we suppose we have the full dossier, at least at one level—an unsurpassably complete record of what he says and hears, all that he does and all that is done to him—whereas with Shakespeare we feel sure that more evidence may always come to light and that, furthermore, however much is included, with him as with us the dossier can never approach completeness.

With real persons the availability of information varies considerably in degree and kind, as is made clear by a moment's reflection about the vastly different ways we develop a sense of the characters of acquaintances, public figures, and historical figures such as Shakespeare and Elizabeth I. The similar and perhaps commensurate variety of accessibility that obtains with fictional personages is exemplified by the two with which the present study has been concerned. Mercury like all gods has a long and only partly recoverable history of communal production and modification, a history that includes denials of his fictionality. To Shakespeare, as to us, Mercury is accessible in the manifold treated above, a manifold that is distinctive to Mercury among gods in innumerable ways, including in particular the fairly distinctive combination of his great popularity, the nearly complete absence of ecclesiastical bodies instituted for the canonization and promulgation of his story, and the exceptional complexity of his own array of characterizing traits. The avenues of Mercury's accessibility to us, as perhaps also to Shakespeare, include the other fictional character with which this study is concerned, the modes and degrees of whose accessibility to us differ in turn in countless ways from the god's.

The foregoing study seems to bear especially on two determinants on Mercutio's accessibility to us. I wish briefly to postpone review of one of these determinants, Mercutio's authorship, as we look back for a moment at the other, his dramaticality.[6] And here, among the (again) innumerable ways in which the exigencies of genre make dramatic personages distinctive, two are of particular note, and both are functions of the performability of drama.

First, there is the foregroundedness that dramatic characters seem not to share with fictional personages of any other sort. It derives from the fact that we have direct access to nothing more of an entirely fictional dramatic character than the things said and done in the character's play(s), of which the most significant are obviously the speeches assigned to the character himself by his name in the speech headings. In narrative, the other mega-genre with significant room for character (character in lyric being generally variously diffused, displaced, or otherwise absent), the narrator may provide many sorts of additional information about a fictional personage, and may provide the information with various colorings and degrees of specificity or summary, so that of necessity a fictional personage in narrative has at least a potential—and therefore actual, in the paradoxical logic operative here—kind of depth or penumbra denied dramatic characters. A dramatic character by contrast is quite determinate. Since no narrator stands between Mercutio and us, we may witness his story immediately.

But on the other hand Mercutio varies from performer to performer, indeed from performance to performance, and he is meant for performance.

Herein a dramatic character is more endlessly mutable, and so more indeterminate, than any other sort of fictional personage. Received as he was meant to be received, in performance, Mercutio appears only as played in a certain way by a particular actor in a given production of *Romeo and Juliet*. Thus the actor and the production have a mediating role in the constitution and transmission of fictional character analogous to that of the narrator in narrative, but arguably still more interventionist. While in a narrative the narrator stands apart from the character presented in various ways including the fact that the narrator generally has an existence independent of the characters presented, in performed drama an absolute linkage between character and mediating performer makes the performance so interventionist as to seem constitutive. At the same time, actors in plays act as you sing prick song, speaking the already written part, enacting the written gestures and acts. The hierophantic and scribal Mercury seems to hover over the fact that the authorial strings of written characters that make up a part, a dramatic character, efface themselves in any realization of the part in performance. And yet at the same time, at least in so literary a medium as Shakespearean drama, the writtenness of the spoken words, their authoredness, calls attention to itself steadily, as is not the case, for instance (except inadvertently) with such other scripted spoken words as those we may hear in television soaps and sitcoms.

These distinctive attributes of dramatic character seem to make Mercutio more susceptible than nondramatic characters to the kind of poststructuralist consideration undertaken above. The notion of character operative here is poststructuralist inasmuch as, while availing itself of structuralist methods and insights, it does not bind itself by them. The structuralist (and modernist) component of the study treats Mercutio as a product of the contrastive relations distinguishing him from other characters in his play. This mode of conceptualization of characters derives, of course, from Saussurean synchronic linguistic analysis as well as from both modernist and new-critical assumptions about the unity and integrity of the individual work of art. It serves in some of the contrastive descriptions of Mercutio's characterizing speech acts and his characterizing bawdy, and more generally in the prevailing sense of him as mutually determinative with the rest of his play. But I have hardly been bound to the structuralist axiom that would make Mercutio inseparable from—that is, meaningless apart from—his play. The poststructuralist (and postmodernist) component of the foregoing does treat Mercutio as separable from, meaningful apart from, his play. In a sense the poststructuralism of the notion of character operative here manifests itself most conspicuously in an absence—the absence of any programmatic corresponding attention to the rest of the cast list.[7] The poststructuralism of the foregoing is, incidentally, closely analogous with its postfeminism: here too the method aims to incorporate insights and discoveries of a preceding critical moment even as it moves beyond limitations inherent in that moment.

Poststructuralist separability and isolatability of dramatic character as conceived here figures importantly in one additional feature of the foregoing consideration of Mercutio. Indeed separability would seem a precondition for the treatment of Mercutio as a diachronic entity. The linguistic model is very apt: just as a lexical or a syntactic unit of a language may be described diachronically, more or less separately from the rest of its language, as a single evolutionary history of which all parts are invoked, so with "Mercutio" as described here. The diachronic Mercutio manifests the operation of numerous, perhaps innumerable, general principles and other determinants governing his history, determinants that may similarly govern many other such histories, as with the nineteenth-century sentimentalization and bowdlerization, or that may govern relatively few, as with the mercurial deathliness shading Mercutio's ongoing corporeality. The sum of those determinants, however, must surely be unique for any so substantial a character as Mercutio.

When I was beginning this study and described to a colleague the little I could then see of what it was I wanted to find out, she asked whether what I envisioned wasn't simply a source study. Even though she hastened to assure me that there was nothing wrong with source study, I resisted concurring, without then being able to justify the resistance beyond saying that the phrase didn't quite seem to mark the route I expected to be traveling. A clearer explanation seems possible now. The term "source study" seems wrong for the present inquiry for two particular reasons, each having to do with one extremity of the history I have been writing considered as a determinate line. On the one hand the Derridean deconstruction of the Western story of origination has variously discredited the old notion of the source as point of origin. On the other hand, while a source study generally takes a particular point in a history—1595, 1988—as its terminus and culmination, the end of the voyage and the vantage point for its survey, the present study's preconceptions are somewhat different. It is true that I have dwelt more on 1595 than on any other moment in the history, and that the present moment of Shakespeare study in the 1980s has also frequently been in view. But the diachronic Mercutio here in view is no more stable now than he ever was. This study is itself one part of an evolution that will continue well after it, if anything does.

Finally we may consider briefly wherein the Shakespeare entailed and revealed by this Mercutio seems distinctive. One need not have any particular Shakespeare study in hand to be aware that, as with Mercutio, so with "Shakespeare": the entity in question is highly variable. At present, one need only have an ear to the ground for an awareness that Shakespeare seems to be in a state of flux proceeding with unusual rapidity and depth. Furthermore, while some research projects might imaginably insulate one from awareness of the flux, the present study seems to have had rather the opposite effect on me. I wish therefore in the space remaining briefly to address the subject of Shakespeare's diachronicity, and then finally to look momentarily at some of the ways the creator of this study's Mercutio differs from other Shakespeares.

A significant part of the current general historicization of all semiological systems including, in particular, those most of us were taught to think of as literary and more or less canonical, has been the historicization of Shakespeare. Jonathan Dollimore and Alan Sinfield (*Political Shakespeare*, 1984), John Drakakis (*Alternative Shakespeares*, 1985), and Terence Hawkes (*That Shakespeherean Rag*, 1986) come to mind as but three notable works among many that have lately helped lay bare the contingent and diachronically variable constitutedness of "Shakespeare," as well as some of the forces and stakes involved in his constitution. It seems unlikely that in the foreseeable future Shakespeare will regain the semblance of immutability and immediacy that attends him through nearly all of his preceding history, and that happens to gain greatest strength and confidence just when (as now seems) his transformations are most extreme, as in the nineteenth century. It also seems unlikely that we have yet made available to consciousness or brought into question all we need about Shakespeare's diachronicity.

The Mercutio surveyed here provides a good index of Shakespeare's diachronic variation. Across the range of Shakespearean characters there is, of course, no uniformity of degree of variation through time. Alongside such comparatively stable characters as Rosalind and Macbeth, others vary appreciably. Isabella, Hal, and Shylock come immediately to mind as examples of comparatively protean beings who pull their plays, and their plays' author, after them in their transmutations. Shylock's transmutations, the best known of these, certainly outdo Mercutio's in terms of elicited or hypothesized general public attitude toward him, but the two cases resemble each other in terms of generic conventions supposed appropriate. And in fact the amplitude of Mercutio's swing between near-vanishing marginality and essential centrality as the unique exemplar of the genre named in his play's title exceeds anything comparable with Shylock or, I believe, with any other Shakespearean character. Thus while Rosalind or Macbeth or, to name cases closer to hand, Romeo and Juliet, contribute (to date at least) to the stability of "Shakespeare," Mercutio is an outstanding member of that smaller band of characters who catalyze change there.

With respect to the question of Shakespeare's own stability or his instability of whatever form, all parties are of course interested. Recent Marxists, feminists, and deconstructionists have in their various ways brought forcefully to our attention the complex of interests and interested assumptions that determine the repeated denial, from Jonson's "not of an age" down to the present, of Shakespeare's contingency and diachronic variation. In its present form that complex comprises most of the various sorts of investments made in maintaining the Shakespeare "industry" much in its present form, as well as a number of predictable philosophical and political commitments. On the other hand, those showing us the undisinterestedness of proponents of an invariant Shakespeare are themselves interested, as they more or less readily admit. They have their own various sorts of investments in decisive change in the Shakespeare industry, as well as their own more or less predictable philosophical and political commitments. Similar states of affairs obtain with other literary texts, but the battle being joined in Shakespeare studies is exceptional in at least two related respects. The stakes are higher because of the very size of the Shakespeare industry. More important, the stakes are also higher because in Anglophone culture Shakespeare's works are the most canonical of the received canon of literary texts.

One particular kind of change in Shakespeare that seems possible, and is even being forecast by some, is his displacement from the centered position he still generally holds in Anglophone culture, and even his marginalization. Some general benefit would necessarily attend such a change, but I (interested as anyone) must here record my sense that the general cost would very far outweigh any benefit. And, without arguing for the case, I do wish to suggest how part of such an argument might be mounted. It seems to me that the marginalization of Shakespeare would have one regrettable effect shared by the denial of his diachronic variation: in both cases some of the valuable history, not only of Shakespeare but also of Anglophone culture as a whole, is suppressed. A fundamental tenet of all the foregoing is the partial legibility of Shakespeare as a palimpsest, the partial recoverability of his diachronic mark. Because of the continuity and centrality of that mark, then, to see or read Shakespeare is to track who we ourselves have been for the past four hundred years, and also well before. The linguistic metaphor is helpful again. Some words in our language seem more or less key or central, and, although they may always be used as if there were no etymology, and they may always be shunted out of a vocabulary, still they seem to me to serve us best when kept in use, and used with a consciousness of their histories.

But should the marginalization of "Shakespeare" come to pass,[8] it may be that the Shakespeare of this study's Mercutio has already faced such an eventuality better than, say, Garrick's or Gentleman's or Barrymore's Mercutio's Shakespeare, and better than the Shakespeares of the corresponding Romeos and Juliets. Our Mercutio's Shakespeare of 1595 has in fact himself not yet quite found his way to the sovereignty he very soon begins to exercise, but Mercutio blooming in his mind is showing him the way there. That way lies past the gilded monuments of princes and the gold effigies of lovers, past institutional sanctions and pieties, and beyond authoritative determination. This Shakespeare's way to sovereignty is a never quite complete withdrawal, from fratricide and perhaps from friendship too, a withdrawal already far advanced in Mercutio's play, where Shakespeare's will already can give way to the conjuring, the call to the wild margins, and the welcome there.

Notes

1.   There would be considerable agreement in the seventeenth, eighteenth, and nineteenth centuries as well, although numerous factors, notably including the establishment of the chronology of the canon, and Bradley's *Shakespearean Tragedy,* would tend to make twentieth-century agreement with Leech's general estimation more substantial. In the middle-to-late nineteenth century, when *Romeo and Juliet* seems to have had its best track record in the Shakespearean sweepstakes, it may have nosed past *Othello* and *King Lear,* but there was always *Hamlet.* The nineteenth-century ending of the play with Juliet's death, incidentally, could be seen as an attempt (which now looks abortive) to make the lovers' tale of woe more tragic by removing the "long-drawn-out ending" whose moralizing Leech, p. 73, finds antitragic.

2.   "But we can guess that the speech prefigures the death [of Mercutio] and that Shakespeare knew . . . that its speaker was soon to die. That does not excuse the crassness of some recent directors who have made the actor of Mercutio's part show a trepidation of his own when, near the end of the speech, he refers to a soldier's dream: our anguish at his death is all the more poignant if he does not show fear or anticipation" (Leech, "Moral Tragedy," p. 74). As I read Zeffirelli's handling of the moment, however, Mercutio's trepidation is nothing like so self-centered as Leech suggests. Rather he seems to have a kind of passing premonition of all the woe to come.

3.   Titularity and marginality converge similarly, and actually, in *The Merchant of Venice* with its other important resonances with *Romeo and Juliet.*Conceived as *The Tragedy of Mercutio,* Mercutio's play of course has a still longer drawn-out ending after the hero's death, an ending whose length is paralleled in Shakespeare only in *Julius Caesar.* While the length, in Leech's eyes, might be antitragic, the "ending" that follows Mercutio's death has an authentically tragic absence of rationalization and an equally authentic demonstration of deleterious effects of the hero's fall in his world.

4.   The model of Victorian England could have affected Mercutio outside the empire as well as inside. A detailed comparison of what happens to him concurrently in the United States would be of interest.

5.   Jehlen, "Archimedes," considers the importance for feminist criticism of this familiar difficulty faced by all movements born in reaction to a prevailing injustice. "Denial always runs the risk of merely shaping itself in the negative image of what it rejects" (pp. 585–86). The current dichotomy in assessments of Mercutio derives not only from the nineteenth- and early-twentieth-century one apparent in the manifestations of Mercutio treated in chapter 7 but also from the dichotomy apparent in the criticism surveyed in McArthur, "Friend," p. 40: "If we . . . survey as a whole the field of criticism . . . we see that . . . the boundaries . . . are oriented about the Johnson-Dryden polarity of Shakespeare the immutable genius versus Shakespeare the clever but antiquated Elizabethan poet." With Johnson McArthur places Schlegel, Coleridge, Bernard Shaw, L. L. Schücking, E. K. Chambers, H. B. Charlton, and Dover Wilson; on Dryden's side stand Voltaire, Goethe, and Tieck. McArthur's own position is a sentimental recuperation of the "unity" of *Romeo* by demonstrating that "even the Queen Mab scene may be read as part of the whole" (p. 44; cf. Henley, "Mab").

6.   These remarks about character and drama carry forward the inquiry begun in my *The Drama of Speech Acts,* pp. 162–66. Indeed the present study's general concern with the entity named Mercutio has many affinities with the earlier study's treatment of dramatic language as verbal action performed by actors such as Mercutio.

7.   I have paid especially little attention to Paris. More than once, having given a colleague some account of the present study, I have then been asked, "But what will you do with Paris?" But the assumption that to do something with any character(s) in a play means that one must do something with all of them is a structuralist and modernist assumption that is unnecessary.

8.   Considering these matters is a bit like "thinking the unthinkable" in some secluded room of the White House or the Pentagon. The occasional vague forecasts of Shakespeare's marginalization that I have encountered have for the most part been off-the-record, but it is easy to find their traces in print, as when Jehlen, "Archimedes," p. 579, claims that any feminism or protofeminism must automatically be devalued and discounted if it is discovered in Shakespeare since "from a feminist standpoint, he was a misogynist." Although the marginalization of Shakespeare does not seem to me particularly likely, it is certainly thinkable and there is precedent in the Western tradition, perhaps most notably in the effective marginalization of Virgil.

THE TEXT SEXED

◆

From the first stages of his career Shakespeare often foregrounds the written-ness—the textuality—of his plays, perhaps most notably in *Titus Andronicus,* the one tragedy preceding *Romeo and Juliet.* In *Titus Andronicus,* in fact, the effect—as with the overlong displays of elaborate figuration—is so pronounced as to seem inadvertent to some.

In *Romeo and Juliet,* Shakespeare has the effect much more under control as he incorporates an ambient hyperliterariness—this being his most literary play to its date, and in some respects the most literary in his canon—in vivid evocations of the quickness of the desirable, vulnerable, sexual body. Hence the play has proven peculiarly germane in recent explorations of what might be called the sex-text nexus.

Gayle Whittier, "The Sonnet's Body and the Body Sonnetized in *Romeo and Juliet,*" addresses the play's use of its Petrarchan and sonneteering inheritance. Finding dramatic and tragic reductions and materializations both of word and spirit, Whittier takes into new territory a thematic reading of a topic that figures prominently in earlier commentary.

In Catherine Belsey, "The Name of the Rose in *Romeo and Juliet,*" metaphysical perplexities in the desire of the young lovers forecast Enlightenment mind-body dualism, and at the same time, by belying that simplification, open ways into postmodern understanding of the human organism's inextricability from culture. In passing, Belsey shows how fundamentally Shakespearean are some of Jacques Derrida's most influential insights.

Jonathan Goldberg, "*Romeo and Juliet*'s Open Rs," turns a Derridean and Shakespearean appreciation of the instability of signification to the service of demonstrating the inadequacy—the present untenability, Goldberg maintains—of prescriptively heterosexist accounts of the play. Goldberg shows how the play's open and unruly identifications across gender, as manifest in verbal play, ground the most bracing and liberating reassessments.

Current Shakespearean interests of Gayle Whittier, Associate Professor of English at Binghamton, include the iconography of Elizabeth I.

Catherine Belsey chairs the Centre for Critical and Cultural Theory at the University of Wales, Cardiff. Her books include *The Subject of Tragedy: Identity and Difference in Renaissance Drama, John Milton: Language, Gender, Power,* and *Desire: Love Stories in Western Culture.*

Jonathan Goldberg, Professor of English at Duke, is the author of *Sodometries: Renaissance Texts, Modern Sexualities, Writing Matter: From the Hands of the English Renaissance, Voice Terminal Echo: Postmodernism and English Renaissance Texts,* and other studies of early modern writing. He is the editor of *The Sodomy Reader* and *Queering the Renaissance.*

The Sonnet's Body and the Body
Sonnetized in *Romeo and Juliet*

GAYLE WHITTIER

When Mercutio names Romeo's inherited malady—"Now is he for the numbers that Petrarch flow'd in . . ." (2.4.38–39)[1]—he places Petrarch as Romeo's literary "father," the poetic counterpart of the dynastic father whose verbal legacy Juliet sees as dangerous: "Deny thy father and refuse thy name . . ." (2.2.34). In Mercutio's allusion, renewal remembers inheritance; there is no escape, familial or poetic, from the influence of a preexisting word. This was true for Shakespeare as for Romeo, since he wrote at or near Petrarch's English zenith, though after the time of Petrarch's greatest Continental influence. That realizing Petrarchan conventions can be fatal is a familiar argument, but in *Romeo and Juliet* the inherited Petrarchan word becomes English flesh by declining from lyric freedom to tragic fact through a transaction that sonnetizes the body, diminishes the body of the sonnet, and scatters the terms of the *blason du corps*.[2]

In fact *Romeo and Juliet* opens with a Petrarchan inheritance in the reliquary of the Prologue's English sonnet, an inheritance that endures structurally but endures emptied of its traditional lyric treasures—the lovesick persona, dense metaphor, emotional extremity, song itself: all these have been supplanted by public narrative. "Two households," not "two lovers," opens the poem; "story" rather than lyric is the genre to be dramatized. Even the liquidity of Petrarchan time—liturgical, natural, personal, and aesthetic—cramps to an explicit reckoning of "two hours," reducing the brief lifespans of the lovers and their even briefer love to countable theatrical "traffic." The surviving sonnet itself sustains a narrative burden more fitting for an entire sequence. No longer a poetic end in itself, the sonnet serves as a means to a dramatic issue. Some Petrarchan verve lingers in the loose and ironic paradox of "civil blood making civil hands unclean" and in the tighter oxymoron

Gayle Whittier, "The Sonnet's Body and the Body Sonnetized in *Romeo and Juliet*," *Shakespeare Quarterly* 40 (1989): 27–41. Reprinted with permission of *Shakespeare Quarterly*.

"fatal loins," but the closing couplet emphasizes a triumph of the prosaic over the lyrical, bequeathing its tired theatrical appeal in wooden prosody:

> The which if you with patient ears attend,
> What here shall miss, our toil shall strive to mend.
> (Prologue, ll. 13–14)[3]

If sonnet form has lost its furor, however, the living volatility of the word, freed from it, erupts in the play's first dialogue, Sampson and Gregory's inelegant chain of "coals," "colliers," "choler," and "collar" (1.1.1–5). Were these four terms contracted, they might comprise a quadruple pun. Unlike a true pun, the sequence evolves in and through felt time. Like a true pun, however, it generates meaning out of sound, setting the phonetic shape of language above the intentionality of the speakers. They do not choose their words; the words, in a sense, choose them. Their talk of love and war, a kind of displaced contest, becomes deliberate and active only at the sight of the Montagues: "My naked weapon is out. Quarrel, I will back thee" (1.1.34). Though the counterword of the law, formal and written, is briefly acknowledged, gesture preempts language: "I will bite my thumb at them, which is disgrace to them if they bear it" (1.1.42–43). And on the airy word "better"—Gregory's emphasis lifts the word from its syntactic matrix and, in a kind of verbal bas-relief, half-objectifies it—the negotiable word yields to fact: "What, drawn and talk of peace?" (1.1.70). A pattern of negative incarnation has taken place against which the prince's spoken decree comes, as usual, too late.

The play's opening, then, establishes the fact that the sonnet form, even when exhausted, will generate dramatic event;[4] that there is a sovereignty in language that subordinates the intention of the speaker and precipitates fact; and that the human word, unlike God's in Genesis, destroys, and destroys in the warp of syntax, the process of dialogue over time. To what degree, then, does this residual and fatal power live on in the inherited poetic word? And to what degree is the body of the poetic word subject to entropy and destruction?

Romeo himself springs forth from the mouth of his father as a recitation inherited from the pages of a courtly miscellany, described but not seen as the topos of the languishing lover.[5] In this persona he suffers less from love than from his desire to live out artistic imitation, to make himself "an artificial [k]night," in worried Montague's pun (1.1.140). Petrarch's is the book he kisses by, but LaRochefoucauld perhaps makes the better case for him: "There are people who would never have fallen in love but for hearing love discussed" (maxim 136).[6] (Juliet, too, is first presented verbally, but as an object of exchange between her father and Paris.)

As apprentice lover-poet, Romeo yearns for a suitably unattainable lady. Rosaline, always a word rather than a presence, bears a name that might entitle a sonnet cycle and that resonates with the love tradition (the *Romance of the Rose,* the rose-form vision of the *Paradiso,* and the ubiquitous symbol of feminine beauty). Like the rose in her name, she will be nominal and brief. When, practicing before Benvolio, Romeo composes his love for her, he produces something itself misshapen, juvenile, resembling a sonnet truncated and inverted:

> Why then, O brawling love! O loving hate!
> O any thing, of nothing first create!
> O heavy lightness, serious vanity,
> Misshapen chaos of well-seeming forms,
> Feather of lead, bright smoke, cold fire, sick health,
> Still-waking sleep, that is not what it is!
> This love feel I, that feel no love in this.
>
> (1.1.176–82)

His "O brawling love" perhaps refers to the brawl he has narrowly missed; almost at once, however, he leaves the world of referentiality as he heaps oxymoron on oxymoron, setting even a Continental record. Romeo's poetic excess reveals emotional deficiency; perhaps his true confession comes last: "I . . . feel no love in this." He himself is aware of being slightly ridiculous. "Dost thou not laugh?" he wonders (1.1.183).

Yet he improves with practice (1.1.185–94) and even achieves some stereotypical poetic balance in his encomium on Rosaline's chastity, a portrait without fleshly detail except for an unPetrarchan "lap" which will not open even to gold (1.1.205–15). In this respect Romeo's praise is as bodiless as his love itself. Still, he looks to the flesh, faltering in his poetic fathers' footsteps and perhaps even borrowing from Shakespeare's own (perhaps concurrent) sonnets urging a young man to marry:

> O, she is rich in beauty, only poor
> That, when she dies, with beauty dies her store.
>
> (1.1.215–16)

Unlike the earlier and feebler "is" / "this" rhyme (1.1.181–82), this later attempt at a closing couplet, though trite, at least achieves the firmness of a sonnet's *pointe.* Significantly, Romeo does not attain poetic mastery at the sight of Juliet; his apprenticeship begins before he sees her, reaches some perfection, and requires sequentiality, subjugation to the world of time, to an influence Juliet catalyzes but does not beget.

Beyond poetic forms, Romeo seeks to become the *author* of the persona he imitates, an artificer born out of an artifact. That is, he would create his own pre-creation, and so preempt inheritance. Appropriately, Romeo's subsequent legacy to his real father will be a letter, written—as is the Petrarchan script in which he first reads his borrowed poetic being. For the moment, innocently and awkwardly, he tries out the difficult and dangerous Petrarchan word. It is difficult in that, while all poetry, if not all language, balances the dream of transcending time and space over the referential facts of limitation, separation, and death (". . . the poet, he nothing affirms and therefore never lieth. . . ."[7]), the Petrarchan word is especially non-referential, with its obvious hyperbole, celestial compliments, and paradox. It is dangerous in that, where the word is performative, Romeo lives out its terms in a referential way, ultimately converting himself from life to "story." When Romeo falls in love with a love already *scripted* as otherworldly and then seeks to dramatize that script, he falls into the living power of an inherited word, which, like fleshly inheritance, bestows *both* life *and* death. Nor will the poetic word submit to a patient Veronese domestication.

Romeo probably fails to recognize the performative and potentially deadly power of poetry because he is so drawn to *its* beauty (not Rosaline's, whose specific physical qualities he scarcely mentions). Lady Capulet, less poetic but at least as naive, wrongly trusts in her own power over the word, wresting it from subject to subject—"Marry, that 'marry' is the very theme / I came to talk of . . ." (1.3.63–64)—and concealing a family commandment under the gracious inquiry, "How stands your dispositions to be married?" (1.65). Advertising Paris, she pays romance its poetic due badly and briefly, turning him from flesh to word and getting stuck midway, at the conceit of a "book of love" (1.3.81–94). Her dominant image betrays her poetry's borrowed source, for it surely does not arise out of lived experience: her carefully coupled rhymes and labored wit ("married lineaments," for example) sound stilted and rehearsed, a collusion between art and dynasty. She speaks, in effect, a written poem.[8] Yet even in her derivative, imperfectly wrought lines, the poetry itself takes metrical revenge, reversing abruptly from masculine to feminine rhyme on the double entendre of "lover" / "cover." Momentarily, Lady Capulet jolts off course, resorting to a new, unintegrated image—"The fish lives in the sea. . . ."—then, recovering the covered book, she descends from the clasp of saints' legends, Golden Story, to a dynastic gold which matters more when the couplet couples: "So shall you share all that he doth possess, / By having him, making yourself no less." Unlike Romeo, she believes a virgin not only may, but *must* open her lap to gold. Gold proves as portable, as instrumental, as is poetry itself to this lady. Its associations are carried even lower by the Nurse, from book to treasure cache to body: "No less! nay, bigger: women grow by men" (l. 95). As for Juliet, she, like her mother and old Capulet, who casually advises Paris to "get her heart" (1.2.16), has no proper fear of the transformative power of either Eros or the poetic word. Her promise, "I'll look to like, if looking liking move" (1.3.97), rattles on the ear like the child's nonsense that it is. She, too, plays with the deadly arrows of Petrarchan metaphor, but sees herself immune: ". . . no more deep will I endart mine eye / Than your consent gives strength to make it fly" (ll. 98–99).

Yet if Romeo and Juliet are naively attracted by Petrarchan conventions, they move in a world where Shakespeare transmutes those conventions to serve the dramatic conspiracy between word and world.[9] For instance, he bends the courtly relic of antithesis so that its opposing terms reciprocate. When Romeo declares that Juliet "seems [to hang] upon the cheek of night / As a rich jewel in an Ethiop's ear" (1.5.45–46), the simile is a Shakespearean original (as if to imply that visionary inspiration has placed Romeo beyond imitation altogether). The jewel simultaneously "shines" because of its dark foil and metaphorizes that foil, for the "rich jewel" both symbolizes Juliet's beauty and gives her name. Not only does the jewel require the backdrop of darkness, then, it reciprocates with it *through* the metaphor, flesh to flesh. Romeo sees Juliet as a word, her name ("Jule" / Jewel) juxtaposed to body, but arising from it. While antithesis is usually the core of Petrarchan dilemma, its terms here, so displaced yet locked, enforce our consciousness of the conjunctive bond, the mysterious cooperation, between good and evil, the beating heart of tragic sensibility. As an extreme verbal condensation of antithesis, oxymoron, an important figure in this play, even serves as an index to characters' tragic educations.[10]

Romeo's celebrated collection of oxymorons in Act 1, already cited, defines a love that is spoken but unlived—the very speed of the sequence prevents the experience of any single trope in it—as well as an overabundance of figures in quest of form. Yet the oxymoron ultimately defines the carnal knowledge of a love in which life and death intertwine. Therefore Juliet expresses contradiction only after she meets Romeo: "My only love sprung from my only hate!" With contradiction comes a recognition of time: "Too early seen unknown, and known too late" (1.5.138–39). After Romeo murders Tybalt, Juliet learns the full power of antithesis, moving from contradiction to oxymoron and then out again (3.2.73 ff.). It is her movement out of the oxymoronic knot that rebuilds the comic possibility for her marriage, but the shadow of the past falls over the dialogue. Juliet's "Was ever book containing such vile matter / So fairly bound?" (3.2.83–84) recalls her mother's librarianship of Paris's image—recalls, in fact, that earlier time when Juliet herself had not yet "dreamed" of marriage, when time itself was imprecisely innocent. Now "what day is that?" Juliet asks of her proposed marriage to Paris, and the day is fixed: "Marry, my child, early next Thursday morn" (3.5.111–12). Not without irony, in the scene where Juliet loses her linguistic innocence, the Nurse echoes Juliet's own innocent denial of the power of the word in Act 2, scene 2: "O Romeo, Romeo! / Who ever would have thought it? Romeo!" (3.2.41–42). The oxymoron's concentrated verbal form empowers contradiction to enter the tragic world of time. Shakespeare not only moves the Petrarchan oxymoron from the decorative to the thematic, but he also makes of it the figure for tragic sensibility itself, and, indeed, for the very structure of the play, since Mercutio's death provides the generic pivot between its oxymoronic halves of the comic dream of a freely creative word and the tragic fact of *things*.[11]

As the Shakespearean oxymoron forces poetry into the world of "uncomfortable time," so Shakespeare also spatializes and embodies the metaphors and situations of the Petrarchan inheritance. They, too, cannot survive purely and verbally on the stage of the world or of the playhouse, for both theatres demand a referentiality at odds with unworldly and transcendent metaphor. Shakespeare translates the courtly exchange of sexual identities—for example, the lady as "lord" whose eyes shoot fatal arrows, etc.; the lover as pining, lamenting, flowing sufferer—into dramatized psychology and setting. He thus risks moving a symbolic transaction from lyric concept (the sublime androgyne) to dramatic embodiment (the grotesque).[12] The Nurse urges, "Stand up, stand up, stand, and you be a man" (3.3.88), while the Friar perceives more of the grotesque than the sublime when he upbraids Romeo: "Art thou a man? Thy form cries out thou art; / Thy tears are womanish . . ." (3.3.109–10). Even Juliet, about to sue for Romeo's hand as Paris does for hers, recognizes her maiden modesty as circumstantial: "Thou knowest the mask of night is on my face, / Else would a maiden blush bepaint my cheek" (2.2.85–86). In the epithalamic soliloquy of Act 3, scene 2, Shakespeare assigns Juliet a poetic form traditionally sung by a man, one that shows an atypical, unblushing, eager bride.[13] Her soliloquizing itself (here and at the beginning of Act 2, scene 5, in Act 4, scene 3, and elsewhere) further indicates a sexual role reversal, since Shakespeare customarily reserves the soliloquy for the male protagonist in a tragedy.[14] The poetic forms that Juliet uses, then, draw attention to her gender, to her body; in lyric poetry, both sexes may fit "to one neutral thing," but drama embodies and temporalizes. Only in the lovers' deaths is sexual decorum restored when Juliet follows Romeo's lead as he has followed her false one. With that, the androgynous dream of poetry is over. The body must be reacknowledged. But the displaced Petrarchan poetic word meanwhile has turned into Shakespearean dramatic flesh.

Shakespeare also materializes customarily worshipful Petrarchan attitudes in setting and architecture, locating Juliet literally above and/or beyond Romeo in the night garden: ". . . for thou art / As glorious to this night, being o'er my head, / As is a winged messenger of heaven . . ." (2.2.26–28). Although Romeo claims to have entered the walled garden on a metaphor, "with love's light wings" (2.2.66), the geographical gap between him and Juliet silently reminds us that we are not in a world of poetic transcendence, but in a world of finite things. Imaged as his "sun," Juliet in fact vacillates in terms of both her philosophical and her physical position. As the scene ends, her literal instability increases. She appears, disappears, reappears—at best an inconstant body, no fixed star. In embodying the Petrarchan word, Shakespeare warps it into the referentialities of the world and of the Globe.

That Juliet is, in fact, *seen* violates poetic custom and must realign Petrarchan metaphor. Traditionally, the spiritualized lady, even when she has a real-life counterpart, is "seen" only through the poet's selective presentation of her in a redeeming *blason du corps féminin,* her body heraldized. But the *blason,* which seems to honor the body, in fact appropriates it, dismembers it,[15] and often fragments flesh and blood into the metaphoric flowers and minerals of "cheeks like roses," "lips like rubies," etc. The *blason* therefore removes the woman from the human realm, which is, after all, the Platonic lover's aim. (Against this dehumanization Shakespeare wrote "My mistress' eyes are nothing like the sun. . . ." The aesthetic joke, however, is on him: in order to dismiss "false compare," he had to include it.)

In *Romeo and Juliet* the *blason* does occur but never in reference to Juliet herself. In 2.1 it is Rosaline's poetically dismembered form that Mercutio enumerates in a brief and naughty parody of the genre. Where the courtly lover contents himself with the beloved's upper parts and makes poetic use of them (as Lady Capulet sought to do with Paris's face), Mercutio moves from the top down, then from the ground up, ending in the generative midst of things:

> I conjure thee by Rosaline's bright eyes,
> By her high forehead and her scarlet lip,
> By her fine foot, straight leg, and quivering thigh,
> And all demesnes that there adjacent lie. . . .
>
> (2.1.17–20)

Falling as it does between the lovers' encounter sonnet (1.5) and the garden scene (2.2), Mercutio's bawdy, intended to reclaim Romeo to himself and the "real" world, exposes a poetry that has forgotten the flesh. Since he has neither seen nor known Juliet, Mercutio does not take mock-poetic liberties with her. But his anatomical "ascent" is, like Romeo's climb to Juliet's chamber, a philosophical descent. Presently he falls to indecency:

> O Romeo, that she were, O, that she were
> An open-arse, thou a pop'rin pear!
>
> (2.1.37–38)

Nor has he worn out the parodic possibilities of courtly description, animalized in his comment on the Nurse—

> An old hare hoar,
> And an old hare hoar,
> Is very good meat in Lent;
> But a hare that is hoar
> Is too much for a score
> When it hoars ere it be spent. . . .
>
> (2.4.134–39)

—vulgarity he underscores with the satiric refrain of "lady, lady, lady" (1.144). The Nurse, in turn, plays off her unerotic bodily ailments against the verbal news of Romeo's wedding plans, then undercuts the *blason*'s hyperboles with a variation in prose: "Romeo! no, not he. Though his face be better than any man's, yet his leg excels all men's, and for a hand and a foot and a body, though they be not to be talk'd on, yet they are past compare" (2.5.39–43).

Juliet herself negatively blazons Romeo in her famous "What's Montague? It is nor hand nor foot, / Nor arm nor face, nor any other part / Belonging to a man" (2.2.40–42). In dismissing his name, she scatters his body, even as she later sees his corpse cut into complimentary stars for heaven (3.2.22). For Juliet, the body is not idealized through words. It supersedes words, as she herself both is and symbolizes embodiment in the tragic arena. (We might see the play as Romeo's [the poem's] search for Juliet [the flesh].) Significantly, she specifically unlinks reality from the word "rose," a standard courtly symbol for *feminine* beauty. Although she becomes more reverently poetic as the play goes on—Romeo and Juliet contract pragmatism and lyricism from one another, respectively—she begins as a disperser of poetic convention and "form" itself.

Where Juliet undercuts Petrarchan compliment, Romeo exceeds it. Juliet's sheer visibility ought to limit the freedom of poetic metaphor by inviting despoiling comparison with physical fact; but when the hyperbolic and the explicit collide, Romeo does not forego, but rather surpasses, even Petrarchan hyperbole.[16] If tradition calls the lady's eyes celestial bodies, then Romeo removes the very sun from the sky: "It is the east, and Juliet is the sun" (2.2.3). Similarly, her eyes are not *like* stars, nor have the heavens bent down to her; rather, "Two of the fairest stars in all the heaven, / Having some business, do entreat her eyes / To twinkle in their spheres till they return" (2.2.15–17). The effect is to remove the celestial point of comparison by a kind of poetic imperialism that substitutes the lady for it. Though the verbal shape of a comparison remains, Romeo's is less an exercise in metaphor than a displacement of heaven by Juliet. In his poetic vision she is the body of the cosmos.

Romeo's earlier saint/shrine metaphor comes nearer earth and is one of the variant *blasons* of the play. Scripturally the body is a temple, but in order for hers to be a shrine, Juliet must first die (this is the prerequisite to canonization). A shrine typically contains a saint's relics, *fragments* of the hallowed body, as a *blason* contains poetic fragments of the living form it elevates. By a kind of dramatic metonymy, the "shrine" makes Juliet both "the container and the contained."[17] As symbol and symbolized in one, Juliet imitates Logos, but a human logos, the word of death. Shakespeare's reworking of Petrarchan metaphor, then, should perhaps be expected, for metaphor is the world's body imagined in the poem, even as the poem's body is a metaphor for the world outside it. In a play that treats the fatal negotiation between voice and flesh, metaphor itself must negotiate its place.

Only briefly, in the lovers' co-created encounter sonnet (1.5.93 ff.), do voice and flesh reciprocate, both through the bodies of the lovers and the body of the poem they speak. Yet even here, while seeming to elevate it to a religious mystery, the poetic word actually deals on behalf of the flesh. Romeo's "mannerly devotion" hides the English "manly" and the French word for hand, *la main,* while his possible desecration of his saint's body ("If I profane with my unworthiest hand . . .") seeks penance in a deeper trespass, "My lips, two blushing pilgrims, ready stand / To smooth that rough touch with a tender kiss" (1.5.93–96). It is Romeo, of course, who takes the poetic initiative, opens the sonnet, and determines its dominant conceit. Juliet responds, but ultimately loses this poetic contest as, in Act 3, scene 2, she determines to "lose a winning match, / Play'd for a pair of stainless maiden-hoods" (ll. 12–13). But if Romeo's words seem to win out over Juliet's momentary (and socially correct) reluctance, it is in her more material medium, flesh itself, that the sonnet concludes with a pair of kisses. As A. J. Earl observes, "the kiss that the troubadours and their latterday heirs, the Elizabethans, had yearned for, is granted in this sonnet" (p. 116). More precisely, the kiss is granted after the sonnet concludes, but in Romeo's voice, as if extended in a fifteenth sonnet line: "Thus, from my lips, by thine, my sin is purg'd." Romeo's "thus" requires that we actually see what he refers to: we cannot simply hear it as a poetic conceit. And, of course, kissing puts out speech. Since a poem's seeming autonomy depends, in Sidney's words, on affirming nothing, this moment marks both the silencing of the poetic speaker and the *sonnet's* corruption into the world of substance and time. (One reader even finds that another, abortive, sonnet follows the first kiss and ends in a second one.[18])

The past further challenges renewal as Shakespeare casts the shadow of its Italian pre-existence over the English sonnet, Romeo delivering eight lines (a broken octave) to Juliet's six (the sestet). Furthermore, the whole of the sonnet is seamed by its antiphonal structure as dialogue rather than mono-logue. The sonnet weds inheritance and exuberance, poem and body, only for the moment. Then its context, the room of interruptions and other public voices, impinges on the private ceremony. Poetic form itself begins to disinte-grate, and a greater tension between poem and flesh subsequently shapes the dialogue in the garden (2.2). There the lovers' betrothal, itself bridging the night when Juliet proposes it and the day when Romeo responds, potentiates (but does not fulfill) the physical consummation of marriage. Promising to supplant language with the new body of matrimony, "one flesh," the dialogue first disrobes Petrarchan poetry, fiery disembodied fragments of which, uncontained by poetic form, radiate as if from the force of their encounter.

In Act 2, scene 2, then, against the backdrop of a Petrarchan situation made geographical, form gives way to a beautiful and unbound shower of fig-ures of speech in which Romeo lifts improbable comparison to impossible identity, then inaugurates his play-long descent from the sun to the angelic messenger and downward into the tomb. Himself wordbound—he would be satisfied with "th' exchange of thy love's faithful vows for mine" (2.2.127)— he is nevertheless ironically inspired by a lady who herself first appears both mute and speaking, then speaks to deny the referential force of language.

Juliet discloses what we all secretly know, that names are both arbitrary *and* consequential. Though she proposes a facile solution ("Doff thy name . . ." in exchange for her flesh), her linguistic dilemma is obvious: in order to dismiss the power of words, she must speak them. And in her desire to separate the name from the body, the Montague family history from Romeo, she goes too far, as Harry Levin observes: "[Juliet] calls into question not merely Romeo's name, but—by implication—all names, forms, conventions, sophistications, and arbitrary dictates of society, as opposed to the appeal of instinct directly conveyed in the odor of a rose."[19] Significantly, when she assigns Romeo the *unnamed* attributes of the flower associated with the lady in courtly custom, she defies the effectiveness of language even to name the body (much less to shape it), and, with that defiance, she rejects even the fragments of the *blason du corps* as a verbal possession of the beloved's flesh. She supplants words with her own body in "take all myself," but the exchange is untenable. Within lines, Juliet fears an oath that will be negatively performative: "O, swear not by the moon, th' inconstant moon, . . . / Lest that thy love prove likewise variable" (2.2.109–11). As the scene ends, she addresses Romeo by the very name she thought he should doff, the "fair Montague" she means to share and to become. Although love's furor inspires her to create the poetic body of a verbal paradox—". . . the more I give to thee, / The more I have, for both [sea and love] are infinite" (2.2.134–35)— her "infinite" comes up against the Nurse's vocal reminder of interrupting finitude. Juliet's ultimate position places her within her antipoetic family. She readily harnesses Eros in social form: "If that thy bent of love be honorable, / Thy purpose marriage, send me word to-morrow," and on a secular schedule, "Where and what time thou wilt perform the rite" (ll. 143–44, 146). Romeo, in turn, will have her loyalty—and her dowry. Her denial of words and Romeo's faith in them are equally extreme; locus and fact will correct both exaggerations in the tomb.

For each of the virgin lovers, a new tragic knowledge intervenes between the vows (word) and the consummation (body) of their love—that is, the knowledge of death and death's companion, time. We sense its imminence in the compression of Juliet's epithalamion, for, despite its classical elements, her soliloquy has the pacing, if not the sentiment, of a *carpe diem* poem. Romeo, meanwhile, discovers that talk of peace cannot prevent the action of violence, even his own violence in recompense for verbally witty Mercutio, the man who played with language and in whose revenge Romeo slays Tybalt, who "hate[d] the word" (1.1.70). Juliet, in her turn, finds that the poetic word of paradox, which she first learned at the feast and in the night garden, must itself be resolved divisively in the world: she opts for Romeo over Tybalt, for the name she would have had Romeo put off in 2.2. If to age means to know the end of language's illusory transcendence, then in this interval the lovers age, a verbal loss of innocence preceding and paralleling their physical loss of innocence. Both must confront the word in its public, inherited, and negative form as "banished," against which poetry itself frays, even ruptures.

After the consummation of their marriage, the lovers become each other's body, "one flesh," but their aubade in response to sunrise has, unlike the sonnet, no predestined body of its own, though it does share, with flesh, an inexorable occasion. On the morning after their wedding night, they relearn the divisive method by which God creates, the separation of light from darkness, as opposed to the poetic synthesis of "day in night" they sought, for they experience the separation of husband from wife. They therefore do not co-create the aubade harmoniously, as they did the sonnet: they argue its terms. The seams in the dialogue are wider; reality wins out. "It is, it is! . . . / It is the lark that sings so out of tune" (3.5.26–27). For while the social world has always impinged on their poetic co-creation, they are now adversaries of a higher, external, and indifferently turning universe, that very cosmos that Romeo metaphorically appropriated and Juliet displaced earlier (2.2).

Juliet's body next *incorporates* antithesis, day and night as correlatives of her "living death." The floral metaphors of the courtly tradition materialize in the potion the Friar has concocted from "baleful weeds and precious-juiced flowers" (2.3.8). When, on entering Juliet's chamber on the morning of her wedding to Paris, the Nurse briefly begins an epithalamion appropriate to the waking of the bride, the form aborts into a cacophonous lament.[20] As body preempts voice, the properties for a wedding—instruments and flowers— prove interchangeable with those for a funeral, but poetic form does not.

Out of the operatic competition of voices,[21] Capulet structures an epitaph:

> O son, the night before thy wedding-day
> Hath Death lain with thy wife. There she lies,
> Flower as she was, deflowered by him.
> (4.5.35–37)

Capulet is not an original man, though he shows traces of the poetic, as if he were an aged Romeo. His epitaph is more translation than invention, derived from models in the Renaissance sourcebook *The Greek Anthology*, where the high number of epitaphs on dead brides suggests a strange Hellenic epidemic.[22] Capulet's classical borrowing underscores his own advancing years, the death of his dynasty, and the continuum of death through which poetic influence may run unchanged from ancient Greece to the Italian Renaissance. It announces the continuity of verbal influence and inheritance (the legacy of the word), opposing it to the broken legacy of the flesh (the Capulet dynasty).

In the tomb the lovers' linguistic and fleshly debts fall due. Drawn by report (rather than by the more incorporated writ that sent him to the

Capulets' feast), Romeo encounters the brutal fact of applied mortality, though it is, of course, false fact (in that Juliet is not really dead) or the fact of the body's falseness (in that she will die). Juliet's formerly poeticized uniqueness is undercut by her presence in a common tomb, no fine and private place, but a grisly parody of the communion of the saints, wherein the dead, the living, and the unborn coexist. Here the dead fester in their several ages of corruption. Against this bodily spectacle Romeo resorts to the topoi of the siege of love and the tempest-tossed lover to resurrect his poetic vision, transposing a victory by Petrarchan conceit between himself and Juliet's corpse: "Death . . . / Hath had no power yet upon thy beauty: / Thou art *not conquer'd, beauty's ensign* yet / Is *crimson* in thy *lips* and in thy *cheeks*" (5.3.92–95; my emphasis).

Ironically, the poetic vision is now *true:* Juliet is not dead. But Romeo no longer trusts bodily appearance, and he therefore does not test word against flesh, appearance against touch. His use of "crimson" inevitably evokes the rose as a symbol of brief beauty, appropriate for the scene (Paris, we recall, arrives to strew literal flowers on the corpse); but even the metaphors of beauty have vanished, the "rose / By any other word" (2.2.43–44) now a nameless rose. Were it not for the precedents of tradition, which so often liken cheeks and lips to this specific flower, we would not imagine it. The spectral rose, like the "honey of thy breath," is the vestige of a *blason du corps.* For Romeo, too, the rose bears an *unspeakable* association because he has never seen his beloved as brief and mortal. She is an eternal principle of wholeness to him. But now her body has *parts,* "lips" and "cheeks," and the poetic "crimson" darkens into the real and mortal stain of Tybalt's body in its "bloody sheets."[23]

With Juliet's death, Romeo also discovers the otherness of his own body, a final *migration du coeur.* In a ghostly *blason du corps* he addresses those very parts that Juliet sought to divorce from names in Act 2: "Eyes, look your last! / Arms, take your last embrace! and, lips, . . . seal with a righteous kiss / A dateless bargain to engrossing death" (5.3.112–15). Juliet then wakes, as Adam did, from a profound sleep—only to find her bridegroom dead. Against the promissory word of transcendence, she—and we—witness the irrevocable referential fact of the unglorified body. Juliet has seen this death before, in a waking vision that inverts courtly custom (3.5.55–56). (The male lover usually imagines the female beloved's death, and that in a dream.) Romeo, too, in an inversion of Petrarchan convention, has envisioned himself dead (5.1.6–9). But where Juliet's graphic vision proves true, Romeo's more hopeful one is only half prophetic, for, though he does die, Juliet's restorative kiss cannot resurrect him.

What of the sonnet's body? Inherited as a strewing—Petrarch named some of his works strewn or scattered, *Rime sparse*—the sonnet undergoes further disintegration in *Romeo and Juliet,* where it is weakened by a disequilibrium between narrative and lyrical impulses.[24] The narrative impulse, dominating the prologues to Acts 1 and 2, is historical in direction, stylistically prosaic rather than lyrical, choric in tone, and theatrically referential, addressing events we will see or have seen staged. The lyrical impulse, dominating the lovers' encounter sonnet (1.5), is prophetic in direction, spiritual and erotic in transcendent metaphor, emotional in tone, and intrinsically non-referential, though pressed into the service of incarnation. Where the dominantly narrative sonnet enforces a documentary distance from the artistic imagination, with the Prologue cautioning the audience that Verona is a fiction "where we lay our scene" and that the time frame of the play itself is artificially compressed into "two hours' traffic," the private song boldly intercedes on behalf of poetic fantasy enfleshed as passionate fact.

Narrative and lyricism balance only briefly, in the encounter sonnet of 1.5. Thereafter, lyricism fragments into glowing figures of speech that, perhaps because of their very ultra-Petrarchan extremity, escape any structural confinement (2.2). The more narrative sonnet sustains form (Chorus, Act 2) but, despite its few oxymoronic acknowledgements, falls short of Petrarchan transcendence. It is as if flesh (the narrative sonnet, bound to time and fact) ruptures from spirit (the lyric impulse of the sonnet, unbound even by the linear shape of its predetermined form) and engages in a Neoplatonic negotiation. Both flesh and spirit prove mortal, however. The narrative sonnet is absorbed into the drama to which it refers, subsumed by referentiality; the lyrical content, after exploding into the fiery tropes of the night garden dialogue, fades, undergoing a resurrection only in the Petrarchan relics of Romeo's eulogy in the Capulets' tomb (5.3). Ultimately, narrative structures a sonnet's body lacking a spirit, while extreme lyricism ensouls without form.

Whether dominantly narrative or lyrical, however, the sonnets in *Romeo and Juliet* recollect anatomy, each verbal body reflecting the fleshly, mortal one. The hands and lips of Romeo's encounter sonnet exist both as poetic word and as visible parts of his and Juliet's flesh. The play's Prologue contains a more general evocation of "civil blood" on "civil hands." And the two bodies reciprocate in "fatal loins," an oxymoron that may be heard as a pun on the close Elizabethan pronunciation of "fatal lines." "Fatal," derived from the past participle of the Latin "to speak," suggests, then, *spoken* lines.[25] In fact the "spoken lines" of the Prologue predestine the plot of the play to be tragic from without, even as the spirit of Petrarchan poetry spoken by Romeo to Juliet finally necessitates their tragic deaths from within. "Fatal lines" lies in the surviving sonnet's body, as death, the original inheritance, lies in the "fatal loins" of our conceptions.

A corresponding dispersal displaces the metonymic *blason du corps,* in which human anatomy itself is strewn as poetic word. In a circular configuration, the sonnet has yielded to partition much like that the *blason* imposes on the blazoned woman's parts. Juliet herself is never explicitly blazoned—contrary to tradition—precisely because to describe her would embody (or disembody) her twofold function as actual person and as the *source* of the poetic word. But the sonnet form "breaks" against her body or, to state it otherwise, against her embodiment and embodying of the poetic spirit, which she comes to symbolize.[26]

Following the deaths of the lovers, the Veronese survivors briefly glimpse the tragic nexus of contraries, not in words, but in the bodies found still warm and, in Juliet's case, still bleeding: an ambiguous but nevertheless fixed boundary between the antitheses of life and death. Yet recognizing and voicing the tragic nexus is not socially useful. As the prince commands, "Seal up the mouth of outrage for a while, / Till we can clear these ambiguities, / And know their spring" (5.3.216–18). His focus is on causality, not mystery: *What happened?* A piecemeal documentary reassembles the facts of the plot, almost as bare now as in the Prologue's "story." For the prince's purpose is not to endorse ambiguity in the fragile equilibrium of poetic paradox but to insure social order. This requires that the lovers be interpreted in terms of public fiction, namely, the claim that their deaths were "not in vain," and that they are (presumably deliberate) "sacrifices of [their parents'] enmity" (5.3.304). (Romeo and Juliet themselves never entertain such a notion, though the pious Friar does. If anything, they overestimate parental enmity to increase the erotic dare.)

The play concludes, then, on the social or dynastic use of language in a marriage contract decreed between the households, though there is no dowry but only a jointure, or widow's portion, to distribute. Unlike the poetry co-created by the lovers, the social poetry at the end of Act 5 is meant to seal, to *close* experience, not to open the speaker to the full force of a lived metaphor. Thus the lyric spirit of the sonnet expires with the lovers, and even its structural remains undergo a kind of amputation in the prince's solemn shaping of the last lines into a foreshortened and vestigial sonnet of one quatrain and a closing couplet. In his verse, social interpretation undercuts both tragic sentiment and poetic fantasy:

> A glooming peace this morning with it brings,
> The sun, for sorrow, will not show his head.
> Go hence to have more talk of these sad things;
> Some shall be pardon'd, and some punished:
> For never was a story of more woe
> Than this of Juliet and her Romeo.
>
> (5.3.305–10)

The marriage of poetic word and flesh remains promissory as the surviving fathers, linking hands in poignant parody of the lovers' first meeting, agree to set up the images of Romeo and Juliet as golden effigies. Perhaps these effigies symbolize "gods of idolatry" in a love religion; certainly they are false, unregenerative bodies. But in them the ancient dream of a poetic word made flesh returns: the lovers' bodies and the metaphors of light through which the lovers beheld them are conjoined, stilled, in the medium of public, solid gold.

Notes

This essay is in memory of Philip Friedheim.

1. This and all references to the text of *Romeo and Juliet* follow *The Riverside Shakespeare,* ed. G. Blakemore Evans (Boston: Houghton Mifflin, 1974). To avoid confusion with my own occasional use of square brackets within quotes, the Riverside brackets have been removed.

2. For the purposes of this essay, "Petrarchan" refers to the general conventions of courtly love rather than to Petrarch's specific poems, since Shakespeare was probably not directly acquainted with Continental models. In this sense, what I call "Petrarchan inheritance" is really the *image* of an influence widely disseminated by Shakespeare's time. For general background, see Leonard Forster, *The Icy Fire: Five Studies in European Petrarchism* (London: Cambridge Univ. Press, 1969), esp. pp. 50–51. More specifically on *Romeo and Juliet,* see Nicholas Brooke, *Shakespeare's Early Tragedies* (London: Methuen, 1968), pp. 80–106; Rosalie Colie, *Shakespeare's "Living Art"* (Princeton, N.J.: Princeton Univ. Press, 1974), pp. 135–67; A. J. Earl, "*Romeo and Juliet* and the Elizabethan Sonnets," *English,* 27 (1978), 99–119; Winifred Nowottny, "Shakespeare's Tragedies," in *Shakespeare's World,* eds. James Sutherland and Joel Hurstfield (London: Edward Arnold, 1964); and Jill Levenson, "The Definition of Love: Shakespeare's Phrasing in *Romeo and Juliet,*" *Shakespeare Studies,* XV (1982), 21–36. For the *blason,* see Nancy Vickers, " 'The blazon of sweet beauty's best': Shakespeare's *Lucrece,*" in *Shakespeare and the Question of Theory,* eds. Patricia Parker and Geoffrey Hartman (New York and London: Methuen, 1985), pp. 95–115; and "The Body Re-membered: Petrarchan Lyric and the Strategies of Description," in *Mimesis: from Mirror to Method, Augustine to Descartes,* eds. John D. Lyons and Stephen G. Nichols, Jr. (Hanover and London: Univ. Press of New England, 1982). Joel Fineman emphasizes the exhaustion of the sonnet form in his *Shakespeare's Perjured Eye* (Berkeley: Univ. of California Press, 1986), in which he notes that the "sonneteering tradition" that precedes Shakespeare, based as it is in England on "a poetic mode already done and overdone elsewhere . . . is fully aware of the fact that epideictic 'likeness' is translated into something different when subjected to excessive repetition" (pp. 188–89).

3. See Levenson, p. 23, for a different sense of the Prologue sonnet: "It stands at the beginning of the tragedy as a replica in little of the familiar story–the cliché clichéd. In a poetic tour de force, Shakespeare reduces that verbose narrative to the exacting form which served as the main vehicle of Petrarchism." In any case, the sonnet *as a form* of poetic fashion was well past its prime in the 1590s, though fashionable in England, where Petrarch was both lauded and parodied. Perhaps it is that very decadence Shakespeare meant to indicate before the poetic resurrection of the form (and even the form's spirit) in the play itself. Nicholas Brooke suggests this resurrective movement: "The opening movement of the play is recapitulated in a rapid development from bustling prose to lusty verse to the full dance and Romeo and Juliet encountering in a full-blown sonnet" (p. 95). Ultimately he finds the play ". . . a highly perceptive exploration of the love-death embrace of the sonneteering tradition, which regards both its superiority and its inferiority to the world of common day" (p. 106).

4. My reading parallels Rosalie Colie's sense of the "unmetaphoring" of the play: ". . . we can see very plainly the problem of expression: Petrarchan language, *the* vehicle for amorous emotion, can be used merely as the cliché which Mercutio and Benvolio criticize; or, it can be earned by a lover's experience of the profound oppositions to which that rhetoric of oxymoron points" (p. 143); and, ". . . *Romeo and Juliet* makes some marvelous technical manipulations. One of the most pleasurable, for me, of Shakespeare's many talents is his 'unmetaphoring' of literary devices, his sinking of the conventions back into what, he somehow persuades us, is 'reality,' his trick of making a verbal convention part of the scene, the action, or the psychology of the play itself" (p. 145).

5. See Earl, pp. 103–8.

6. *The Maxims of LaRochefoucauld,* trans. Louis Kronenberger (New York: Random House, 1959), p. 136.

7. Sir Philip Sidney, *An Apology for Poetry*, ed. Geoffrey Shepherd (Edinburgh: Thomas Nelson and Sons, 1965), p. 123.

8. Writ generally functions in a negative way in Shakespeare's tragedies. It *seems* to maximize the transcendental potential of all language, since one can carry a letter farther than a human voice carries, and since a document may outlast its scribe. But ultimately its triumph over time and space proves provisional: by being material, the writ *resubjects* language to the accidents of time and space. Tybalt, then, a man of destructive action, sends a letter of challenge to Romeo; because he has seen the name of Rosaline inscribed on a guest list, Romeo attends the Capulets' feast, where he will meet death; and the Friar's letter to Romeo in Mantua is not delivered (it *returns* rather than transcends). When Romeo adopts the Petrarchan conventions, he falls in love with a kind of writ.

9. See Earl for a larger treatment of Shakespeare transmutations of Petrarchan conventions.

10. See Robert O. Evans, *The Osier Cage: Rhetorical Devices in Romeo and Juliet* (Lexington: Univ. of Kentucky Press, 1966), especially his chapter "*Oxymoron* as Key to Structure," pp. 18–41. It is Brooke, however, who sees Mercutio's death as pivotal: "The whole play is challenged and re-directed by this scene. The genre in which it is conceived is set sharply against a sense of actuality as Mercutio dies the way men do die—accidentally, irrelevantly, ridiculously; in a word, prosaically. . . . The shock of this scene is used to precipitate a change of key in the play: it becomes immediately more serious, and decisively tragic where before it had been predominantly comic" (p. 83).

11. Inescapably, one notices that properties begin to proliferate in this play as Romeo's "love's light wings" are replaced by actual ropes—ladders to the literal act of the wedding night's physical consummation. In Act 5 Paris appears with real flowers to strew Juliet's grave, while Romeo, in turn, comes with spade and crowbar, and the Friar brings a mattock and crowbar himself. The dramatic movement is not simply towards materialization, but the material world as *agency* and as *nonpoetic agency*. See Richard Fly, *Shakespeare's Mediated World* (Amherst: Univ. of Massachusetts Press, 1976), especially Chapter 1, "Tempering Extremities: Hazardous Mediation in *Romeo and Juliet*," pp. 1–26, for a full discussion of this interesting aspect of the tragedy.

12. Marie Delcourt, *L'Hermaphrodite* (Paris: Presses Universitaires de France, 1958), p. 68, specifically distinguishes between the sublime (conceptual) and the grotesque (actual) types of the androgyne.

13. For a persuasive definition of the epithalamion's "runnawayes eyes" as Cupid's, and for a more detailed analysis of the poem itself, see Gary M. McCown, " 'Runnawayes Eyes' and Juliet's Epithalamium" in *Shakespeare Quarterly*, 27 (1976), 150–70. His reading of the transmutations in the classical imagery, attitudes, and situations of the epithalamion enlarges and augments what Earl notes in "*Romeo and Juliet* and the Elizabethan Sonnets."

14. See Linda Bamber, *Comic Women, Tragic Men* (Stanford: Stanford Univ. Press, 1982), pp. 7–8.

15. See Nancy Vickers, "Diana Described: Scattered Woman and Scattered Rhyme," *Critical Inquiry*, VIII, 12 (1981), 265–79.

16. See Earl. esp. pp. 108–11.

17. Barbara L. Estrin ("Romeo, Juliet and the Art of Naming Love," *Ariel*, 12 [1981], 31–49, esp. p. 35) includes a fascinating comparison of 2.2 with Genesis, the other "Book" by which the lovers kiss.

18. "The four lines immediately after the kiss form the beginning of another sonnet. . . . It is, however, interrupted after the first quatrain by the Nurse, who comes to call Juliet to her mother. . . . It is also curious that both the complete and the incomplete sonnet end with a kiss, the first imaged as a prayer of the lips, the second imaged as both purgation of sin and the sin itself . . ." (Gideon Rappaport, "Another Sonnet in *Romeo and Juliet*," *Notes and Queries*, n.s. 25 [1978], 124).

19. "Form and Formality in *Romeo and Juliet*," *SQ*, 11 (1960), 3–11, esp. p. 4.

20. For a full treatment of this scene, see Thomas Moisan. "Rhetoric and the Rehearsal of Death: The 'Lamentations' Scene in *Romeo and Juliet,*" *SQ,* 34 (1983), 389–404.

21. The "operatic" concept of the scene originates with Harry Levin, "Form and Formality in *Romeo and Juliet,*" p. 9.

22. See *The Greek Anthology,* eds. A.S.F. Gow and D. L. Page, 2 vols. (Cambridge: Cambridge Univ. Press, 1965), Vol. I, 87 (Aniphanes III), 237 (Diodorus VI), 291 (Paimenion III), 313 (Philip XXIV), and 379 (Thallus III).

23. It is difficult not to associate Tybalt's bloody shroud with the blood-stained sheets of a consummated wedding. (Elizabethans had a more celebratory view of that blood than do we moderns.) Such a reading enhances the tomb scene as a consummation of the marriage, as influenced by Petrarch, the otherworldly terms of courtly love always containing this end. The fact that Juliet's body is found still bleeding in death when it has so recently bled in love further emphasizes this connection.

24. Over *Romeo and Juliet* as a whole, then, poetic form, increasingly *incorporated* into dramatic scenes, tends both to disintegrate and to regress historically. The historical regression accelerates as the referentiality of the poetic form increases. Romeo's encounter sonnet, for example, is less determined by external occasion than is the aubade; the aubade, in turn, responds to a cyclic movement in nature, whereas the subsequent epitaph recited by Capulet arises from the fixed and immutable fact of a human death. What is more, while both the aubade and the epitaph require appropriate *tones,* neither constructs a predestined (inherited) body as does the sonnet form.

25. I am indebted to my colleague J. David Walker for this insight.

26. Juliet's very age suggests that she both represents and defeats a translation of sonnet into flesh. At *almost* fourteen (and not sixteen, as in Brooke's earlier *Romeus and Juliet*), she has years almost equal to the completed form of the sonnet's fourteen-lined body.

The Name of the Rose in *Romeo and Juliet*

CATHERINE BELSEY

I

Is the human body inside or outside culture? Is it an organism, subject only to nature and independent of history? Or alternatively is it an effect of the signifier, no more than an ensemble of the meanings ascribed to it in different cultures, and thus historically discontinuous? Or, a third possibility, is this question itself reductive, a product of our wish to assign unambiguous causes and straightforward explanations?

When it comes to sexual desire, our culture is dominated by two distinct and largely contradictory models, both metaphysical in their assumption that we can identify what is fundamental in human nature. One metaphysic proposes that sex is a matter of the body, originating in the flesh and motivated by it, however people might deceive themselves with fantasies about romance. The other holds that love is a marriage of true minds, and that sex is (or ought to be) the bodily expression of this ideal relationship. Both models take for granted a dualist account of what it is to be a person, a mind on the one hand, and a body on the other, one of them privileged, the two either in harmony or in conflict. This dualism is associated with the Enlightenment and the moment of its crystallization is the Cartesian *cogito*.[1]

But in practice desire deconstructs the opposition between mind and body. Evidently it exists at the level of the signifier, as it imagines, fantasizes, idealizes. Desire generates songs and poetry and stories. Talking about it is pleasurable. At the same time, however, desire palpably inhabits the flesh, and seeks satisfaction there. Desire undoes the dualism common sense seems so often to take for granted.

The human body, we might want to argue in the light of our postmodernity, is subject to the imperatives of nature, but at the same time it does not exist outside culture. It owes to the differentiating symbol its existence as a single unit, with edges, limits. Psychoanalysis adds the presence of the symptom, evident on the body, the mark not of organic disease but of disorder at the level of the signifier, and psychoanalysis identifies the 'talking cure' as the disorder's remedy.[2] Desire, it urges, is an effect of difference, in excess of the reproductive drive. Furthermore, it knows itself as desire to the degree that it reads both the signifying practices of the body and the cultural forms in which desire *makes sense*. It is not possible to isolate the human body as natural organism, even methodologically: such a body would precisely not be human.

Romeo and Juliet is a play about desire. It is also a text poised on the brink of the Enlightenment, and it can be read, I want to suggest, as engaging with some of these issues, putting forward for examination in the process paradoxes that, for all the historical difference, a postmodern moment can find sympathetic. The bodies of the lovers are inscribed and, crucially, tragically, named. Their own account of love, while it displays a longing to escape the constraints of the symbolic order, reveals in practice precisely the degree to which it is culture that enables love to make sense. In *Romeo and Juliet* desire imagines a metaphysical body that cannot be realized.

II

Though there can be no doubt that Renaissance culture was profoundly and distinctively patriarchal, one sphere in which Shakespeare's women are perfectly equal to men is their capacity for experiencing sexual desire. Venus, Cleopatra, Portia in *The Merchant of Venice*,[3] and, of course, Juliet, are presented as sharing with their near-contemporaries, Alice Arden, the Duchess of Malfi, Beatrice-Joanna and Ford's Annabella, for example, an intensity of passion which is not evidently exceeded by that attributed to the men they love. These women are shown as subjects and agents of their own desire, able to speak of it and to act on the basis of it.

Meanwhile, Thomas Laqueur's *Making Sex* assembles persuasive documentation from the Greeks to the Renaissance of similar assumptions among European analysts of physiology and anatomy. Laqueur finds in this distinct sphere of knowledge, which is also, of course, a distinct discursive genre, what he calls the "one-sex" model of the human body. The one-sex understanding of the body prevailed, he argues, until modern science redefined women and men as *opposite* and antithetical sexes. In the one-sex body the sexual organs are understood to be similarly distributed among men and women, though externally visible in men and internal in women. Thus the vagina commonly corresponds to the penis, the uterus to the scrotum, and so on. Laqueur is clear about the implications of this account for the understanding of erotic impulses themselves: both sexes were capable of intense sexual pleasure; both sexes experienced desire. Indeed, it was widely held that female pleasure was necessary to conception, and this was consequently seen as an important proj-

ect of male sexual activity. Desire was not in any sense a masculine preroga-
tive. On the contrary,

> The process of generation might differ in its nuances as the vital heats, the
> seeds, and the physical qualities of the substances being ejaculated differed
> between the sexes—but libido, as we might call it, had no sex.[4]

Some Renaissance physicians would have gone even further. Jacques Ferrand,
for example, whose second treatise on lovesickness was published in Paris in
1623, argues that, being less rational than men, women are correspondingly
more subject to violent erotic desires, and less able to resist their own
impulses. A woman, according to Ferrand, "is in her Loves more Passionate,
and more furious in her follies, then a man is."[5]

Laqueur does not, of course, imply that the one-sex body was the product of a less patriarchal culture. On the contrary, the male body represented
the ideal of perfection; the female body, meanwhile, differed from it because
women possessed less of the vital heat which pushed the sexual organs out-
wards. But the difference was one of degree, Laqueur insists, not kind.
Women, less perfect than men, were in consequence less entitled to power
and prestige. But they were not men's opposite, passive and passionless where
men were active and desiring. That antithesis belongs to a later epoch.

Renaissance medical knowledge is neither a source of the plays nor a
guarantee of their meanings. It is too easily supposed that we can read off the
true meaning of fictional texts from the other knowledges of the period, as if
the culture somehow shared a single, homogeneous account of the world, and
was in that respect simpler, less diverse than our own.[6] We should not now
expect popular romance to depict the world in the same way as psychoanalysis, and even current pornography frequently takes precious little account of
elementary anatomy. I invoke Laqueur's extremely valuable work here simply
as additional evidence that it was possible in the sixteenth and seventeenth
centuries to imagine female desire, and even to take it seriously.

But there are also significant generic differences between Renaissance
anatomy and Renaissance fiction. In the medical treatises libido had no necessary moral implications: this was a knowledge which set out to record the
world it found in the authorities and in experience. The drama, however,
makes no attempt at value-free analysis. It cannot avoid showing the implications of the passions it depicts, and consequently it tends, whether incidentally or as its main project, to offer an assessment and evaluation of female
desire. But the judgements it makes are by no means univocal or monolithic.
As my examples suggest, desire may lead women into bad ways (*Arden of
Faversham*, *The Changeling*); it may be radically misdirected (*'Tis Pity She's a
Whore*), or innocent in itself but unfortunate in its consequences (*The Duchess
of Malfi*); its moral status may be profoundly ambiguous (*Antony and Cleopatra*); it may be seen as lyrical but at the same time absurd (*Venus and Adonis*).

But alternatively, desire reciprocated may be the foundation of conjugal marriage and (we are invited to assume) the nuclear family, as it is in Shakespeare's comedies. It was the Enlightenment, according to Laqueur, which insisted on the two-sex model of male and female bodies, the woman's lacking what defined the man's. And it was also the Enlightenment which tended to polarize male erotic activity and female passivity. Not until the nineteenth century was it established as a fact of nature that good women had no sexual feelings at all. The oppositional stereotypes of sexless virgin and voracious whore are not helpful in making sense of the work of Shakespeare and his contemporaries.

III

There was of course a convention, not that women should feel nothing, but that they should appear aloof in order to intensify male desire. This is the convention that Juliet unwittingly breaks when she declares her love at her window, only to be overheard by Romeo. It is quite late in their discussion, however, that she alludes, perhaps rather perfunctorily, to the proprieties of female behaviour: "Fain would I dwell on form, fain, fain deny | What I have spoke, but farewell compliment!" (*Romeo and Juliet,* II.2.88–89). The moment for observing the conventions has clearly passed, and propriety itself soon becomes matter for a teasing romantic overture on her part: "If thou thinkest I am too quickly won, | I'll frown and be perverse, and say thee nay, | So thou wilt woo, but else not for the world" (II.2.95–97).

At the heart of the play it is Juliet who speaks most eloquently and urgently to define, perhaps on behalf of both lovers, the desire experienced in the secret life of the body:

> Gallop apace, you fiery-footed steeds,
> Towards Phoebus' lodging; such a waggoner
> As Phaeton would whip you to the west,
> And bring in cloudy night immediately.
>
> (III.2.1)

The opening imperative, in conjunction with the image of the pounding, burning hooves, suggests the speeding pulses and the impatient ardour of desire, as well as its barely controlled power, and the allusion to Phaeton that follows evokes the boy's failure to manage Apollo's unruly horses, and so implies a surrender of what remains of restraint. Juliet's speech is entirely explicit in its invocation of love performed, acted, possessed and enjoyed. Their wedding night will be "a winning match | Play'd" between a symmetrically and reciprocally desiring couple "for a pair of stainless maidenhoods" (ll.

12–13). This necessarily clandestine love—perhaps the more thrilling because it is clandestine, because the fear of discovery intensifies the danger and the excitement[7]—is to be enacted in secret, in total darkness, and in silence:

> Spread thy close curtain, love-performing night,
> That [th'] runaways's eyes may wink, and Romeo
> Leap to these arms untalk'd of and unseen!
> Lovers can see to do their amorous rites
> By their own beauties.
>
> (l. 5)

The (bed-)curtain of the dark is to exclude all outsiders, and the runaway god of love himself will close his eyes,[8] so that no one sees their union, not even the lovers. If "see" is a metaphor (l. 8), they are to be guided in the performance of their amorous rites by the beauty of each other's bodies. Love, the conceit implies, has no need of light, since its mode of "seeing" is tactile, sensational. And the syntax here might lead us to suppose that if the lovers are "unseen" by themselves as well as other people, so too, perhaps, the act is "untalk'd of" by the lovers, since speech is also superfluous. Indeed, night is invited to obscure even the signifying practices of the virgin body. "Hood my unmann'd blood, bating [fluttering] in my cheeks, | With thy black mantle" (ll. 14–15). It is as if Juliet imagines the presence of the desiring bodies as pure sensation, sightless, speechless organisms in conjunction, flesh on flesh, independent of the signifier. A rose by any other name, she had earlier supposed, would smell as sweet (II.2.43–44): the same gases, emanating from the same petals, striking the same nostrils, its physical being separable from the word that names it. The name, the signifier, and the symbolic order in its entirety are to be relegated to a secondary position, the place of the merely expressive and instrumental.

But these isolated, unnamed bodies (and roses) are only imaginary. The human body is already inscribed: it has no existence as pure organism independent of the symbolic order in which desire makes sense. In the sixteenth-century text Juliet's imagined act of love is paradoxically defined in a densely metaphoric and tightly structured instance of signifying practice. The speech depends on invocations repeated with a difference ('Come civil night [. . .] Come night, come Romeo [. . .] Come gentle night, (ll. 10, 17, 20)), framing an elaborate conceit in which the love-performing darkness both is and is not synonymous with Romeo himself, the lover who is ultimately to be perpetuated in little stars (l. 22). The text specifies a wish in a tissue of formally ordered allusions, comparisons and puns, which constitute a poem, the zenith of signification, self-conscious, artful, witty. In order to bring before us its imagined bodies, the play here invokes a long poetic and rhetorical tradition, and in the process the lyricism which conjures up the act of love necessarily supplants it too. Moreover, this is a set piece, an epithalamion, though it is spoken, ironically, not by the assembled wedding guests, but by the bride herself, and in solitude.[9] What is enacted within it is desire imagining its fulfillment, and not the event itself, nor even any possible event. Love is inevitably performed within culture, within, indeed, a specific culture: bodies do not exist outside the cultural moment which defines them, and experience cannot be identified beyond the meanings a cultural tradition makes intelligible. What we call a rose might take any other name, but if it were name*less,* outside difference, who is to say that its smell would be "sweet"? Here too a whole cultural tradition underlies the recognition (re-cognition) of this sweetness—and its association with love.

Romeo and Juliet is about desire. It is also one of Shakespeare's most evidently formal, conventional texts. As Rosalie Colie points out, the play draws on the traditions of Roman comedy, with its young woman and two suitors, one of them approved by her father. The garrulous nurse belongs to the same genre. Meanwhile, the Prologues to Acts I and II are sonnets, and the lovers converse in Petrarchan imagery. Mercutio, on the other hand is an Ovidian figure. When the lovers are together they perform in joint and reciprocal set pieces: first a sonnet (1.5.93–106) and then an *aubade* (III.5.1–36). But there is no necessary contradiction, Colie proposes, between convention and desire: on the contrary, the effect in the text is precisely to naturalize the familiar forms. "One of the most pleasurable, for me, of Shakespeare's many talents, is his 'unmetaphoring' of literary devices, his sinking of the conventions back into what, he somehow persuades us, is 'reality.'" The Petrarchan convention of love at first sight, she goes on to argue, "is here made to seem entirely natural [. . .] its conventionality forgotten as it is unmetaphored by action."[10]

In this respect, Colie might have added, Shakespeare's text is no more than a superlative instance of culture in general, which works precisely by unmetaphoring the device and naturalizing inherited forms. There is no unmediated experience located entirely outside the existing semiotic repertoire, though there are, as the play demonstrates, unexpected deviations, juxtapositions, turns, and resistances. In the play Ovid disrupts Petrarch; comic form leads to tragic denouement; choric narrative appropriates the lyric voice of the sonnet. Culture imagines the symbol as truth, and "proves" its case by novelty, demonstrating that it is constantly possible to formulate something new, surprising or unexpected.

In a brilliant discussion of the formality of *Romeo and Juliet* Gayle Whittier argues that the play shows how the inherited word declines "from lyric freedom to tragic fact."[11] She points out that the poetic mode in which Romeo falls in love precedes him, and that he longs to be the author of the lover he becomes. But in Whittier's account the narrative mode of drama displaces the abstract and timeless paradoxes of Petrarchan poetry. It endows the word with flesh, and in the process necessarily subjects it to time and death. Poetry, Whittier argues, is transcendent: love is referential. The bodies of the lovers exist in time, and confront death: the poetry which precedes them also survives them.

The argument is extremely convincing, and it is eloquently presented. If in the end I put a slightly different case, the distinction between us is perhaps no more than a matter of emphasis. I want to stress the degree to which the letter invades the flesh, and the body necessarily inhabits the symbolic. This above all is the source of the tragedy of *Romeo and Juliet*. Petrarch, their names and the word of the Prince ("banished") are all decisive for the protagonists, but the symbolic order is not external to their identities: on the contrary, it is exactly the element in which they subsist. On the other hand, they exceed it too. The body which it defines is not contained by the symbol, and desire seeks to overflow the limits imposed by the differential signifier.

IV

In recognizing that the name of the rose is arbitrary, Juliet shows herself a Saussurean *avant la lettre,* but in drawing the inference that Romeo can arbitrarily cease to be a Montague, she simply affirms what her own desire dictates.

> O Romeo, Romeo, wherefore art thou Romeo?
> Deny thy father and refuse thy name;
> Or, if thou wilt not, be but sworn my love,
> And I'll no longer be a Capulet [. . .]
> 'Tis but thy name that is my enemy;
> Thou art thyself, though not a Montague.
> What's Montague? It is nor hand nor foot,
> Nor arm nor face, [nor any other part]
> Belonging to a man. O, be some other name!
> What's in a name? That which we call a rose
> By any other word would smell as sweet;
> So Romeo would, were he not Romeo call'd,
> Retain that dear perfection which he owes
> Without that title. Romeo, doff thy name,
> And for thy name, which is no part of thee,
> Take all myself.
>
> (II.2.33–49)

Identity, the speech acknowledges, exists in the symbolic as the Name of the Father. Juliet imagines a succession of (im)possibilities: that Romeo should repudiate his father's name, or she hers; that he should be named differently; and finally that he should simply remove his name, as if it were extrinsic, separable from identity. In place of Romeo's name Juliet offers her "self," implying that beyond their names, as beyond the name of the rose, the lovers could exist as unnamed selves. This move to transcend the signifier, however, the play at once makes clear, is precisely a contradiction. In offering to take what she urges *literally,* Romeo can only propose punningly to assume another *name,* to adopt a different location in the symbolic:

> I'll take thee at thy word
> Call me but love, and I'll be new baptiz'd;
> Henceforth I never will be Romeo.
>
> (l. 49)

But the signifier, however arbitrary, is not at the disposal of the subject. Romeo's name precedes him, makes him a subject, locates him in the community of Verona. It is not optional. Later Romeo will offer to excise his murderous name, but he cannot do so without killing himself:

> O, tell me, friar, tell me,
> In what vile part of this anatomy
> Doth my name lodge? Tell me, that I may sack
> The hateful mansion.
>
> (III.3.105)

Unlike hand or foot, Romeo's name is not something that he can lose and retain his identity, continuing to be the specific, differentiated Romeo that Juliet loves.

Lovers are prone to perceive the imaginary essence of the object of desire, to identify a "self," a presence which subsists beyond the symbolic order, the "dear perfection" of the loved one independent of the public and external name. This is the evidence of their idealizing passion. A lover who might be expected to know better, the author of Jacques Derrida's sequence of postcards, also affirms something of this kind:

> you will never be your name, you never have been, even when, and especially when you have answered to it. The name is made to do without the life of the bearer, and is therefore always somewhat the name of someone dead. One could not live, be there, except by protesting against one's name, by protesting one's non-identity with one's proper name.[12]

Here too, the letter kills, we are invited to suppose, but desire gives life. The name is a trapping, inessential, inherited or given, a reminder that the individual's autonomy is always imaginary, the effect of a place allotted by others, by the family, by a whole culture.

But Derrida's amorous-philosophical text is not naïve (of course!).[13] The name is dead because it is ancestral; it is dead because in differentiating the person that it names, it constitutes a reminder of all the other possible objects of desire, and the arbitrariness that singles out *this* one; and it is dead finally because it stands in for the person it names, and thus supplants the being who elicits so much intensity, intervening between the lover and the loved one. But there is no suggestion that it is possible to do more than protest against the imposed identity, to insist on non-identity with *that,* to refuse the imposition. Though it imagines it in an oxymoron ("I am calling you [. . .] beyond your name, beyond all names,"[14] the text does not in the end suppose that the person could exist independently, a free-floating essence beyond nomenclature, which is to say beyond difference.

Nor, indeed, is Shakespeare's text naïve. The name of Montague, imposed, ancestral, *is* Juliet's enemy, the text as a whole makes clear. If Romeo's non-identity with his name legitimates their love, the repudiated name returns, nevertheless, to ensure their tragedy. Even though his name is no part of the man Juliet loves, the play at once draws attention to the impossibility of discarding the name which differentiates him. Hearing in the darkness a voice reply to her musings, the shocked Juliet demands, "What man art thou?" (l. 52), and how else can Romeo indicate who he is but by reference to a name which precisely cannot be specified without identifying an opponent of all Capulets:

> By a name
> I know not how to tell thee who I am.
> My name, dear saint, is hateful to myself,
> Because it is an enemy to thee.
>
> (II.2.53)

In the event, Juliet recognizes his voice, a property of the lover like hand or foot, or any other part, and promptly puts her recognition to the test—by naming him:

> My ears have not yet drunk a hundred words
> Of thy tongue's uttering, yet I know the sound.
> Art thou not Romeo, and a Montague
>
> (l. 58)

The question of names recurs at intervals throughout Derrida's "Envois" to *The Post Card.* The text is at least in part an engagement with Oxford philosophy and its distinction between "use" and "mention" ("Fido is my dog"; " 'Fido' is a possible name for a dog"). But this issue is part of a larger debate in Western philosophy concerning the question whether proper names have meaning. The answer to this question has implications for our understanding of the relationship between language and the world,[15] and this in turn is the problem Derrida has addressed throughout his work. Proper names imply that words may be no more than substitutes for things, labels for the objects they refer to, without meaning in themselves. What, after all, does "Smith" mean? If names have no meaning, however, but only reference, what are we to say when the name is Medusa, and the referent does not exist? And is "Homer" meaningless? Or does "Homer" precisely *mean* the anonymous author(s) of the *Iliad* and the *Odyssey,* who must have existed, but probably not as Homer? If so, is meaning independent of what goes on in the world, a matter of shared, inherited knowledge, which may be false? Who does Homer's name belong to? To an individual? Or to a culture? What *gives* it its meaning?[16]

The "Envois" to *The Post Card* consists of a series of love letters to an unnamed person, addressed poste restante "because of all the families" (p. 45). The epistolary form throws into relief the problems of "communication," and the story of a passionate clandestine love makes evident how much is at stake in the process of writing. The secret love letter is a paradigm case of the urgency and the impossibility of meaning as immediate, transparent, individual, exclusive *presence.* All language is subject to what Derrida calls "the Postal Principle as differantial relay" (p. 54). The message is always differed and deferred (differantiated), since the intervals and the distance, the delays and relays, separate the people it was designed to unite. Much of Derrida's love story concerns a critical, definitive, "true" letter which fails to arrive. Instead it is eventually returned unopened, and remains for ever unread by the addressee, unopened by the sender, though it goes on to haunt the relationship, since its existence cannot be forgotten. This "dead letter" is at once outside the living love affair and formative for it. In response to Lacan's account of *The Purloined Letter,* Derrida's text insists that the letter never arrives at its destination.

At the same time, *The Post Card* proposes, the letter can never ensure its own secrecy. However cryptic it is, however coded, designed exclusively for the recipient, if the message is intelligible, it is always able to be intercepted, read, misread, reproduced. Since it is necessarily legible for another, who does the letter belong to? To the sender, the addressee, or an apparently irrelevant unspecified third party, representative of the symbolic order in all its (dead) otherness? Their secret love does not belong exclusively to Romeo and Juliet. To the degree that it inhabits the symbolic, to the extent that it is relayed in messages and letters, even when the messages in question are those of the signifying body itself, love is tragically not theirs to control.

Derrida's text refuses to name its object of desire, the secret addressee of the love letters, though it plays with a succession of possible names (Esther, Judith, Bettina (pp. 71–73, 231)). It names others, however, who feature in the itinerary of the lover (Neil Hertz, Hillis, Paul, Jonathan, and Cynthia, and a woman who seems tantalizingly, comically, to be called Metaphysics (p. 197)). It thus keeps the reader guessing, about the identity of the beloved, and about whether the named and apparently non-fictional figures can be ruled out (p. 223). It names the writer, but only (punningly?) as acquiescent, as *j'accepte* ("this will be my signature henceforth [. . .] it is my name, that *j'ac-cepte*" (p. 26)), leaving in doubt whether the whole story is fictional, or in some disguised and elusive way referential, "true," and problematizing in the process those terms themselves. But though it withholds the name of the loved one, it substitutes a pronoun, "you": a shifter, certainly, but no less differential for that. The amorous project is to locate the living object of desire beyond the inherited, dead signifier, to invest it with a transcendent existence outside mortality. At the same time, of course, *The Post Card* recognizes this impulse as imaginary, "metaphysical," and perhaps in the process offers another clue—or possibly a red herring—which might lead us to identify the object itself:

> You have always been "my" metaphysics, the metaphysics of my life, the "verso" of everything I write (my desire, speech, presence, proximity, law, my heart and soul, everything that I love and that you know before me). (p. 197)

The beloved is not named, but is not nameless either, for the lover or the world:

> I have not named you while showing you to others, I have never shown you to others with the name they know you by and that I consider only the homonym of the one that I give you, no, I have called you, yourself. (p. 219)

"Yourself" is not an unmediated self. It is not a name, but at the same time it is not independent of the signifier. And as a shifter, it patently does not belong to the unnamed object of desire.

Romeo and Juliet are not reducible to their proper names, but they are not beyond them either, though in their idealizing, transfiguring imagery they repeatedly locate each other outside mortality, in the heavens, among the inauspicious stars, not at their mercy (II.2.2; 15–22; III.2.22–25). And their names are not their property: they do not belong to them in the same way as hand or foot, or any other part. As subjects, the lovers aspire both to love and to immortality only by virtue of the differentiating, inherited signifier, which subjects them, in the event, to death itself.

V

What is at issue in the *aubade* is the name of the lark.

> Wilt thou be gone? it is not yet near day.
> It was the nightingale, and not the lark,
> That pierc'd the fearful hollow of thine ear.
> (III.5.1)

The referential truth is available here, but it is not what matters. The debate is about the significance of the birdsong that the lovers hear, its meaning: not ornithology, but the time of day. The same bird known by any other name would make the same sound, but it would be of no interest unless a culture had already invested the song with the meaning of dawn. It is the lark: Romeo proves it on the evidence of other signifiers:

> Look, love, what envious streaks
> Do lace the severing clouds in yonder east.
> Night's candles are burnt out
>
> (l. 7)

The lark is already inscribed as "the herald of the morn" (l. 6), and while the time of day is also referential, a matter of fact, it too is in question here in its meaning, as the signifier of the moment when Romeo's banishment takes effect, separating, because of their names, the desiring bodies of the lovers. The world of nature, of birdsong and morning, is already invaded by culture, even though it also exceeds it, and the knowledge that it purveys is necessarily at the level of signification.

Juliet's epithalamion is uttered, ironically, in the direct shadow of the Prince's sentence, immediately after it is pronounced (III.1.186–97), but thanks to the Postal Principle she does not yet know it. When the message that Romeo is banished is finally delivered by the Nurse, her account initially obscures the truth, and Juliet believes that Romeo is dead (III.2.36–70). Juliet's premature lament for Romeo here finds a parallel in the family's lamentations for her apparent death (IV.5). Both are displaced, inappropriate, and yet not wholly irrelevant, since they anticipate the events of the play, as if the signifier lived a life of its own, partly but not entirely independent of the referent. Meanwhile, Friar Lawrence's letter fails to reach its destination and Romeo, in possession of another narrative, the public account relayed by Balthasar, tragically returns to act on Juliet's supposed death.

The Prince speaks the sentence of banishment, but it is to be carried out on Romeo's body, causing either his absence or his death. Romeo's absence is a kind of death for Juliet too, she affirms:

> Some word there was, worser than Tybalt's death,
> That murder'd me; I would forget it fain,
> But O, it presses to my memory
> Like damned guilty deeds to sinners' minds:
> "Tybalt is dead, and Romeo banished."
>
> (III.2.108)

The insistent signifier is determining for the bodies of the lovers, and yet at the same time it is not definitive, in the sense that its implications are not contained by its meaning. " 'Romeo is banished': to speak that word, | Is father, mother, Tybalt, Romeo, Juliet, | All slain, all dead." (ll. 122–24). The signifier, which differentiates, specifies limits and imposes boundaries, also evokes an unspeakable residue, boundless and unlimited: "There is no end, no limit, measure, bound, | In that word's death, no words can that woe sound" (ll. 125–26). The woe exceeds the word because no word can make it present. Supplanted by the signifier, it exists as an absence hollowed out within the utterance—just as it does within the corresponding signifying practice of the body, the weeping which is to follow (ll. 130–31).

In the same way, the signifier cannot exhaust desire, since desire inhabits the residue that exceeds what can be said. Challenged to "unfold" in speech the happiness of her marriage, Juliet replies:

> Conceit, more rich in matter than in words,
> Brags of his substance, not of ornament;
> They are but beggars that can count their worth,
> But my true love is grown to such excess
> I cannot sum up sum of half my wealth.
>
> (II.6.30)

Love, Juliet claims, like the unnamed rose or the untalked of act, is more substantial than mere words. For this reason, she continues, its substance cannot be counted, cannot be summed up in words. And she makes the affirmation in an ornamental metaphor, an analogy between love and wealth familiar to us from the *Sonnets* and from Theseus's opening speech in *A Midsummer Night's Dream.* The comparison, which brings the intensity of the love before us, simultaneously has the effect of supplanting it, replacing it by the signifier, so that the speech demonstrates precisely the impossibility it affirms of putting love into words. This excess of love over the signifier is what invests desire with metaphysics, and at the same time, if Derrida is to be believed, the metaphysical with desire. As speaking subjects, we long for the unattainable verso of signifying practice—proximity, certainty, presence, the thing itself. Lovers long to make present the unspeakable residue that constitutes desire.

VI

Shakespeare's play ends with death, the golden statues—and names again. At the beginning of the final scene Paris decorously strews Juliet's tomb with flowers and sweet water, in a gesture appropriate to a man who would have been her bridegroom. He is interrupted by her actual bridegroom, whose intentions, in contrast, are excessive, in every sense of the word: "savage-wild,

| More fierce and more inexorable far | Than empty tigers or the roaring sea" (V.3.37–39). Alan Dessen makes the point that modern productions commonly include a structure which represents the tomb. This, he argues persuasively, is not necessarily how the scene would have been staged in the 1590s. On the contrary, the tomb might well have been no more than a stage door or a trap door in the stage, and Juliet's body might have been thrust out on a bier at the point when the scene shifts to the inside of the tomb. Including the tomb, as they do, Dessen says, modern productions often leave out Romeo's mattock and crowbar. In consequence, they fail to do full justice to the emblematic contrast the scene sets up between Romeo and Paris, the one sprinkling scented water on the grave, and the other violating the tomb with an iron bar, forcing open what he himself calls this "womb of death" (l. 45).[17] When Romeo, who is beside himself with passion, offers to *strew* the churchyard with the interloper's limbs, the contrast is surely complete.

Explaining his purpose, Romeo "lies" to Balthasar:

> Why I descend into this bed of death
> Is partly to behold my lady's face,
> But chiefly to take thence from her dead finger
> A precious ring . . .
>
> (l. 28)

The lie is also intelligible as a coded truth, a cryptic declaration of a real purpose, not intended to be legible to Balthasar, of re-enacting his clandestine marriage by a second exchange of rings. In the grotesque parody of the wedding night that follows, Romeo seeks a repetition in the tomb of the original darkness, silence and secrecy invoked so eloquently in Juliet's epithalamion, though once again these amorous rites are to be lit by beauty, as Juliet, who once taught the torches to burn bright (I.5.44), now "makes | This vault a feasting presence full of light" (V.3.85–86).

This time, too, the body signifies. There is blood in Juliet's face once more, to the point where Romeo seems almost to read the message it puts out:

> O my love, my wife,
> Death, that hath suck'd the honey of thy breath,
> Hath had no power yet upon thy beauty:
> Thou art not conquer'd, beauty's ensign yet
> Is crimson in thy lips and in thy cheeks,
> And death's pale flag is not advanced there.
>
> (l. 91)

But because his understanding at this moment is constructed in accordance with another narrative, he cannot read the story of Juliet's living body. Again he turns to her, this time with a question: "Ah, dear Juliet, | Why art thou yet so fair?" (ll. 101–02). The audience could have told him the answer (and perhaps did in early productions?). But Romeo, in the light of what he thinks he knows, produces another hypothesis:

> Shall I believe
> That unsubstantial Death is amorous,
> And that the lean abhorred monster keeps
> Thee here in dark to be his paramour?
>
> (l. 102)

(It is tempting, especially in the context of Georges Bataille's current popularity, to find an erotics of death in this conceit, but it is worth bearing in mind that from the point of view of the audience, the account is ironic, since it represents precisely the wrong answer.)[18] The re-enacting of the wedding night remains in consequence imaginary. They die, as Juliet performed their epithalamion, separately. "These lovers of the night remain," as Kristeva puts it, "solitary beings."[19]

Their grave is not, however, a private place. On the contrary, it is the family vault of the Capulets, a memorial, precisely, to the name, which is all that remains of their ancestors, but which lives on to shadow the present so tragically. Moreover, no sooner has he established the close-curtained secrecy of this second wedding night, than Romeo interrupts his address to Juliet to recognize the dead body of Tybalt in its bloody sheet (l. 97). Once again Tybalt, who insisted on the importance of Romeo's name and the "stock and honor" of his own kin (I.5.54, 58, 61), and who for that reason fatally sustained the feud, intervenes between the lovers, as an emblematic third party, representative of the inherited symbolic order in all its dead—and deadly—otherness. Finally, the whole community crowds in, the community which is ultimately responsible for the arbitrary and pointless ancestral quarrel, and which is powerless to reverse the effects of a violence carried on in the names of Montague and Capulet, and enacted on the bodies of the new generation.

VII

Romeo and Juliet are immortalized as signifiers. The promised golden statues are, of course, a metamorphosis, effigies of their bodies, beautiful, precious, and lifeless. Metamorphosis enacts something of the project of the signifier, arresting, and stabilizing the object of desire, fixing it as possession—and supplanting it in the process. Like metaphor, metamorphosis offers an image in place of the thing itself, but the image is precisely *not the same*. Venus is able to hold the flower that Adonis becomes, but the flower is no longer Adonis. The reconciling golden statues appear too late to interrupt the fatal invasion of the signifier into the living organism. Verona will recognize the effigies of Romeo and Juliet, but the effigies will signify concord, not desire.

And yet finally, as is to be expected of signifiers, the lovers are incorporated into a love story, foretold by the Prince, dramatized by Shakespeare. The play closes, appropriately, with their names, which are not synonymous with the lovers themselves, but which are not independent of them either. The play, and the legend of love that the play has become, have been astonishingly popular from the Restoration period on. The text has been performed, adapted, cut, reinterpreted, rewritten as a musical, filmed,[20] and now produced as a movie starring cats. Even in death, therefore, the record of the lovers' desiring, inscribed bodies is preserved in the archive, filed, appropriately enough, under their names:

> For never was a story of more woe
> Than this of Juliet and her Romeo.
> (V.3.309)

Evidently it was possible, before the dualism of the Enlightenment separated us all neatly into minds and bodies, to identify another relationship between the organism and the culture in which it becomes a human being. *Romeo and Juliet* dramatizes the sexual desire which is produced at the level of the signifier and inscribes the body of the lover. The play also acknowledges the slippage between the signifier and the world it defines and differentiates. But above all, it puts on display the hopeless longing to escape the confines of the signifier, to encounter directly, im-mediately, the rose that exists beyond its name. And to this extent *Romeo and Juliet* suggests the degree to which the named, differentiated lover is always only a stand-in for something which cannot be embraced, a reminder, as Plato proposes, of "an ideal that is out of sight, but present in the memory."[21]

Does the continued popularity of the play, even in a predominantly Enlightenment culture, perhaps suggest a dissatisfaction with the neat Cartesian categories by which we have so diligently struggled to live?

Notes

I am grateful to Alan Dessen and Cynthia Dessen for their incisive comments on an earlier version of this essay.

1. The dualism of the Enlightenment differs from Plato's and Augustine's. Both Platonic and medieval souls are immortal and their affiliations are divine. But the Cartesian mind is predominantly secular and human. Nor is its relation to the body always one of superiority. Enlightenment science, paradoxically, had the eventual effect of reversing Descartes's hierarchy.

2. Charles Shepherdson, "Biology and History: Some Psychoanalytic Aspects of the Writing of Luce Irigaray," *Textual Practice,* 6 (1992), 47–86. I owe to the clarity of that essay the theoretical framework of my argument here.

3. *The Merchant of Venice,* III.2.108–14. Shakespeare references are to *The Riverside Shakespeare,* ed. by G. Blakemore Evans and others (Boston: Houghton Mifflin, 1974).

4. Thomas Laqueur, *Making Sex: The Body and Gender from the Greeks to Freud* (Cambridge, MA: Harvard University Press, 1990), p. 43.

5. Jacques Ferrand, *Erotomania,* trans. by Edmund Chilmead (Oxford, 1640), p. 214. Female desire was widely taken for granted in the Middle Ages, and natural philosophy commonly presented women as more libidinous than men (Mary Frances Wack, *Lovesickness in the Middle Ages: The "Viaticum" and its Commentaries* (Philadelphia: University of Pennsylvania Press, 1990), pp. 110–25.

6. The New Historicism sets out to break with this version of the Elizabethan world picture by insisting on the single anecdote which is not offered as "representative." But though it produces acute insights, the New Historicist juxtaposition of fiction with quite different knowledges, as if it could be taken for granted that they illuminate each other, risks repeating Tillyard's unifying and simplifying gesture. In "Fiction and Friction," for example, after a number of disclaimers Stephen Greenblatt goes on to identify Renaissance England as "a culture that knows, as a widely accepted physical truth, that women have occulted, inward penises" (*Shakespearean Negotiations: The Circulation of Social Energy in Renaissance England* (Oxford: Clarendon Press, 1988), pp. 66–93, p. 87). He then uses this medical knowledge to explain the transvestite theatre, female cross-dressing in Shakespeare's comedies, and homoerotic desire in the period. All this is suggestive, inventive, and challenging, but it fails to take account of the counterknowledge, evident in the bawdy jokes of the theatrical tradition itself, that women lacked what men possessed. Greenblatt himself cites Viola's "a little thing would make me tell them how much I lack of a man" (*Twelfth Night,* III.4.302–03). Gratiano's "would he were gelt that had it" is comic if Nerissa is understood to be "gelded" (*The Merchant of Venice,* V.1.144). See also: " 'That's a fair thought to lie between a maid's legs.' 'What is?' 'Nothing.' " (*Hamlet,* III.2.118–21), and David Wilbern, "Shakespeare's Nothing," in *Representing Shakespeare: New Psychoanalytic Essays,* ed. by Murray Schwarz and Coppélia Kahn (Baltimore: Johns Hopkins University Press, 1980), pp. 244–63.

7. Julia Kristeva, *Tales of Love,* trans. by Leon S. Roudiez (New York: Columbia University Press, 1987), p. 211.

8. Gary M. McCown, " 'Runnawayes Eyes' and Juliet's Epithalamium," *Shakespeare Quarterly,* 27 (1976), 150–70, pp. 156–65.

9. McCown, " 'Runnawayes Eyes,' " p. 165.

10. Rosalie Colie, *Shakespeare's "Living Art"* (Princeton, NJ: Princeton University Press, 1974), pp. 135–67, p. 145.

11. Gayle Whittier, "The Sonnet's Body and the Body Sonnetized in *Romeo and Juliet,*" *Shakespeare Quarterly,* 40 (1989), 27–41, p. 27.

12. Jacques Derrida, *The Post Card: From Socrates to Freud and Beyond,* trans. by Alan Bass (Chicago: University of Chicago Press, 1987), p. 39.

13. See Derrida's own reading of *Romeo and Juliet:* "Aphorism Countertime," *Acts of Literature,* ed. by Derek Attridge (New York: Routledge, 1992), 414–33.

14. Derrida, *The Post Card,* p. 130. Compare: "But it is you I still love, the living one. Beyond everything, beyond your name, your name beyond your name" (p. 144).

15. See J. R. Searle, "Proper Names and Descriptions," *The Encyclopaedia of Philosophy,* ed. by Paul Edwards, 8 vols (London: Collier Macmillan, 1967), VI, 487–91.

16. I am grateful to Andrew Belsey for a discussion of the problem of proper names.

17. Alan C. Dessen, "Much Virtue in 'As' " in *Shakespeare and the Sense of Performance: Essays in the Tradition of Performance Criticism in Honor of Bernard Beckerman,* ed. by Marvin and Ruth Thompson (Newark, NJ: University of Delaware Press, 1989), pp. 132–38.

18.   See Georges Bataille, *Erotism: Death and Sensuality,* trans. by Mary Dalwood (San Francisco: City Lights Books, 1986); and *The Tears of Eros,* trans. by Peter Connor (San Francisco: City Lights Books, 1989).

19.   Kristeva, *Tales of Love,* p. 216.

20.   See Jill L. Levenson, *Romeo and Juliet,* Shakespeare in Performance (Manchester: Manchester University Press, 1987).

21.   Kristeva, *Tales of Love,* p. 269.

Romeo and Juliet's Open Rs

Jonathan Goldberg

Over the past twenty years, *Romeo and Juliet* has become the Shakespeare play assigned to more U.S. high school students than any other. *Julius Caesar* has been usurped; the sexual revolution has replaced the civics lesson. Yet, given the conservative nature of most high school curricula, one can only assume that the play is taught in formalist terms (the young vs. the old, night vs. day, love vs. society, etc.) and toward a valuation of a kind not limited to high school lesson plans. Typical in this regard might be these sentences from Brian Gibbons's "Introduction" to his Arden edition of the play (1980): "The lovers are from the outset withdrawn in an experience of sublime purity and intense suffering which renders them spiritually remote from other characters and the concerns of the ordinary world. The single clear line of ideal aspiration in love is set against the diversified complex intrigues which proliferate in the ordinary world, and contact between the two has tragic consequences."[1] In such an estimation (it recurs as the thesis in the thirty-five pages of his "Introduction" given over to—ominously—"The Play"), Gibbons would seem to be doing little more than echoing the closing lines of the play, in which the prince intones, "never was a story of more woe / Than this of Juliet and her Romeo" (5.3.308–9) as his response to the offer of Montague and Capulet to raise a monument to the dead pair of lovers:

> *Mont.*   For I will raise her statue in pure gold,
> That whiles Verona by that name is known,
> There shall no figure at such rate be set
> As that of true and faithful Juliet.
> *Cap.*   As rich shall Romeo's by his lady's lie,
> Poor sacrifices of our enmity.
>
> (298–303)

Predictably enough, Gibbons finds in this moment that the "artifice of eternity" (74) is being erected, the statues symbolizing for him "the alchemical

Jonathan Goldberg, *"Romeo and Juliet's* Open Rs," *Queering the Renaissance,* ed. Jonathan Goldberg (Durham, N.C.: Duke University Press, 1994): 218–35.

transmutation of worldly wealth, property, earth, into the spiritual riches of the heart and the imagination" (76).

In such estimations of the "purity" and transcendentality of their love, and, by extension, of Shakespeare's art, mystifications are set up to obscure what can as easily be read in the lines: that the corpses of Romeo and Juliet continue to have a social function, indeed that they make possible the union of the two opposing houses; moreover, this is as long lasting as the name of the city in which their monument is erected, while the material value of the statues, insisted upon as Montague and Capulet vie in their offers, is tied to that contingent temporality, to a future that cannot be predicted or controlled however much these grasping and still rivalrous fathers would do so. Reading the lines this way, one can hear them echoing against the concerns in the play, voiced over and again, about the possibility that names and words might be unmoored and uncontrollable, subject to accidents and to determinations that no artifice of eternity can secure. One could also see that the three men speaking at the end of the play are bent upon securing the social through the dead couple, and one could extend this back to the entire play, reading the love of Romeo and Juliet as imbricated in rather than separated off from "ordinary" life. The idealization of the lovers, to be brief, serves an ideological function. The marriage of their corpses in the eternal monuments of "pure gold" attempts to perform what marriage normally aims at in comedy: to provide the bedrock of the social order. Or, to speak somewhat more exactly, the heterosexual order.

Yet, what is solidified in this final set of gestures is indicated just before, when Capulet offers his hand to Montague and calls him "brother" (295). For, to speak more exactly, what the ending of the play secures is a homosocial order,[2] and it is that configuration that continually triangulates the relation of Romeo and Juliet, adding in every instance a third term that gives the lie to the shelter of their love. Romeo and Paris as possible husbands, still fighting over the body of Juliet in the final scene of the play; Capulet and Paris as the patriarchal couple trading Juliet between them; Romeo and Tybalt as enemies and yet as lovers, joined and divided by Juliet. The functioning of the patriarchy (the "brotherhood" of Montague and Capulet at the end of the play, the surrogate sonship that extends from Capulet to Paris), as well as its misfunctioning (if rivalry and enmity are that—an easily disputed point), is tied to the love of Romeo and Juliet. Indeed, what makes their love so valuable is that it serves as a nexus for the social and can be mystified as outside the social. The sexual revolution replaces the civics lesson indeed: with the myth of love as a private experience the personal is disconnected from the political.

One would think, therefore, that feminist criticism that has engaged the play would speak against the formalist project that I have conveniently fetched from the account offered by Gibbons; to a certain extent it has, and valuably, by excoriating patriarchal violence in the play. But it too dreams of the ideal world that Gibbons imagines. I take as typical the opening sentences of Coppélia Kahn's discussion of the play: "*Romeo and Juliet* is about a pair of adolescents trying to grow up. Growing up requires that they separate themselves from their parents by forming with a member of the opposite sex an intimate bond which supersedes filial bonds."[3] This seems ready for high school use; the play is translated effortlessly into modern (at any rate 1950s) terms. The tragedy of the play implied in these opening sentences has to do with the failure of Romeo and Juliet to grow up into the mature couple that has separated itself from parental bonds. Mystified, thereby, is the fact that at the end of this ideal trajectory lies the transformation of the couple into its parents; what they rebel against is also what they become. These blandly descriptive sentences reek of prescriptiveness, most notably when growing up is allowed, indeed required to have, a single heterosexual trajectory. How far this might be from *Romeo and Juliet* the term "homosocial" has already begun to suggest, and Kahn's rewriting of the play to suit her normalizing plot couldn't be clearer. For rather than breaking the filial bond, Romeo and Juliet reensure it; it is the brotherhood of Montague and Capulet that they secure. And such would have been the case too had the play been the comedy Kahn desires, in which boys would arrive at manhood free of the phallic aggression and fear of women that deform the patriarchy, for even in this benign state they would not leave behind the institutional site of marriage upon which patriarchy rests. Were the social order to work properly, Kahn implies, it would effortlessly produce heterosexuality. Shakespeare, she believes, critiques patriarchy because it does not make growing up easy; his art is on her side.

In the pages that follow, I do not seek to enlist Shakespeare for the projects of a formalist and heterosexist agenda, but rather, following Eve Kosofsky Sedgwick, to suggest that the homosocial order in the play cannot simply be reduced to a compulsive and prescriptive heterosexuality; that sexuality in the play cannot be sheltered from sociality; that sexuality in the play cannot be found enshrined in an artifice of eternity because neither the social work that the play performs nor the play itself (a formalist phantasm) can be thought of in those terms.

Accounts of the sort that I have been invoking rest upon the value of the love between Romeo and Juliet, treating it as a unique manifestation, the locus of all kinds of intensities and transcendentalities (the perfection of the individual and, concomitantly, of the work of art). So doing, critical estimations could be said to follow a path that the play itself marks out, for, at the opening of the play, Romeo is in love, but not, as it happens, with Juliet, rather with Rosaline, and from the opening of the play, Romeo is being solicited to forget her and pass on to some more responsive object. The critics, that is, manage to do what Romeo is told to do. "Forget to think of her" (1.1.223), the peace-mongering Benvolio counsels his friend—his "fair coz" (1.1.205)—

a lesson he reiterates in less than exalted terms: "Tut man, one fire burns out another's burning" (1.2.45). It is a lesson Romeo learns; to Friar Laurence's worried query, "Wast thou with Rosaline?" Romeo replies, "I have forgot that name, and that name's woe." "That's my good son" his "ghostly father" returns (2.3.40–43): Benvolio and Friar Laurence have been preaching Romeo the same sermon, a lesson in forgetting that, at least in the first scene of the play, Romeo protests that he cannot learn, a lesson which, once accomplished, involves, arguably, the very transformation that Benvolio counsels, not so much a forgetting as a replacing, a substitution. Seen in that light, Juliet as replacement object is inserted within a seriality rather than as the locus of uniqueness and singularity. The play offers reasons to think about the relationship in these terms, not least when Juliet on the balcony ponders Romeo's name and likens it to the rose that remains itself whatever it is called (2.2.38–49). Is Juliet that rose, and, thereby, Rosaline renamed? What would the consequences be of thinking of her as the newest avatar of Rosaline in the play? What, moreover, would follow from the other identification implied in Juliet's lines, one which locates Romeo in the place of the rose, and thus also in Rosaline's place? At the very least, a recognition that desire might not be determined by the gender of its object, that the coupling of Romeo and Juliet is not a unique moment of heterosexual perfection and privacy but part of a series whose substitutions do not respect either the uniqueness of individuals or the boundaries of gender difference.

These implications can be read from the start, in Benvolio's gentle solicitations of his "fair coz"; as the play opens, Benvolio knows where to find Romeo because he shares with him a like condition, "measuring his affections by my own" (1.1.124), keeping his distance as Romeo keeps his, weeping at his sorrows, displaying thereby a "love . . . that . . . / Doth add more grief to too much of mine own" (186–87); one heart vibrates to the other's:

> *Romeo.* Dost thou not laugh?
> *Ben.* No coz, I rather weep.
> *Romeo.* Good heart, at what?
> *Ben.* At thy good heart's oppression.
> *Romeo.* Why such is love's transgression.
> (1.1.181–83)

"Love's transgression" here refers indifferently to the effects of Rosaline upon Romeo, dividing him from himself, and the affection, the love of Benvolio for him, marked as it is, at once, by the strongest indications of identification and distance. His counsel, that Romeo forget Rosaline, is tantamount to a desire for him to remember himself and his friend; his counsel to replace Rosaline with some other flame is undertaken in the belief that a happy Romeo would be a happier companion.

The situation with Rosaline can't help but recall the initial sequence in Shakespeare's sonnets, where the sonneteer urges the young man to marry in order to further solidify bonds between men. In those poems, as Sedgwick astutely observes, the woman is barely present, no more than the conduit for firming up the patriarchy and guaranteeing the young man's place within a social order in which all the most heavily invested relations are those between men. The woman in these poems is no one in particular, simply anyone whom the young man would marry, and she poses no threat to the men or to the love that the sonneteer proffers. Rosaline would seem to be in much the same situations; she has no lines in the play and if she ever is onstage—at the ball at the Capulets' to which she has been invited, for example—her presence is unmarked and unremarked. Benvolio's desire that Romeo replace Rosaline with some more willing young woman seems to operate within the assumption that such a woman could occupy the position of the woman in sonnets 1–17, a nonentity that would guarantee that Romeo fulfilled his debt to society and yet remained available for the comforts of friendly solicitations. Such assumptions, it might be supposed, are at play too when Friar Laurence breathes a sigh of relief that his "son" has not transgressed with Rosaline, and he hastens to legitimate the relation with Juliet by arranging their marriage. If these plans presume a smooth transition from one love to another, they also make clear that from the start Romeo's condition is not one in which love exists in the privatized domain to which commentators assign it. Romeo's absence is remarked by his parents as the play begins; his friend's counsels make clear that love affects their relation too; and Friar Laurence moves quickly to legitimize the relationship through the institution of marriage.

In this context it is worth noting that Romeo's initial oxymoronic descriptions of love are occasioned by the signs of the street fight that opens the play; that is, he reads his emotional state as the reflection of the public brawl. This is only to say from another vantage point that love, from the start of the play, is implicated in the social, not separate from it. Thus if, from one vantage point, it might appear that in moving from Rosaline to Juliet, Romeo moves from an unproblematic love to a disruptive one, the plot of replacement would seem rather in either case to recognize the sociality of desire. The difference between Romeo's two loves—of comfort and despair?—is crossed from the start, and both loves work to secure and to disrupt the social; both loves are "transgressive." Both loves are forbidden, a fact made clear when we recall the moment when Rosaline is first named in the play; her name appears on the list that Romeo reads of those invited to the Capulets' ball; she is Capulet's "fair niece" (1.2.70). "My only love sprung from my only hate" (1.5.137): Romeo may be, for Juliet, her first transgressive desire, but she is, for Romeo, the second in his pursuit of forbidden loves. When Juliet delivers her speech about Romeo and the name of the rose, she inserts him into the series in which she already participates as Romeo's substitute love, a new Rosaline with a different name (it is worth noting that the Rosaline figure in Shakespeare's source has no name).

Placing him in her place, however, Juliet follows a textual track marked out earlier. For while it is arguable, as I have argued, that the negotiations around Rosaline resemble those in the initial sequence of Shakespeare's sonnets, one moment in which those poems are recalled might suggest that the configuration is not quite the one I have already described. Romeo's complaint about Rosaline is that she is unresponsive, chaste as the moon; refusing to be "hit / With Cupid's arrow" (1.1.206–7), she is armed against love, even against "saint-seducing gold" (211): "O she is rich in beauty, only poor / That when she dies, with beauty dies her store" (213–14). These are recognizable complaints from the initial sonnets, but there they are directed at the young man who threatens by a kind of usury to make waste. These charges are laid at Rosaline as well in the lines immediately following those quoted above, when to Benvolio's query, "Then she hath sworn that she will still live chaste," Romeo replies, "She hath, and in that sparing makes huge waste." In these respects Rosaline duplicates the young man who seems to have a patent on a beauty that the sonneteer cannot imagine located anywhere but in him and a progeny of young men who will duplicate and keep forever in circulation his unmatchable beauty.

> Looke what an unthrift in the world doth spend
> Shifts but his place, for still the world injoyes it
> But beauties waste hath in the world an end,
> And kept unusde the user so destroyes it.[4]

If Rosaline is, in this respect, in the place of the young man of the sonnets, the connection is furthered by her name, for it is possible to suspect that in the sonnets her name is his; in the very first poem he is named "beauties *Rose*" (1.2). Hence, when Juliet ponders the name of the rose—a name that might as well be hers or his—her lines operate in this sphere of gender exchange too.

On the one hand this could explain why the figure of Rosaline is so unthreatening in the play, how easily Romeo's grief over her can be incorporated in homosocial relations; she is so little a woman that she might as well be a man, so little a woman that all she does is to consolidate relations between men and serve as a conduit for them. Yet before one endorses this reading, one would also have to add: she is a forbidden love, as much as Juliet is, and as threatening too. If, that is, Rosaline, and the infinite replaceability of the rose, intimate the smooth workings of a homosocial order that gives women a place only in order to erase them, the transgressive danger spied in this love—even if it is between men and so secured—is what the period might call *sodomy*. Moreover, that transgression—of alliance, of the ties of the patriarchal organization and distribution of property and entitlements—

while usually thought to occur between men, can also take place between a man and a woman. Locating Rosaline as the young man, in short, might as easily place her in the sphere of the homosocial as in the space of less containable and less socially approved desires. It's here that one might suspect that the name of the rose—like the name Rosaline as it travels in Shakespeare's plays to characters in *Love's Labours Lost* and *As You Like It,* where Rosalind's other name, of course, is Ganymede—plots a trajectory from the fair young man to the dark lady. For it is of course the case that the threatening sexuality that the dark lady represents—outside marriage and promiscuous and dangerous to the homosocial order—is closer to sodomy than almost anything suggested in the poems to the young man. Yet one must think of these sets of poems in a complementary and displaced relationship rather than, as in Joel Fineman's account, as marked by the uncrossable diacritical markings homo and hetero.[5] Just as the threat to Romeo's masculinity that Juliet represents when he declares himself effeminized by her—valor's steel gone soft (3.1.111–13)—might be read not only within the dynamics of the dark lady sonnets (Juliet assuming Rosaline's guise in that transformation), but also as suggesting another movement across gender: if Romeo is feminized by her, she perhaps is masculinized. Hence, at the moment when Romeo spies Juliet on the balcony, he declares that the sun has replaced the moon; the moon earlier is Rosaline's celestial counterpart, mythically allying her to Diana. Is the sun, then, male, and is Juliet Romeo's Apollo? Such a question returns us to the position of Rosaline as fair young man and to the possibility that Juliet's gender is equally destabilized, and thereby leads us to ponder desires that are not governed by the gender of objects and which are not allied to the formations of gender difference as the homo/hetero divide imagines them.[6]

Such a way of reading the play is anathema to heterosexualizing readings of *Romeo and Juliet* and of Shakespeare in general. Thus, when Janet Adelman, for example, declares that the tragedy begins at the moment in which Romeo announces his effeminization ("O sweet Juliet, / Thy beauty hath made me effeminate / And in my temper soften'd valour's steel" [3.1.115–17]) because it signals the breakup of male-male relations in the play, solidified by their aggression toward and fear of women, this marks a tragedy that she regards as inevitable when comedy takes the form of male bonding or, worse, as it seems in Adelman's account, when male bonding can extend itself to the transvestite actor.[7] In those instances, Adelman opines, Shakespeare's plays indulge in the supposition "that one need not choose between a homosexual and a heterosexual bond" (91), a belief that she terms a fantasy that stands in the way of maturity and male development, which must culminate in heterosexuality. Otherwise, the plays might suggest "the fantasy that the relationships [with transvestite actors] are simultaneously homosexual and heterosexual—a simultaneity that threatens to become uncomfortable when, for example, in *As You Like It* we hear that Orlando has kissed Ganymede-Rosalind" (86). We, it is presumed, don't like it, and the reason seems to be that anything other than heterosexuality is repellent.

However much arguments like Kahn's or Adelman's expose the misogyny of Shakespeare's plays, their enforcement of heterosexuality and gender difference belies energies in the plays that cannot be reduced to the erasure of women. For if one thinks of Rosaline or of Juliet assuming the place of men, or of Romeo taking up a feminine position, those differences only read invidiously within the logic of a compulsory heterosexuality. When Rosaline is imagined as hoarding herself, and refusing to open her lap to gold, she is, like the young man and like the dark lady, imagined as sexually autonomous and sexually self-fulfilling. Insofar as Juliet takes up the position of Rosaline, their difference is marked by a single word. The woman who says no has become the woman who says yes; "Ay" is Juliet's first reported word (1.3.43), her first word in the balcony scene (2.2.25), and the locus of her subjectivity is her assent to desire, her active solicitation of sexual experience (see, in this respect, her play on "Ay" and "I" in 3.2.45–51). When she thinks about having sex with Romeo, she imagines cutting him up into little pieces (3.2.21–25); whether this marks her as (in the favored terms of Kahn's analysis) phallically aggressive or not, it suggests that the diacritical markings of gender are transgressed in the play, something to be seen as well earlier in the same soliloquy, in which the solicitation of night, a maternal figure, is transformed into the scene of an enactment of a "strange love" (3.2.15) in which Romeo first is night and then lies "upon the wings of night / Whiter than new snow upon a raven's back" (18–19). In this "purification" and masculinization of her beloved not only has he become—as she was—the brightness of day, but he also takes Night from behind; strange sex indeed.

It is, of course, arguable that the transgressions of gender that masculinize Juliet (or Rosaline) participate in misogyny (either by way of erasure or by excoriating active sexuality, as occurs most often in the play through attacks on the nurse), but this move across gender also allows a subject position for women that is not confined within patriarchal boundaries. That is to say, it is only by seeing the energies in the plays that are not dictated by a compulsory heterosexuality and gender binarism that one can begin to mark their productive energies. In the case of *Romeo and Juliet,* as I have been suggesting, this means to put pressure on the heterosexualizing idealization of the play and on the magical solution it arrives at over the corpses of the young lovers. It is, in short, to make them available for forbidden desires that really do call patriarchal arrangements into question. Readings of the plays, written from whatever position, that seek to enforce a compulsory heterosexuality must be complicit with the domestication of women and with the scapegoating of men (often by palming off the ills of heterosexuality on homosexuality). Such readings need to be opposed, and not merely on ideological grounds; hetero- and homosexuality are profound misnomers for the organization of sexuality in Shakespeare's time. As this essay has been suggesting, gender and sexuality in *Romeo and Juliet* do not subscribe to the compulsions of modern critics of the play.

So much Juliet's lines on the name of the rose prompt us to think, especially, as I have been suggesting, in the identifications across gender that they allow, and for the ways in which they open trajectories of desire that cross gender difference. If the rose is most literally Rosaline's name respelled, it is, with only the slightest metaphorical force, Juliet's as well, since she is not only Romeo's newest rose, but is herself locked within "orchard walls . . . high and hard to climb, / And the place death" (2.2.63–64), a dangerous flower to be plucked, dangerous, as I have been suggesting, and as this description does too, because the desires she represents are closely allied to forbidden sexual acts more usually thought of as taking place between men. Juliet is most explicitly a flower when she has apparently been taken by death. "The roses in thy lips and cheeks shall fade" (4.1.99), Friar Laurence tells her, and this is what her father sees; "the sweetest flower of the field" (4.5.29), he tells her husband-to-be, has been taken already, not, as is the case, by Romeo, but by death: Death has "lain with thy wife. There she lies / Flower as she was, deflowered by him" (36–37). Such imaginings of the sexual act as taking place in the wrong place ("the place death") and with the wrong partner only further the sense that the sexual field in which desire operates in the play is the forbidden desire named sodomy. The ungenerative locus of death allies the sexual act to the supposedly sterile and unreproductive practice of usury associated with the young man and with Rosaline's self-hoarding and waste, themselves as suggestive of sodomy as they are of masturbatory activities as well.

If the living-dead Juliet is the flower deflowered, the usual deformations of the signifier that works to make these connections in the play—the name of the rose—find a further point of transformation (of nominal difference and identification) at her funeral. Friar Laurence orders rosemary to be strewn on her supposed corpse (4.5.79) and the stage direction at line 96 suggests that it is done: *"Exeunt all but the Nurse and musicians, casting rosemary on Juliet."* Juliet's living-dead status could be taken to prevaricate in bodily terms between the generative and ungenerative desires whose paths cross each other in the play; much as she has and has not been deflowered by death, her union with Romeo is, from the end of the second act of the play, legitimated by marriage and continues to summon its allure from the unspeakable terrain of sodomy. If, in her balcony speech, Juliet joins herself to Romeo through the name of the rose—the name that connects them both through the cross-gendered figure of Rosaline as well—at her funeral the name has been transformed to rosemary. But this too has been anticipated by the vagaries of the signifier, or so the nurse reports in lines that seem to have misheard the balcony declaration and to send those lines about the rose along the route to the rosemary cast upon Juliet:

Nurse. Doth not rosemary and Romeo begin both with a letter?
Romeo. Ay, Nurse, what of that? Both with an "R."
Nurse. Ah, mocker! That's the dog's name, "R" is for the—No, I know it begins with some other letter; and she hath the prettiest sententious of it, of you, and rosemary, that it would do you good to hear it.

(2.4.202–8)

The circuit of desire moves through the letter R, linking Romeo, the rose, Rosaline, rosemary, and Juliet, whose name begins with some other letter but is not misspelled in this sequence, proper and improper at once like the name Rosemary attached by her to Romeo and through the rosemary to her living-dead body, or like the forbidden fruit (whose other proper name we will, in a moment, confront) that can be domesticated behind the orchard walls.

The nurse's lines deform the lovely alliteration of the letter R; she hears in it not only the growling of a desire that is less than transcendentally human—the bestial bark—but also something else. In his note on lines 205–6, Brian Gibbons allows Phillip Williams to complete the nurse's unfinished sentence: "the Nurse just stops herself from saying the word *arse*—'with a somewhat unlooked-for show of modesty.' "[8] Another name for alliteration, apt here: assonance; another name for the movement of the letter R and the cross-couplings it allows, the *open Rs*. Gibbons goes where the nurse does not, immodestly allowing the unspeakable, and not just in the margins; the word is pronounced outside the garden walls as well:

> *Mer.* If love be blind, love cannot hit the mark.
> Now will he sit under a medlar tree
> And wish his mistress were that kind of fruit
> As maids call medlars when they laugh alone.
> O Romeo, that she were, O that she were
> An open-arse and thou a poperin pear!
>
> (2.1.33–38)

The medlar, whose other name, open-arse, is this secret now pronounced, is a member of the rose family (check Webster's if you don't believe me).[9] Gibbons allows the open-arse into his text (it appears in no quarto nor in any early edition of the play), an instance, in which, as he puts it in the textual introduction of his edition, he has "retained" an "archaic" form (25) unwarranted by his copytext.[10]

I don't want to be detained here by the textual crux of 2.1.38, much as it would communicate with the other moment that has animated this discussion—the passage on the rose, which also has a famous textual problem around the very issue of the proper name or word which makes possible the open Rs of this text; or the nurse's assonance, available only in Q2, a text of the play remarkable for its self-remarking textuality.[11] Rather, I would simply notice that in this scene Mercutio begins by conjuring Romeo, naming him by his proper—which is to say, entirely generic—names: "Romeo! Humours! Madman! Passion! Lover!" (2.1.7), and that when these (im)proper names fail to raise him, Mercutio tries a more (in)direct approach, naming him by calling him up in the name of Rosaline: "In his mistress' name / I conjure only but to raise up him" (28–29). If the lines imagine Romeo rising to occupy this place, they deal at once in an identification between Romeo and Rosaline and with Romeo's desire for Rosaline. These meet in that conveniently open place that the Rs mark, the open-arse that also hits and deflects the mark (much as both Q1 and Q2 fail to deliver what Gibbons and most modern editions now allow Mercutio to say). Mercutio's lines about a blind love that does and does not hit the mark recall Benvolio's counsels earlier about the deflection of Romeo's desires from Rosaline (1.1.203–5), and they too suggest that the path of the deformations of desire away from her never leaves the spot that she marks, which is precisely the unnameable crossing here (in the modern text) not left blank or marked out or marked over. The locus of anal penetration, of course, is available on any body, male or female. Mercutio's conjuring also conjures him into the magic circle, an O that is not, as most commentators would have it be, the vaginal opening, for this is how Mercutio voices—through Rosaline—his desire for Romeo, his version, that is, of Benvolio's more benign voicing of the place she can occupy between men.[12] Mercutio is calling Romeo up for him, as he does throughout the opening acts of the play, a deflection of Romeo's desire from the unresponsive beloved, to one who, as much as Juliet later, wants to share a bed with Romeo (where Mercutio would lie is suggested by the solitary bed he goes home to, the "truckle-bed" [2.1.39] that lies under one placed above it).

As Mercutio conjures up Romeo in his generic names, and then deflects those names through the name of Rosaline, he calls up his relationship to Romeo. The secret name of Romeo in the play, as Joseph Porter has convincingly argued, is Valentine, the otherwise nonexistent brother of Mercutio named only in the list of those invited to the Capulet ball that the illiterate servant cannot read, and that Romeo does: "*Mercutio and his brother Valentine*" (1.2.68).[13] It resonates (assonates) with another name down the list, "*Signior Valentio and his cousin Tybalt*" (71). This second Valentine, as invisible elsewhere in the play as the first, participates in a cousinship that, like the brotherhood of Mercutio and Valentine, may name properly what cannot be said. This male couple resounds when Tybalt charges Mercutio with being Romeo's "consort" ("Mercutio, thou consortest with Romeo. / *Mer.* Consort?" 3.1.44–45), and to Mercutio's dismay at Romeo's declaration a few lines later that he would rather make love than fight with Tybalt. Tybalt, after all, is someone that Mercutio characterizes as ill-equipped to handle a sword; if Romeo is his man, as he declares (3.1.55), then, Mercutio opines, Romeo will follow him, taking him, it would seem, from behind. If Mercutio counsels Romeo to prick love for pricking (1.4.28), it is, it appears, because he fears that his Valentine has received the "butt-shaft" (2.4.16) of love, that Rosaline, armed like Diana, has hit his mark, that the boy love has come to the depth of his tail and buried his bauble in that hole rather than in his (see 2.4.90–100). To return to the scene of conjuring, then, is to register Mercutio's rivalry for a place that anyone might occupy and to recognize his projection into Rosaline's place as his own, as his way, that is, of occupying the magic circle or owning, to vary the metaphor slightly, the desires named by the open Rs in the text.

That these desires can be named variously, and never properly, Mercutio's lines further intimate when the secret name is one that maids trade among themselves in private. Female secrecy is broached in those lines, and appropriated to a secret about transgression that does not respect gender difference. If there is, in this context, something to be said about the textual crux at 2.1.38, it is perhaps best suggested by J. Dover Wilson's gloss in the Cambridge edition of the play (1955) on the reading that is adopted by Gibbons (and by a number of other editions, most recently by Stanley Wells and Gary Taylor in their 1986 Oxford *Complete Shakespeare*). Q1, as noted above, has "open *Et caetera*" at this point while Q2 prints "An open, or thou" (D1v). Wilson argues that a compositor or scribal error is responsible for "or" (as a misreading of manuscript "ers," the presumption that leads Gibbons to "retain" a reading not found in any printed text but assumed to have been in Shakespeare's hand). In writing his note on the crux, Wilson conveniently ignores the comma in Q2 which might, like the unfinished sentence of the nurse's, indicate that Mercutio leaves unsaid what needs not be said (the alternative name for the medlar is about as available as anything, an open secret not to be said more openly). This allows him to dispose of the possibility that "or" means "or" rather than being a misread arse. "He speaks," Wilson opines, "of the fruits [the ripely rotten apple and the popping pear] as complementary not alternative so that 'and' not 'or' is required" (151). "And" introduces, anglice, the "bad" Q1 evasion of the more forthrightly named Rs. For Wilson, this is what is proper and required at this spot, that her arse and his poperin complement each other. In other words, Wilson reads "and" to mean "or" (inserts "and" in his text so that it does so) since "or" might mean "and"; "or," were it to be there, might offer an "alternative" that Wilson will not allow, the possibility that either member of the couple could assume either position. This is perhaps the scandal that the whispering of the maids is about, or that can be heard as Juliet swallows the potion in order to get Romeo in the grave before Tybalt does ("O look, methinks I see my cousin's ghost / Seeking out Romeo that did spit his body / Upon a rapier's point! Stay, Tybalt, stay" 4.3.55–57). In those lines Juliet assumes Mercutio's rivalrous position, while Tybalt functions for her—as he had for Romeo, and as he does earlier for Juliet in a scene that prevaricates over and also enforces the identity of her cousin and her lover (3.5.65–125)—as the switching point for an identification that breaches love and enmity, friend and villain, death and life, the open arse and the open grave of transgressively (un)productive desires. What these moments share—and they structure the trajectories of desire imagined in the play—is the recognition that anyone—man or woman—might be in the place marked by the open Rs of *Romeo and Juliet*.

Notes

1.   Brian Gibbons, ed., *Romeo and Juliet* (London: Methuen, 1980), 70. All citations are from this edition. For further evaluations of this edition, see my review of it in *Shakespeare Studies* 16 (1983):343–48 and Stanley Wells's review in *TLS* 4030 (20 June 1980):710. G. Blakemore Evans in his New Cambridge edition of the play (Cambridge University Press, 1984) devotes pp. 16–20 to "language, style and imagery" in familiar formalist terms.

2.   I take the term from its usage by Eve Kosofsky Sedgwick, *Between Men* (New York: Columbia University Press, 1985), and in the pages that follow depend upon her arguments throughout the book as well as their particular application to Shakespeare in the chapter "Swan in Love."

3.   "Coming of Age in Verona," reprinted from *Modern Language Studies* 8 (1977–78):5–22 in Carolyn Ruth Swift Lenz, Gayle Greene, and Carol Thomas Neely, eds., *The Woman's Part* (Urbana: University of Illinois Press, 1980), 171–93.

4.   1609 text quoted from *Shakespeare's Sonnets,* ed. Stephen Booth (New Haven: Yale University Press, 1978), 9.9–12.

5.   Fineman's account in *Shakespeare's Perjured Eye* (Berkeley: University of California Press, 1986) compulsively reproduces this distinction—even claiming for Shakespeare nothing less than the invention of "the poetics of heterosexuality" (18), yet, as he moves to take up the issue of cross-coupling, and with it the phenomena of the pricked prick and the cut cunt (see, e.g., pp. 275 ff.), as he terms them, the difference between hetero- and homosexuality is breached. Nonetheless, the mode of breaching is by the route of castration and thus operates under the aegis of the oedipal and thereby within the heterosexualizing argument that allows for difference only under that rubric.

6.   Work on the historicity of gender that would lend support to these suppositions would include Stephen Greenblatt's "Fiction and Friction," in *Shakespearean Negotiations: The Circulation of Social Energy in Renaissance England* (Oxford: Clarendon Press, 1988), esp. pp. 73–86; Thomas Laqueur's *Making Sex* (Cambridge: Harvard University Press, 1990); and Ann Rosalind Jones and Peter Stallybrass, "Fetishizing Gender: Constructing the Hermaphrodite in Renaissance Europe," in Julia Epstein and Kristina Straub, eds., *Body Guards* (New York: Routledge, 1991).

7.   See Janet Adelman, "Male Bonding in Shakespeare's Comedies," in Peter Erickson and Coppélia Kahn, eds., *Shakespeare's Rough Magic* (Newark: University of Delaware Press, 1985); pp. 80–81 are on *Romeo and Juliet*.

8.   G. Blakemore Evans also cites Williams at this point in his New Cambridge edition, but then misunderstands the implications of the nurse's speech: "Obviously she can't read or spell, and because of its rude associations she decides that 'Romeo' and 'rosemary' must begin with some other letter" (p. 115). The nurse, however, registers that she stops herself from saying a word that sounds like it begins with an R but doesn't; Evan's swipe at the nurse's illiteracy displaces, one suspects, his discomfort at the associations implicated in the nurse's assonance.

9.   I'm grateful to Natasha Korda for pointing this out to me as well as to a set of notes she prepared on the crux in Mercutio's lines which has helped me think through the points argued here.

10.   For a glance at this "retention" (anal?) and its supposed restoration of an original unavailable in any text that might claim to be close to a Shakespearean original, see Random Cloud, "The Marriage of Good and Bad Quartos," *Shakespeare Quarterly* 33 (1982):430–31. For a defense of the properness of this scandalous reading by the modern editor who first printed it in his 1954 Yale edition of the play, see Richard Hosley, "The Corrupting Influence of the Bad Quarto on the Received Text of *Romeo and Juliet*," *Shakespeare Quarterly* 4 (1953):21. Hosley would rather have *open-arse* than allow his text to be "contaminated" by the "bad quarto," Q1, which reads "open *Et caetera*" (D1) at this spot.

11.   For pursuit of the crux about the name of the rose, up to the point engaged in this essay, I refer the reader to an earlier essay of mine, " 'What? in a names that which we call a Rose': The Desired Texts of *Romeo and Juliet*," written for and delivered at the 1988 session of an annual conference at the University of Toronto on editorial and textual matters and forthcoming in the volume of papers from that meeting, *Crisis in Editing: Texts of the English Renaissance,* ed. Randall McLeod. In that essay I call into question the usual supposition that of the two quarto editions of the play, Q1 (1597) is simply a "bad quarto" (shaped by the memories of actors and the imposition of nonauthorial materials), while Q2 (1599) is authoritative and derived from Shakespeare's hand; rather, I suggest, both texts arise from a theatrical milieu of continual revision and rewriting, and no modern text of the play can fail to consult both or can easily adjudicate differences between the two texts or, as often happens, when Q2 offers more than one version of the same set of lines, in the hope of arriving at final or original authorial intention. I argue that intentionality was never so limited.

The crux involved in 2.1.38 will be unraveled in the discussion that follows; in Q1 the line alludes to an "open *Et caetera*" (D1), which, were one to take that script as depending solely on stage performance, would mean that this reports the line as spoken (i.e., as speaking and possibly evading speaking more forthrightly), though it is also possible to regard the *Et caetera* either as a way of naming otherwise what need not be named any more forthrightly or as an evasion of more direct naming supplied by the printer and not following what the actor actually said.

At this point, Q2 reads "open, or," (D1v), and, it is assumed, as I discuss below, that "or" represents a misreading by the compositor of Shakespeare's hand ("ers" is assumed to have been in the manuscript); the notion that "arse" was once really in the text or spoken on stage is not quite so easily made, however, since the comma in Q2 might indicate that a pause, and not a word, was offered at this spot. Again, one faces the dilemma of whether an unsaying said more than the more forthright reading offered by Gibbons; whether the lines in each earlier text have been censored, and if so, by whom; what, if anything, was actually spoken by the actor at this point; or, indeed, whether there was one way in which this line ever was delivered. Or, finally, whether this massive textual problem does not also correspond to the very nexus of the utterly unspeakable / absolutely commonplace nature of anal sex, in this instance dictated by all the proprieties surrounded by the supposed unbreachable difference between the allowable spheres of male-male intimacy and the excoriated one called sodomy, or between the supposition that the only "good" sex performed by male-female couples is procreative and conducted under the auspices of marriage, everything else being capable of being called, once again, sodomy.

12.   I follow Joseph Porter here, who argues in *Shakespeare's Mercutio* (Chapel Hill: University of North Carolina Press, 1988) that the lines "involve the idea of Mercutio's taking Rosaline's place not only as conjurer but also as container of Romeo's phallus" though I do not follow him in wishing to make this the "fleeting apparently subliminal trace of sexual desire on Mercutio's part" (157) since that assumption implies that homoerotic desire must operate within the regimes of a closet that, I think, more appropriately might be seen as part of the modern apparatus of sexuality with its markers of homo- and heterosexuality. Since these desires are not distinguished and their boundaries are more fluid in Shakespeare's time, there is no need to make them unavailable, which locating homoeroticism as subliminal does. On pp.

160–62, Porter ably dismantles the heterosexualizing readings of this moment, in which even an open-arse is read as a figure for female genitalia, the most extraordinary of such instances perhaps being that of Eric Partridge, *Shakespeare's Bawdy* (London: Routledge, 1990 [1947]): " 'An open *et-caetera*' must here mean 'an open arse.' Yet my interpretation of Shakespeare's 'open *et-caetera*' as 'pudend' is correct, for the opening clearly refers to the female cleft, not the human anus. With the human bottom regarded as involving and connoting the primary sexual area, compare the slangy use of *tail* for the human bottom in general and for the female pudend in particular" (101–2). While Porter valuably insists that Mercutio's lines are about sodomy, his concession that "of course the sodomy is heterosexual" (161) could be seen as complicit with the heterosexualizing of Partridge and other commentators on the line precisely because it differentiates homo- and heterosexual sodomy. The acts are not so distinguishable; moreover, the conceptual range of the term sodomy in the period does not heed the hetero/homo distinction, as Alan Bray makes clear as a starting point in his discussion in *Homosexuality in Renaissance England* (London: Gay Men's Press, 1982), 14. My arguments above about a transgressive sodomy, and its link to cross-gender relations, seek to void this diacritical marker, and the move seems to me important both because it takes account of the history of sexuality but also insofar as it opposes the ways in which the distinction of homo- and heterosexual sodomy was mobilized in the U.S. Supreme Court decision in *Bowers v. Hardwick,* which denied any fundamental constitutional right for acts of so-called "homosexual sodomy" while guaranteeing the legality of the act for heterosexuals.

13.   See Joseph A. Porter, "Mercutio's Brother," *South Atlantic Review* 49 (1984):31–41, and the fuller development of the argument in *Shakespeare's Mercutio,* 1–10, 145–63.

TRACING THE
AUTHORIAL MIND

◆

Earlier generations wrote as if they were intimate with the mind of the Bard of Avon, and in popular culture it is commonplace to hear "Shakespeare says, '. . . ,'" when the speaker quoted is, say, Juliet. Such intuitions were challenged by the notion of the "death of the author," which gained some currency not long ago in general critical discourse. In Shakespeare study that notion has sometimes been associated with the now widely recognized "instability" of Shakespeare's dramatic text. To some, abandoning the presupposition of a unique authoritative version of each play has seemed to drive a last nail into the coffin of the once accessible playwright.

In fact, however, recognition of the instability of Shakespeare's play texts serves precisely, and powerfully, to counter reports of the "death" of this particular author. For, the more we can isolate of, say, scrivener Ralph Crane's interventions in a play text, the more sharply the Shakespearean stands clear. And the more we see of intertextual relations between Shakespeare's texts and others, and among Shakespeare's own texts, including evidences of rethinking and revision, the more we gain unprecedented insight into the mind surpassingly responsible for the value accorded those works.

Amy J. Riess and George Walton Williams, " 'Tragical Mirth': From *Romeo* to *Dream*," address what has been something of a crux in commentary on *Romeo and Juliet*, the question whether this play precedes or follows *A Midsummer Night's Dream*. Earlier commentators have noted links between the two plays, perhaps more closely affiliated via formal and lexical repetitions and echoes than any other pair in the canon. Riess and Williams, noting many more, illuminate relationships between these texts (and with others, such as Ovid), most of which "must have been unconscious in Shakespeare's mind," and so provide persuasive new grounds for placing the tragedy first.[1]

E. Pearlman, "Shakespeare at Work: *Romeo and Juliet*," surveys, in the second quarto of *Romeo and Juliet*, "vestiges both small and large" of Shakespeare's progress of revision. He tracks an authorial play of mind in the heat of composition, attending to evident revisions of single words and lines and also such large-scale architectural changes as the interpolation of Mercutio's Queen Mab speech. Whereas editors generally have treated these textual discrepancies as annoyances to be discounted or swept away, Pearlman, writing in the new climate of recognition of textual instability, finds these moments invaluable for the vantages they open into Shakespeare's process of composition.[2]

The collection concludes with the newest and perhaps the most revolutionary essay, Donald W. Foster, "The Webbing of *Romeo and Juliet*." As Foster shows, using *Romeo and Juliet* as a test case, his Shaxicon, itself on the verge of public debut, enables advances in dating and attribution that would have been undreamed-of a mere 15 years ago. In Foster's hands, furthermore, electronic scholarship—the way of the future, according to him, and to many others—provides startlingly detailed panoramas of the workings and habits of Shakespeare's mind.

Amy J. Riess Kaz graduated from Duke in 1993, is completing a Master's degree in English from Emory as she teaches at Holy Names Academy in Seattle, and hopes to pursue doctoral studies in the near future.

George Walton Williams is Emeritus Professor of English at Duke, where he has taught courses in Shakespeare for many years. He has published articles critical and textual in diverse periodicals, edited *Romeo and Juliet* in 1964 and again (with Robert K. Turner Jr.) in 1970, is currently preparing the edition of *Henry V* (with T. L. Berger) for the Variorum Series, and is associate Editor of the Arden Series.

E. (Elihu Hessel) Pearlman was educated at Cornell and Harvard; he teaches in the department of English at the University of Colorado at Denver. He is currently studying Shakespeare's craftsmanship.

Donald W. Foster, Jean Webster Professor of Dramatic Literature at Vassar College, is the author of *Elegy by W. S.: A Study of Attribution,* and of various articles on Shakespearean, classical, and biblical literature. Shaxicon, his text data base, is being reformatted for access on the World Wide Web.

Notes

1.   The question of priority may of course be complicated by new grounds for assuming revision of both plays. While Riess and Williams do not address this matter, their analysis would seem to hold good for sequencing the first versions of the two plays. Their evidence, such as verbal reprises, is generally called internal, as opposed to such external evidence as data from the surrounding culture, or topical allusions within the text in question. Foster, in the essay here, marshals a new and powerful sort of evidence, which might also be called internal.

2.   Future probes may conceivably go still deeper into the quick forge and working-house of Shakespeare's thought. For instance, much—perhaps most—"rewriting" happens before anything at all is set down. With instruments now becoming available—critical instruments and also the technology of electronic texts—it may be possible to track more of those mental cancellations, displacements, and amendments than heretofore.

"Tragical Mirth": From *Romeo* to *Dream*

Amy J. Riess and George Walton Williams

Perhaps Queen Mab gallops through critics' brains, and then they dream of the chronology of Shakespeare's plays—especially the sequence of *Romeo and Juliet* and *A Midsummer Night's Dream*. Editors of either of these two plays are inclined to consider the play that they are editing the later play. Harold F. Brooks surmises in the Arden *A Midsummer Night's Dream* (1979) that *Romeo and Juliet* preceded; Brian Gibbons intimates in the Arden *Romeo and Juliet* (1980) that *A Midsummer Night's Dream* preceded. R. A. Foakes's New Cambridge *A Midsummer Night's Dream* (1984) posits the precedence of *Romeo and Juliet;* and G. Blakemore Evans's New Cambridge *Romeo and Juliet* (1984) suggests the precedence of *A Midsummer Night's Dream*. Stanley Wells and Gary Taylor, editors of both plays, in the *Complete Works* (1986) place *A Midsummer Night's Dream* before *Romeo and Juliet* but in the *Textual Companion* (1987) explain why *Romeo and Juliet* should precede *A Midsummer Night's Dream*.[1] These and other critics have argued for dating on the basis of natural events, such as earthquake, flood, and marriage, or of rhetorical elements, such as rhyme and vocabulary, but their efforts seem not yet to have settled the argument to everyone's satisfaction. This paper will argue from internal evidence that *Romeo and Juliet* is the earlier play, and that in writing *A Midsummer Night's Dream,* Shakespeare used the events and the language of tragedy to increase the mirth of comedy. Whether or not he did so deliberately is beyond our knowledge, but some relationships are inescapably demonstrable. Most of these must have been unconscious in Shakespeare's mind; a few—as we see the matter—would seem to derive significance from a conscious awareness of the effect that the familiar knowledge of the earlier play would have on an audience in its response to the later play, such a knowledge perhaps shaping, certainly enriching, that response.

Though many of the relationships between *Romeo and Juliet* and *A Midsummer Night's Dream* have been noted, some merit further consideration, particularly those concerning the playlet "Pyramus and Thisby," a text derived from Golding's version of Ovid's *Metamorphoses,* Book 4, lines 55–166. The

Amy J. Riess and George Walton Williams, " 'Tragical Mirth': From *Romeo* to *Dream*," *Shakespeare Quarterly* 43 (1992):214–218. Reprinted with permission of *Shakespeare Quarterly*.

first of these is the relationship between the parents of the young lovers, represented in the performance before the court in Athens by the erecting of a wall, symbolizing the parents' hostility, and by the later removal of that wall, symbolizing their reconciliation—a reconciliation effected by the deaths of their children. However, as C. L. Barber argued many years ago, "There is nothing in Ovid about a reconciliation, but there is a great deal at the end of *Romeo*."[2]

In the original casting of the playlet, in Act 1, scene 2, of *A Midsummer Night's Dream,* Peter Quince announces that he will take the part of Thisby's father, and he assigns the part of Pyramus' father to Tom Snout, the tinker.[3] In Act 3, scene 1, the two mechanicals assigned the parts of the fathers, the counterparts of Capulet and Montague, are the first to refer to the wall. Quince (Thisby's father) recognizes that there must be "a wall in the great chamber; for Pyramus and Thisby, says the story, did talk through the chink of a wall" (ll. 54–56), and Snout (Pyramus' father) retorts, "You can never bring in a wall" (l. 57).[4] But in the performance, those parents do not appear; and hence there can be no hostility between them. Nevertheless, Shakespeare retains the wall to divide Pyramus and Thisby as a symbol of the divisive feud between the Montagues and Capulets. Juliet specifically has layered the walls with a mortar of mortality and has linked them with the deaths that results from the feud of the families:

> The orchard walls are high and hard to climb,
> And the place death, considering who thou art,
> If any of my kinsmen find thee here.
>
> (2.2.63–65)

The language and context of passages concerning the wall in the playlet betray the fact that Shakespeare had these fatal "orchard walls" of *Romeo and Juliet* in mind when he fashioned the "witty partition" of "Pyramus and Thisby."

And though there is no need to bring in a wall, in Act 5 Snout himself plays the part of Wall. In giving the part of Wall to Snout, a tinker, Shakespeare may have been taking into account the customary deprecatory attitude toward tinkers as unskilled menders.[5] In such unskillfulness Snout as Wall may represent the continuing hostility (not easily mended) between the feuding families imported from *Romeo and Juliet.* In the wandering Wall of "Pyramus and Thisby," Shakespeare perpetuates the feud of *Romeo and Juliet.* Wall concludes his speaking part: "Thus have I, Wall, my part dischargèd so; / And, being done, thus Wall away doth go" (5.1.202–3). Wall exits, and Theseus indicates symbolically the end of the feud: "Now is the mural down between the two neighbors" (ll. 204–5). But Wall reenters at the end of the playlet, retaining his association with the fatal feud, for Demetrius observes that Wall, along with Moonshine and Lion, will "bury the dead" (ll. 340–41). This observation provokes Lion's assurance, for a second time, that "the wall is down that parted their fathers" (ll. 342–43), and that the feud has come to an end. The barrier between feuding parents—not in Ovid, not in *A Midsummer Night's Dream,* not in "Pyramus and Thisby"—must allude to a situation that the audience would have recognized: the "Pyramus and Thisby" playlet deconstructs the wall of *Romeo and Juliet* hostility and ends with *Romeo and Juliet* reconciliation.

Another link between the tragedy and the playlet which may indicate precedence is the alteration of Quince's prologue so that in details it agrees with the prologue of *Romeo and Juliet.* In Act 3, scene 1, Quince announces, "Well, we will have . . . a prologue, and it shall be written in eight and six" (ll. 21–22), and Bottom offers the alternative meter of eight and eight (ll. 23–24); but neither form is used for the prologue of the actual "Pyramus and Thisby" performance in Act 5. Quince writes in ten and ten (iambic pentameter) and so conforms the "Pyramus and Thisby" prologue to the metrics of the *Romeo and Juliet* prologue.[6] Quince's prologue begins and ends with units of ten lines, each consisting of two quatrains and a final couplet (5.1.108–17, 141–50). (After the first of these units, courtly conversation intrudes and interrupts [ll. 118–25].) But between these two "stanzaic" forms occurs a section of fourteen lines (plus one), replicating the rhyme scheme of the Elizabethan sonnet that constitutes the prologue of *Romeo and Juliet,* with, however, an extra line (unrhymed) interpolated before the final couplet, thereby "improving" on the standard sonnet form: "This grisly beast (which Lion hight by name)" (l. 138). Perhaps Quince adds this extra lion-line to accommodate Snout, who declared at the rehearsal, "Therefore another prologue must tell he is not a lion" (3.1.29–30). Snug, as the Lion, delivers his own prologue later (5.1.216–23).

The opening quatrain of the "Pyramus and Thisby" prologue continues the end rhyme (while reversing the final sentiment) of the *Romeo and Juliet* prologue, which concludes: "The which if you with patient ears attend, / What here shall miss, our toil shall strive to mend" (ll. 13–14). While the prologue of *Romeo and Juliet* ends with the intent "to mend," the "Pyramus and Thisby" prologue begins with the likelihood that the mechanicals' performance will "offend":

> If we offend, it is with our good will.
>> That you should think, we come not to offend,
> But with good will. To show our simple skill,
>> That is the true beginning of our end.
>>>> (5.1.108–11)

The word "offend" initiates the action of the opening line and, as the last word of the second line, sets the *b* rhyme of the quatrain—a rhyme that continues the rhyme of the *Romeo and Juliet* prologue's final couplet. Quince fears the "simple skill" of his players may "offend," while the "toil" of the *Romeo and Juliet* players had "strive[n] to mend."

A third link between *Romeo and Juliet* and "Pyramus and Thisby" occurs in the diction common to both plays. Although not all of these language parallels advance the precedence of either play, some clearly do, demonstrating the priority of *Romeo and Juliet*. The "hempen homespuns" speak the broken yet recognizable language of *Romeo and Juliet* in their farcical rendition of Shakespeare's earlier play, garbling the phrases from the tragedy to achieve grand comedy. In *Romeo and Juliet* the lovers utter the word "come" when haplessly they attempt to circumvent their fates. Romeo says "Come, cordial and not poison" (5.1.85) after he defies the stars (l. 24) and the consequence there hanging (1.4.107) and departs for Juliet's tomb, and Juliet says "Romeo, I come!" (4.3.58) before she drinks her sleeping potion. In the playlet, Pyramus and Thisby embellish the language of *Romeo and Juliet* by twice repeating their calls to "come." At the sight of Thisby's mantle, Pyramus cries, "Approach, ye Furies fell! / O Fates, come, come" (5.1.277–78), and Thisby, in concomitant mawkishness, addresses the Fates: "O Sisters Three, / Come, come to me" (ll. 328–29).[7]

The muddled language of "Pyramus and Thisby" evokes the death scenes of *Romeo and Juliet*. Romeo's "Thus with a kiss I die" (5.3.120) provides a suitable example for Pyramus. Pyramus takes Romeo's simple but dramatic and suggestive "thus" and "die" and with great panache begins and ends his farewell, "Thus die I, thus, thus, thus. . . . Now die, die, die, die, die" (5.1.293, 299).

In what is perhaps an even more telling manifestation of dependence, the seeming deaths of Juliet and Thisby beg comparison. In the tragedy, Capulet mourns what he believes to be the death of Juliet, using the personification of Death as lover, and laments to Paris that Death has lain with Juliet: "Flower as she was, deflowerèd by him" (4.5.37). In ludicrous fashion Pyramus mourns what he believes to be the death of Thisby, using—as it were—the same image: "Since lion vile hath here deflow'red my dear . . ." (5.1.285). The image of Death as lover, borrowed from *Romeo and Juliet* and here associated in "Pyramus and Thisby" with a lion, is absurd: a lion may quail, crush, conclude, or quell a maiden but not, one supposes, deflower her. This "reinterpretation" is the more striking because the word "deflower" is itself a revamping of Golding's word "Devour."[8] That Shakespeare changed "devour" to "deflower" so that Pyramus could echo Capulet seems certain.[9] The word "deflower" occurs nowhere else in the canon except in *Titus Andronicus* and *Measure for Measure*. That rarity unites *Romeo* and *Dream* inextricably, and the inappropriateness of the usage in *A Midsummer Night's Dream* argues strongly that the appropriate usage preceded in *Romeo and Juliet*.

Shakespeare quietly intimates even in the titles of his plays his intention to transform the subdued, penetrating language of *Romeo and Juliet* into the "tragical mirth" of "Pyramus and Thisby." The Second Quarto gives the full title of *Romeo and Juliet* as "The Most Excellent and lamentable Tragedie of *Romeo* and *Juliet*."[10] "The Most . . . lamentable Tragedie" lends its name to its farcical counterpart: "The most lamentable comedy and most cruel death of Pyramus and Thisby," as announced by Peter Quince (1.2.11–12).[11] In Act 5, Theseus reads out another title for the play: " 'A tedious brief scene of young Pyramus / And his love Thisby; very tragical mirth' " (5.1.56–57). Shakespeare may have taken words for this title from Preston's *Cambises:* "A lamentable tragedy mixed ful of pleasant mirth."[12] That Shakespeare had Preston's title in mind when he named his playlet seems likely, since the "pleasant mirth" of the *Cambises* title translates into the "tragical mirth" of the altered title of the playlet. However, it is most probable that this second title of "Pyramus and Thisby" takes its wording from *Romeo and Juliet* as well. At the end of Act 5 in *Romeo and Juliet,* the Prince orders Friar Laurence to state what he knows concerning the tragic deaths of the young lovers. The Friar begins his solemn narrative "I will be brief, for my short date of breath / Is not so long as is a tedious tale" (5.3.229–30).

Words culled from the Friar and placed heavy-handedly beside each other begin the second title of the "tedious brief scene of young Pyramus / And his love Thisby." "Tedious" and "brief" are words linked by Shakespeare in *Richard III,* at 1.4.88–89 and 4.4.28, and in *The Rape of Lucrece,* at line 1309 (as well as, famously, in *Hamlet,* at 2.2.91–92), but the linkage in *Romeo and Juliet* and *A Midsummer Night's Dream* joins the words in each instance at the beginning of the account of the lamentable story of young lovers. Furthermore, in *A Midsummer Night's Dream* the words appear together in the same line twice (and one or the other on three more occasions in the scene). The repetition of "tedious" and "brief" in lines 56 and 58 calls particular attention to the incongruous pairing and perhaps invites us to think of the deaths of those earlier lovers in the Friar's account, briefer than a tedious tale. Thus the Friar's opening words contain more than merely an introduction to his narrative of the tragic lovers; rendered ridiculous in the second title of the playlet, they reveal succinctly Shakespeare's creation from the tragedy of *Romeo and Juliet* the mirth of "Pyramus and Thisby."

That it was fitting for Shakespeare to mock his earlier tragedy in his "Pyramus and Thisby" playlet is reasonable; Shakespeare parodies his own work in just such a fashion in *1 Henry IV,* where the serious scene of domestic banter between Hotspur and Lady Percy in 2.3 is derided through Prince Hal's mockery in 2.4. It would be difficult to argue that these treatments of the same event could be reversed.

In fact, the lovers from Ovid do not participate in Shakespeare's earlier play. Thisby is mentioned in *Romeo and Juliet,* but her actual presence there would be as unsuitable as is the taunting of Mercutio. Ignorant of Romeo's love for Juliet and teasing his friend about his unrequited love for Rosaline—

the wrong lady—Mercutio refers to Thisby as having "a grey eye or so, but not to the purpose" (2.4.42). After that rejection, Shakespeare writes a playlet "to the purpose," a story of more woe, for Thisby and her Pyramus (with eyes as "green as leeks" [5.1.327]) in *A Midsummer Night's Dream.*

Notes

1.   Brooks, pp. xliii–xlv; Gibbons, p. 30; Foakes, p. 2; Evans, pp. 5–6; Wells and Taylor, *Complete Works,* pp. 351–412, and *Textual Companion,* pp. 118–19.

2.   *Shakespeare's Festive Comedy: A Study of Dramatic Form and its Relation to Social Custom* (Princeton, N.J.: Princeton Univ. Press, 1959), p. 152, n. 25.

3.   Surely it is significant in this discussion of sequence to note, as Barber does (p. 152), that the three parents surviving at the end of *Romeo* are the same three that are "alive" at the beginning of *Dream* to be cast in "Pyramus and Thisby." (*Romeo and Juliet* is the only play in the canon to have the full complement of four parents for the two lovers.)

4.   All citations of Shakespeare refer to *William Shakespeare: The Complete Works,* ed. Alfred Harbage (Baltimore: Penguin, 1969). We accept Pope's emendation, "mural," for F1 "morall" (*Dream,* 5.1.204).

5.   Cf. *OED,* definition 1c, "a botcher."

6.   In the same way that Shakespeare changes the meter of Quince's prologue to conform with the iambic pentameter of the *Romeo* prologue, he changes the weapon of Thisby, as G. Blakemore Evans notes (p. 5). In the description given in Quince's prologue, Thisby kills herself with the kind of weapon that Juliet uses, a dagger (*Dream,* 5.1.148; *Romeo,* 5.3.169, 203), though in the performance she impales herself on the sword of Pyramus (5.1.335–36). In his delivery of the prologue, Quince "knows not the stop" (l. 120), we are told—a rhetorical ineptness that may echo Juliet's deliberate deception in her lament for Romeo: "I never shall be satisfied / With *Romeo,* till I behold him. Dead / Is my poor heart" (Q2 *Romeo,* 3.5.94–96).

7.   In *Something of Great Constancy: The Art of "A Midsummer Night's Dream"* (New Haven and London: Yale Univ. Press, 1966), David Young points out that Shakespeare mocks the invocation to the Fates and Furies found in older plays such as *Damon and Pythias* and *Appius and Virginia* (pp. 38–39).

8.   Anthony Brian Taylor, in "Golding's Ovid, Shakespeare's 'Small Latin', and the Real Object of Mockery in 'Pyramus and Thisbe'," *Shakespeare Survey,* 42 (1989), 53–64, notes that Quince misdirects details from Ovid: "For example, in Pyramus' celebrated *apostrophe ad leones,* the detail of the lions 'devouring' [him] ('consumite viscera', 4.113), which is part of his despairing request to them when he thinks Thisbe dead, is transferred to the girl in the equally impassioned address to the beasts [*sic*] by the hero of the [playlet] (5.1.[284]ff.) and, either through Quince's occasionally unhappy way with words or through a particularly infelicitous slip of the tongue on Nick Bottom's part, becomes the grossly unnatural, 'Since lion vile hath here *deflowered* my dear' (5.1.[284], [Taylor's] italics)" (p. 62). Professor Annabel Patterson called this detail to our attention.

9.   An argument might be advanced on the basis of logic or economy that the sequence in this associative system progresses from Ovid's (i.e., Golding's) devouring lion to Pyramus' deflowering lion to Capulet's deflowering Death, but that sequence is finally not tenable; the association stems not from the lion in Ovid but from the flower in Shakespeare, an image natural to young lovers and organic to *Romeo and Juliet.* Romeo hopes that the "bud of love" may prove "a beauteous flower" (2.2.121–22), and Capulet's remarks follow that natural growth as the play develops from the "buds" of 1.2.29 to the "flower" of 4.5.29, 37, deflow-

ered by Death. That deflowering is of the essence of its tragic growth. The associative system moves then from Capulet's flower, Juliet, deflowered by Death, to Pyramus' Thisby, deflowered by the lion (via Ovid's Pyramus and his devouring lion). (Thisby is described as flowers in rehearsal, but not in her apotheosis in performance.) The development rises from the flower to the lion.

10.   There is, admittedly, no incontrovertible evidence that the title of the play the audience came to see in 1595 was the same as that recorded at such length in the Second Quarto four years later in 1599 (sig. A3). But the flyers and hoardings on the Theatre must have had some distinctive and engaging title; why not this one? The First Quarto (1597) entitles the play "An Excellent conceited Tragedie of Romeo and Juliet," arguably—like the rest of Q1—derivative.

11.   Anthony Taylor notes that Ovid introduces the story of Pyramus and Thisby as a "fable" and that the Elizabethans translated *fabula* as "a tale" or "an interlude or a comedie" (p. 62). Quince takes the secondary meaning: "Hence his constant reference to his dramatization of the lovers' story as an 'interlude' (1.2.5 and 5.1.154) and as a 'comedie,' despite its obviously tragic content, as in its title, 'The Most Lamentable *Comedy* and Most Cruel Death of Pyramus and Thisbe' (1.2.11–12, [Taylor's] italics), is an attempt in his own muddled way to be true to what he thinks he has found in Ovid's text" (p. 62).

12.   Thomas Preston, *A lamentable tragedy mixed ful of pleasant mirth, conteyning the life of Cambises* (London: J. Allde, 1569). Harold Brooks also notes this parallel in his edition of *Dream,* p. 107.

Shakespeare at Work: *Romeo and Juliet*

E. PEARLMAN

By the time Shakespeare began to compose *Romeo and Juliet,* he had already established the practice of striking second and subsequent heats upon the muses' anvil. In *Titus Andronicus,* Shakespeare appears to have restructured two scenes (1.1 and 4.3) during the process of composition and added the "fly" scene (3.2), with its striking anticipations of *King Lear,* after the play was drafted.[1] He changed localities, reassigned speeches, and even introduced a new character (Launce) while rewriting *The Two Gentlemen of Verona.*[2] There seem to be extensive revisions in both *2* and *3 Henry VI;* an unusually clear instance is that Richard's vengeful speech on the death of the Earl of Salisbury (2.3.15ff.) has come down to us in very different but equally mature versions in the 1595 *True Tragedie* and in the Folio.[3] Enigmas in the text of *Love's Labour's Lost* can be explained only by revision, and Berowne's great manifesto ("O we have made a vow to study, lords" [4.3.113ff.]) is erroneously printed in both its preliminary and improved forms.[4]

Although *Romeo and Juliet* is not regarded as a play subject to extensive revision, it has long been acknowledged that the authoritative 1599 quarto (Q2) was set not from a theatrical prompt-book or from a transcribed fair copy but directly from manuscript, and that it inadvertently preserves evidence of Shakespeare's changes and corrections.[5] Textual investigators have collected a number of "false starts" in the verse and have hinted at other alterations. A cautious reexamination of the exiguous evidence, coupled with a degree of tolerance for uncertainty and conjecture, reveals that Shakespeare was hospitable to revision and experimentation. He can be found perfecting a line or phrase, re-thinking the architecture of the whole, and even importing into the play incidents that are extrinsic to its initial design. *Romeo and Juliet* may be more occasional, improvisational and perhaps even more collaborative than has generally been allowed.

II

The Most Excellent and lamentable Tragedie, of Romeo and Juliet (the 1599 "good" quarto, or Q2) retains vestiges both small and large of Shakespeare's

E. Pearlman, "Shakespeare at Work: *Romeo and Juliet,*" *English Literary Renaissance* 24 (1994): 315–342. Reprinted with permission of *English Literary Renaissance.*

progress. The most obvious appear almost as a stutter of the pen where a phrase is advanced only to be altered and replaced. In Q2, when Romeo embraces Juliet in the vault, he begins "Why art thou yet so faire? I will beleeve, / Shall I beleeve that unsubstantiall death is amorous" (5.3.102–03; sig. L3).[6] Shakespeare apparently replaced the indicative "I will beleeve" with the interrogative "Shall I beleeve," so that rather than Romeo's answering his question, he now asks another. Romeo's disorientation and puzzlement are conveyed more clearly by the revision than by the draft. In another place, a first version seems to be followed by a second when Shakespeare expands one line into two. Friar Lawrence first succinctly proposes that once Juliet swallows the potion, she will "Be borne to buriall in thy kindreds graue." Inveterately long-winded, he then amplifies: "Thou shall be borne to that same auncient vaulte, / Where all the kindred of the *Capulets* lie" (4.1.111–12; sig. I3v). The friar's additions—"auncient vaulte" and "*Capulets*"—reinforce his point that the loss of Juliet is a blow to both tradition and family. In yet another case, a single thought seems to appear in two successive variant forms: "Earth hath swallowed all my hopes but she, / Shees the hopeful Lady of my earth" (1.2.14–15; sig. B2v).[7] In this instance, the first of the two lines is far richer metaphorically and accords with the play's well-developed stratum of oral imagery (the attention to nursing and weaning; to poisoning; to the "rotten lawes" {5.3.47; sig. L2} of the sepulchre in which Juliet is interred, etc.). The improved version may have been inserted above the original or in the margin and the superseded line imperfectly deleted. Vestiges such as these allow the inference that Shakespeare blotted and revised in order to clarify mood, character, or metaphor.

There is also a pattern of revision in passages in which Shakespeare indulged a 1590s fondness for flamboyant rhetoric. When, for example, Juliet discovers that the newly married Romeo has just killed her cousin Tybalt, she expresses her passion for his person and her hatred for his deed in a series of adjective-noun antitheses that echo the "cold fier, sicke health" (1.1.178; sig. Bv) oxymora so memorably employed by Romeo. Juliet's extended apostrophe contains the two lines "Bewtifull tirant, fiend angelicall: / Rauenous douefeatherd rauē, wolvishrauening lamb" (3.2.75–76; sig. G2v). "Fiend angelicall" is right on the oxymoronic target, and "bewtifull tirant" comes close to the mark (although a more exact rhetorical congruence would seem to call for either "beautiful monster" or "democratic tyrant"), but the untidy conceits in the second of these two lines are far wide—both hypermetrical and repetitive—and modern editors have felt compelled to correct what the author left undone. Shakespeare not only puns on the noun raven—the corvid, and the verb raven—to consume greedily, but he also tried to contrast both the colors and appetites of the voracious raven and pale dove. Even Shakespeare did not find a compact phrase to handle so many variables. While the lamb that ravens down a wolf is as plainly oxymoronic as the angelic fiend, neither the "rauenous dove" of Shakespeare's first stab or the "douefeatherd rauē" of his second (which modern editors print) is quite on target. The awkward manuscript phrase seems to have confused the Q2 compositor. If he had found a hint that a deletion was intended, he would surely have excised one or more words from the line, if only so that he would not need to compress so many letters into a small space (he was even compelled to use a "nasal macron" to indicate an absent "n" and to omit a necessary blank before the nonce coinage "wolvishrauening"). If, as it seems, the compositor meticulously reproduced exactly what his copy contained, then Shakespeare did not find a satisfactory locution while the manuscript still remained in his hands; the record of his indecision stands in the imperfect line.

Shakespeare faced a different but related perplexity in the scene in which domineering Capulet tries to bully his recalcitrant daughter into marrying Paris. A crucial part of Capulet's speech appears in edited texts so:

> God's bread, it makes me mad! Day, night, work, play,
> Alone, in company, still my care hath been
> To have her matched.
>
> (3.5.176–78)

These vigorous sentiments, the core of which is Capulet's triplet of opposed substantives (day-night, etc.), were printed in a less finely honed form in Q2.

> Gods bread, it makes me mad,
> Day, night, houre, tide, time, worke, play,
> Alone in companie, still my care hath bene
> To haue her matcht.
>
> (sig. I1)

Capulet began by simply reciting a list of five items that are, roughly speaking, measurements of time: "day," "night," "hour," "tide" (in the sense preserved in "eventide" and "noontide"), and "time" itself. But the speech does not continue along the path on which it originally seems to have set out. Shakespeare appears to have returned to the beginning of the line and reinterpreted the first two words—"Day, night"—not as nouns at the head of a litany of similar terms, but as antonyms. He then began again and followed "day-night" with two more pairs of opposites—work-play, alone-in company—and by doing so provided Capulet with a more distinct mode of expression. The compositor dutifully followed Shakespeare's manuscript and printed both his initial undeleted and second efforts. But, misled by "houre, tide, time," he did not fully grasp the pattern at which Shakespeare had latterly arrived and he erroneously set the phrase (if it is possible to draw an inference from whimsical Elizabethan commas) that is punctuated in modern texts "alone, in company" as "alone in companie"—as if Capulet were confessing to be a melancholic, solitary even among the busy haunts of men. Q2 therefore preserves as if in amber the moment in which Shakespeare discovered that even old Capulet could speak in figures of contradiction. Moreover, the passage seems to be one on which Shakespeare continued to ponder even after the manuscript that eventually became Q2 left his hands. Q1 preserves a more highly wrought rendering of these lines in which Capulet's first stumblings have been suppressed and his chain of pairs lengthened: "Day, night, early late, at home, abroad, / Alone, in company, waking or sleeping, / Still my care hath beene to see her matcht" (sig. H1).

The trail of Shakespeare's effort to refine his conceits is even more evident in the rhetorically complex passage in which brainsick Romeo laments his banishment from Verona and from his beloved. Friar Lawrence vainly attempts to instill a modicum of temperance in his young charge and patiently explains that Romeo should think himself fortunate that the penalty for duelling in the street, customarily execution, has been commuted to mere banishment. Romeo replies that Friar Lawrence's palliatives only "[cut] my head off with a golden axe" (3.3.22; sig. G3v). His complaint becomes increasingly imprudent and less logical as it gathers momentum. If heaven is where Juliet lies, Romeo contends, then to be separated from Juliet is to be sent to hell. A vision of damnation arises even with the thought of banishment: "O Frier, the damned vse that word in hell: / Howling attends it" (47–48; sig. G4). Romeo's logic, or illogic, is organized around a set of antitheses: on the one hand is Juliet, heaven, and mercy, and on the other hand, banishment from Juliet, torture, death, hell, damnation, howling. But the path from the elysian to the infernal did not prove easy for either Romeo or Shakespeare to negotiate. Even as Romeo, distraught, drops down the chain of being, from cat and dog, to mouse, to fly, so his language becomes more highly figured and artificial.

> Tis torture and not mercie, heauen is here
> Where *Iuliet* liues, and euery cat and dog,
> And little mouse, euery vnworthy thing
> Liue here in heauen, and may looke on her.
> But *Romeo* may not. More validitie,
> More honourable state, more courtship liues
> In carrion flies, then *Romeo:* they may seaze
> On the white wonder of deare *Iuliets* hand,
> And steale immortall blessing from her lips,
> Who euen in pure and vestall modestie
> Still blush, as thinking their owne kisses sin.
>   (33–39; sig. G4)

Romeo juxtaposes the filth of the "carrion flies" to the "pure and vestal modesty" of his beloved. With the gaudy conceit in which Juliet's hand is grasped or her lips kissed by courting flies, Shakespeare dallies with absurdity (his personifications unintentionally evoke the memory of Launce's grieving cat "wringing her hands"[8]). Romeo's oratory, designed to give prominence to the flourishes of rhetoric, comes to an imperfect climax in Q2 when two separate pentameter lines appear in both initial and improved form:

This may flyes do, when I from this must flie,	1
And sayest thou yet, that exile is not death?	2
But *Romeo* may not, he is banished.	3
Flies may do this, but I from this must flie:	4
They are freemen, but I am banished.	5

(4–43; sig. G4)

(Line 4 revises line 1; line 5 revises line 3; line 2 logically concludes the passage and effects a transition to the remainder of the speech. Modern editors customarily but not uniformly discard lines 1 and 3 and print the lines in this order: line 4, line 5, line 2.) It appears that Shakespeare began with a weak pun on the word "fly"—"This may flyes do, when I from this must flie"—but was not satisfied that the opposition he sought was sufficiently emphatic. He therefore rearranged the words to supplement the pun with antimetabole: "Flies may do this, but I from this must flie." After composing, perhaps, an intervening transition, Shakespeare first drafted and then abandoned the curiously detached third-person observation, "But *Romeo* may not, he is banished." This phrasing, he seems to have recognized, diluted and weakened the daring comparison of Romeo to the fly. Shakespeare recast the line to emphasize the almost metaphysical yoking and also to introduce a paradox in which flies are granted the "freedom" of the city from which Romeo has been expelled: "They [i.e. flies] are freemen, but I am banished." After completing these complicated maneuvers, Shakespeare was able to bring the speech to conclusion without leaving behind further traces of revision. However uncongenial to modern sensibility, the garish fly-freeman conceit was devised with scrupulous attention to detail.[9]

Can it be mere coincidence that, in each of these three cases, Shakespeare paused at a moment of rhetorical exuberance? Unable to find the appropriate successor to "fiend angelicall," Shakespeare let stand the muddled ravenous raven. Setting out to create a litany of synonyms for time, he turned instead to a sequence of substantives in opposition ("day-night," etc.). To give voice to Romeo's shattered emotions, he yoked the heaven of vestal Verona to the hell of carrion flies. The intricate rhetorical patterning that is the hallmark of *Romeo and Juliet* was not effortlessly achieved.

III

When Shakespeare revised Romeo's lament to create a moment of ingenious rhetoric, he was exercising and perfecting his poetic technique. Not all the changes in Q2 are of this sort. While the botched or repetitive line poses a problem of craft, other anomalies in the text raise questions of design. The most conspicuous evidence that Shakespeare changed his plan in the course of writing *Romeo and Juliet* is simply that he began with a *Prologue,* supplied another chorus at the juncture of the first and second acts, but then brought the play to conclusion without further choral interventions. If there is a *Prologue,* why is there no mirror *Epilogue?* And if there is to be one chorus, why in the world are there not three others? What would cause Shakespeare to establish a pattern and then immediately forsake it?[10] The purpose of neither *Prologue* nor chorus is perspicuous, and Samuel Johnson's indictment of the one applies equally to the other: "The use of this chorus is not easily discovered; it conduces nothing to the progress of the play, but relates what is already known, or what the next scene will show; and relates it without adding the improvement of any moral sentiment."[11] Although Johnson does not bother to say it, his observation carries the corollary that *Romeo and Juliet* might be a weaker play (as it would certainly be a very different one) if it paused intermittently for choral summary or prediction.

How can the presence of *Prologue* and, even more significantly, the chorus, be understood? It is possible that Shakespeare composed successive choruses, but if he did so, there is no accounting for their disappearance. The circumstances admit only two logical alternatives. Shakespeare either (a) planned to write a full set of choruses and changed his mind, or (b) decided at the outset to begin with one format and then abandon it. Plan (b) seems much too clever and Machiavellian. Plan (a) is altogether more likely, even though it does not explain why, if Shakespeare changed his plan, he never deleted the passages in question, and even more so, why he allowed the *Prologue* (though not, apparently, the chorus) to be retained in performance (as registered by its appearance in Q1). The only credible explanation is that both *Prologue* and chorus are analogous to the vestigial ravenous raven and survive as residue of Shakespeare's first intention. The change of direction in *Romeo and Juliet* ought to provoke the kinds of questions raised by the disappearance of the ambitious frame narrative in *The Taming of the Shrew.*

But why would Shakespeare have begun his play with a prologue and chorus? and why did he not continue down the path on which he had set out? The first of these questions is the easier one to answer. Unsure of his ultimate purposes, Shakespeare was simply conforming to the template established by other English tragedies he had seen or read. Although only a handful survive, tragedies composed for the popular stage between 1580 and 1595 (the year in which *Romeo and Juliet* was most likely to have been written) regularly give prominence to choruses. In the principal exemplar of the genre, Thomas Kyd's *Spanish Tragedy,* Revenge and the ghost of Don Andrea introduce the action, re-appear at intervals, and moralize at the end. The closely related *Soliman and Perseda* gives exactly the same prominence to Love, Fortune and Death, and so does Robert Yarington's *Two Lamentable Tragedies* to its choral trio of Homicide, Avarice, and Truth. *Doctor Faustus* features a prominent pro-logue and epilogue (although corruptions in Marlowe's text make it difficult to speak with assurance about its choruses). *The Jew of Malta* is famously introduced by Machevil. Robert Greene's *Alphonsus* is so much in the mode of *Tamburlaine* that its precedent may not be relevant, but it begins with Venus "let downe from the top of the Stage" to say a prologue and returns her to her place only after she has delivered a last summary speech. In *Locrine,* the choral role is played by Atey (Ate) adept at moralizing ("Lo here the end of lawlesse treacherie . . ." [2269]). Of the surviving tragedies, only the ill-assorted pair of *Titus Andronicus* and *Arden of Feversham* do not employ choruses (although *Arden* offers a brief epilogue spoken by Franklin).[12] When Shakespeare sat down to write *Romeo and Juliet,* nothing would have been more natural than for him to reproduce the pattern of his predecessors.

Shakespeare may very well have found a second precedent in the poem that was his principal source. When Shakespeare returned to Arthur Brooke's *Romeus and Juliet* (a work which, to judge by the occasional near-paraphrase, he kept close at hand during the process of composition), he would have been reminded that Brooke began with a brief moralizing epistle and a summary of the plot—"The Argument"—in the shape of a sonnet. Shakespeare digested some of the material in Brooke's epistle and argument into a *Prologue* that replicates the sonnet form of its model. Brooke began "Love hath inflamed twayne by sodayn sight. / And both do graunt the thing that both desyre. / They wed in shrift by counsell of a frier" and continued to the moment of death: "He drinkes, his bane. And she with Romeus knyfe, / When she awakes, her selfe (alas) she sleath."[13] Shakespeare's *Prologue* also stoops to plot summary: "From forth the fatall loynes of these two foes / A paire of starre-crost louers, take their life: / Whose misaduentur'd pittious ouerthrowes, / Doth with their death burie their Parents strife" (5–8; sig. A2). Shakespeare retained a slight moralizing—in the portentous adjective "star-crossed" as well as in the notion that the deaths of children can be understood as sacrifices to their parents' enmity.

Although Shakespeare may have started with a traditional prologue, once he had pondered his plot or composed a few scenes, he would have been forced to confront and reconcile the clash between the conventional choral frame and the untraditional form that his play had begun to assume. Although the choruses are an inheritance from the past, *Romeo and Juliet* itself is pioneering and experimental. The very groundwork of the play—Shake-speare's transfusion of tragic weight into the motifs of comedy—represents innovation of a high order. But the very first audiences of *Romeo and Juliet* would have known that they were hearing a play that was novel and even revolutionary long before the interpenetration of love and death came to their notice. The almost invariable practice of the tragic playwrights who preceded Shakespeare had been to follow a huffing prologue with a "stately" speech. The first character to hold the stage was conventionally a person of stature or authority, preferably of the highest available rank. Such a speaker would characteristically set the stage in a dignified expository address. *Titus Andronicus,* although lacking a prologue, follows tradition when Saturninus strides on stage to declaim "Noble patricians, patrons of my right. . . ." But in *Romeo and Juliet,* Shakespeare abandoned this well-established convention. He turned aside from the formal address, spurned dignity, and, inverting the ordained hierarchy, chose to generate Verona not from the top down but from the bottom up. He started with the lewdness of the truculent servants and worked his way first through the junior and then through the principal members of the feuding households before at last arriving where earlier plays would have begun—at a formal speech by Verona's prince. Moreover, it is the tendency of choruses to allegorize or simplify. The chorus's announcement that "Now old desire doth in his deathbed lie, / And young affection gapes to be his heire" (2 *Chorus* 1–2; sig. D1) figures human emotions in terms of an abstract tableau; in the body of the play, Shakespeare represents emotions with much greater particularity and subtlety. In like manner, the chorus authoritatively predicts that in the next act "passion lends [Romeo and Juliet] power" (13; sig. D1). In so saying, the chorus reduces the behavior of the young lovers to a static formula far simpler than the richly detailed portrait that Shakespeare so artistically creates. In the context of *Romeo and Juliet*'s up-to-date experimentation, the pious gestures and traditional format of the *Prologue* (and *a fortiori* the chorus) became increasingly dysfunctional, limiting, and obsolete. To the degree that the composition of *Romeo and Juliet* enacts a contention between the traditional and the innovative, the attrition of its choral frame represents a clear victory for the new.

There is another and even more obvious reason for Shakespeare's disenchantment with the scheme of *Prologue* and chorus. When Shakespeare made the decision to dramatize the story of Romeo and Juliet, he committed himself to a plot that was widely believed to be factual. At some point he must have decided to remain faithful to the story and to restrain the impulse to transform or supplement the narrative he had inherited. He held to his purpose even though *Romeus and Juliet* contains some truly intractable plot problems, many of them circling around the implausibility of Friar Lawrence's harebrained potion—suspended animation—vault scheme. When Shakespeare wrote the *Prologue,* he assured his hearers that the play would end with the young lovers linked in death. Yet during the process of composition he discovered that in order to maintain interest in the inevitable, he had to tease his audience with hints that Romeo and Juliet might be reconciled and permitted to prosper at last. He went to great lengths to maintain the viability of what might be called the "comic option." The proliferation of comic characters, dialogue, and themes is momentous, but Shakespeare also sustained optimism by allowing one of the feuding characters to make an oblique gesture at a truce: "tis not hard," says Capulet, "For men so old as we to keepe the peace" (1.2.2–3; sig.

B2v). Shakespeare also invented an episode not in Brooke when he introduced Paris to Friar Lawrence only to raise and then defeat the expectation that friar and suitor would share their information and forestall the inevitable. He followed this disappointment with a second episode (4.1) in which Juliet herself misses the opportunity to be honest with Paris. Paris, in fact, becomes the focus of the comic option; his otherwise gratuitous death in the last scene means that the suitor favored by old Capulet no longer stands as a threat to the young lovers. Even Romeo, usually fatalistic, is provided with a propitious dream that raises the most misleading expectations:

> I dreamt my Lady came and found me dead,
> Strange dreame that giues a deadman leaue to thinke,
> And Breathd such life with kisses in my lips,
> That I reuiude and was an Emperor.
>
> (5.1.6–9; sig. K4)

With such devices, Shakespeare cheered and deceived his audience into hoping against hope that all will turn out for the best and that Romeo will happily embrace Juliet in the tomb at the very moment that she awakens. Shakespeare's contrivances in keeping tragedy at bay are so successful that the play can be transformed into comedy with an absolute minimum of tampering: accordingly, in the Restoration, "when the Tragedy was Reviv'd again, 'twas Play'd Alternately, Tragical one Day, and Tragi comical another; for several days."[14] While his predecessors had employed the chorus to moralize about the operations of an impersonal fate, Shakespeare dispensed with overt moral and instead attempted to beguile his audience into believing that Juliet may have her Romeo after all. As *Romeo and Juliet* evolved into a play bent on prolonging tension, choral interventions that drained the plot of suspense became supererogatory at best and counter-productive at worst. Shakespeare aborted his initial plan because the chorus was old-fashioned in a play that had become modern, because it was moralistic in a play that became indifferent to externally asserted pieties, and because it laid on the table an outcome that Shakespeare had now decided to keep up his sleeve.

Shakespeare therefore seems to have approached different problems differently. On the microcosmic level of the word or phrase, he was certain enough of his conceits to toil over a passage of ornate rhetoric. Yet at the same time, he cavalierly discarded a scheme of prologue and chorus without even bothering with the perfunctory deletions that would make the play all of a piece. He burnished fashionable 1590s gilded rhetoric while abandoning the conventional format of 1590s tragedy. In these revisions, Shakespeare seems to be both conservative and daring—confident of his poetry yet willing to replace his initial and rigid conception of the play with a more flexible design.

IV

In one of the least explicable corners of the play, there are two episodes that modern interpreters either pass over in silence or pause only to express bewilderment. The first is the "lamentations" scene. When it is believed that Juliet has died the night before the wedding morn, her mother and father along with the Nurse and County Paris join to chant a dirge that is so excessively lugubrious that there is no agreement whether Shakespeare has failed as a poet or has composed a hilarious parody of true grief.[15] Following hard at the heels of this lament, the clown/servant Peter appears on stage with the musicians and engages in some undistinguished comic banter. While the lamentations scene is difficult to interpret, it is intrinsic to the plot; the clown episode is extrinsic and there is good reason to consider it to be an interpolation.

To review: a noise of musicians in the employ of County Paris is present during the lamentations. When the wailing concludes, the principal parties are shepherded off the stage by Friar Lawrence:

> Sir go you in, and Madam go with him,
> And go sir *Paris,* euery one prepare
> To follow this faire Coarse vnto her graue
> *Exeunt manet.*
>
> (4., 5., 91–93; sig. K3)

The stage partially empties, leaving only the Nurse and at least two musicians—"*Musi.*" and "*Fid.*" (i.e. Musician and Fiddler)—behind. The scene comes to conclusion when the Nurse delivers herself of a couple of lines of characteristically unconscious bawdy:

> *Musi.* Faith we may put vp our pipes and be gone.
> *Nur.* Honest goodfellowes, ah put vp, put vp,
> For well you know, this is a pitifull case.
> *Fid.* I my {i.e. by} my troath, the case may be amended.
>
> (97–99)

A definitive stage direction—"*Exit omnes*" (*Exit* was corrected to *Exeunt* in Q3)—apparently clears the stage and ends the scene. But Q2 then prints "*Enter Will Kemp.*" It now appears that the stage direction has been of no force, because the musicians have not departed after all but have remained to engage in a quip and a crank with the famous clown.[16] Will Kemp, nominally in the role of Capulet's servant Peter, riddles the musicians with questions about the phrase "musique with her siluer sound" and reveals at last that "Musitions have no gold for sounding." Only then does the stage in fact clear. The erroneous direction—"*Exit omnes,*" or "everybody leaves"—seems in all likelihood to have ended the scene as it was originally conceived. While

Shakespeare originally brought the lamentations scene to conclusion with the phased exit of its principal characters, he has now appended an epilogue of sorts in order to sweeten the part of the celebrity comedian Will Kemp, whom he seems to imagine not as Peter or servant or clown but *in propria persona*.[17]

Kemp's jibes and jests are rarely performed and do not make a strong impression on the modern reader, perhaps because Shakespeare only weakly tethers Kemp's dialogue to the play's major themes. In *Twelfth Night*, the economics of Illyria is a continual concern and Feste's pennies and shillings are therefore thematically momentous, but Verona is not a community concerned with getting and spending and Kemp's worrying of gold and silver is therefore nothing more than a clown's bit. It is true that the popular song that Kemp recites or sings—"When griping griefes the heart doth wound" (123)—comments obliquely on the mourning that precedes it, even as its drab sound complements the stilted lamentations. It is also a truth of Shakespeare's private thematic lexicon that music, silver-sounding or no, can soothe the agitated breast. Yet on the whole, the antics of Shakespeare's clowns speak to modern audiences when they appear in the form of inspired soliloquies after the fashion of Launce, Bottom, and Touchstone, or when clever disputations with members of the established classes—the gravedigger with Hamlet, the fool with Lear, or the fig-bearing clown with Egypt's queen—throw the principal actions of the play into longer perspective. Kemp's performance in this play falls into neither of these categories and does not seem to be either especially relevant or especially clever, at least not to the untuned twentieth-century ear. It is easy to assume that Shakespeare's benefaction to Kemp would have had no major repercussion on the play as a whole. But this obvious inference may be a gross error, for there is collateral evidence that the musicians' scene was neither trivial nor marginal. One of Kemp's great successes was in *A Knack to Know a Knave* (1594)[18]—an old-fashioned moral play, part abstraction and part pseudo-history. Kemp's solitary appearance is quite brief. A Miller, a Smith and a Cobbler (Kemp) are the madmen of Gotham. They disagree about which of them should deliver their petition to the king ("Let us consult among our selues, / How to misbehaue our selues to the Kings worship" [1365–66]). The Smith's argument is odd: "Why (sir) there was a god of our occupation, and I charge you by vertue of his godhed, to let me deliuer the petition" (1374–75). Kemp expands on the blasphemy, "But soft you, your God was a Cuckold, and Godhead was the horne, and thats the Armes of the Godhead you call upon" (1376–78). It is agreed that Kemp/Cobbler should present the petition. The king sweeps in.

> *Cob.* We the townes men of *Goteham,*
> Hearing your Grace would come this way,

> Did thinke it good for you to stay,
> But hear you, neighbours, bid somebody ring the bels,
>   And we are come to you alone to deliuer our petition.
>
> (1400–04)

The madmen ask for a license "to brew strong Ale thrise a week" (1406–07).

> *Kin.*   Well sirs, we grant your petition.
> *Cob.*   We humblie thanke your royall Maiesty. . . .
> *Exeunt omnes.*
>
> (1409–11)

Despite the fact that there is nothing unusual, artistic or witty about these lines (saving the blasphemy), the title-page of the quarto offers unassailable evidence that the scene was a notable success:

> A most pleasant and merie new Comedie, Intituled, *A Knacke to knowe a Knaue.* Newlie set foorth, as it hath sundrie tymes bene played by ED. ALLEN and his Companie. With KEMPS applauded Merriments of the men of Goteham, in receiuing the King into Goteham.

Kemp's triumphs in *A Knack to Know a Knave* may be compared to his very similar performance in *Romeo and Juliet.* Just as in *Romeo and Juliet,* Kemp's appearance is merely a pretext for clowning. There is no organic reason to link the business of the petition either to the Earl of Cornwall's intemperate pursuit of the beautiful maiden Alfrida or to Honesty's stylized fretting. The Cobbler delivers his petition to the King only because Lord Strange's Men has in its employ an unusually entertaining and witty clown who is a favorite of audiences and makes money for the company. While the part of Peter melds more smoothly into *Romeo and Juliet* than the Cobbler's into *A Knack,* its late addition certainly seems to owe as much to external factors as to dramatic necessity. In neither play is the literary quality of Kemp's scene at all material. Without the advertisement on the title-page of *A Knack,* even the most discriminating modern reader would be hard put to discover the glory of Elizabethan popular comedy in Kemp's few flat lines. The basic question remains: if Kemp's merriments were applauded in the one play, why would not his merriments in *Romeo and Juliet* be equally acclaimed? In both plays, Kemp would have put his mobile face and athleticism to good use. There is every reason to believe that in performing *A Knack to Know a Knave,* Kemp/Cobbler said much more than was set down for him and improvised around the playwright's outline (if the phrase "Kemp's applauded merriments" does not in fact suggest that he composed his own lines). While the knockabout folly of the man who was soon to jangle his bells all the way from London to Norwich in nine days is fundamentally unrecoverable, Q1 preserves two shards of evidence that indicate that Kemp spliced some of his own material into the scene. While Q2 gives Kemp only a pair of lines to sing, the compiler of Q1 heard a third: "And dolefull dumps the minde oppresse" (sig. I2v). Secondly, Peter/Kemp changed the name of one musician from the "Hugh Rebick" of the Q2 manuscript to "Mathew minikine" of the Q1 performance. How much of Q2's script of this scene was Shakespeare's and how much was Kemp's is impossible to ascertain. When Shakespeare added this scene, he did not merely interpolate a few inconsequential quips, but exposed his play to a formidable incursion by one of the theater's most notable, recognizable and prominent performers. Modern readers of *Romeo and Juliet* must consider the possibility that at least to some members of the ancient audiences, this corner of the play may have provided the play's most memorable moments.

Moreover, it is generally taken to be the case that the kind of broad robust buffoonery for which Kemp was famous was obsolescent and beginning to pass from the scene. In a few years, Shakespeare himself would turn ventriloquist to criticize it in Hamlet's voice.[19] It is something of a marvel that a play that had become modern and innovative as it took shape was now required to accommodate a traditional and old-fashioned kind of clowning. With the introduction of Kemp's scene, *Romeo and Juliet* became less linear and less coherent, but at the same time much more capacious, varied, and expansive.

V

By all odds the most wondrous of Shakespeare's additions to *Romeo and Juliet* is the Queen Mab speech. Mercutio's excursus is not articulated with the remainder of *Romeo and Juliet* in terms of plot, content, language, or intellection. There is no overlap between the realist, materialist Mercutio and the Mercutio who celebrates Queen Mab in elaborate, imaginative, and romantic terms. The printing of the speech in Q2 is suspicious. There is no harmony between the speech and the play in which it finds itself; its presence in *Romeo and Juliet* is an afterthought. Yet even though the speech is of alien origin, it is so powerful in itself that it forces both the character and the play to surrender to an entirely new conception of theatrical decorum.[20]

When Mercutio speaks the Queen Mab speech, he has already established himself as Romeo's intimate companion. Yet in the course of an extended address, he does not once allude to his friendship with Romeo, or to Romeo himself, to Benvolio, to Rosaline, with whom he suspects Romeo is in love, or to the masque to which the young men are hieing, or to the feud, or to the Capulets or Montagues, or to Verona itself. At the same time that he slights these obvious subjects, he surveys matters that are of no interest either to himself or to any other party elsewhere in the play. At no other moment in

Romeo and Juliet is there a concern with the fairies on whom Mercutio principally dwells. The various personages whom Mab provokes to dream come from another theatrical universe. While it might be possible to argue that as a duellist Mercutio would be interested in things military, there is no real congruence between an urban bully-boy and the professional soldier implied by "breaches, ambuscados, spanish blades" (1.4.82; sig. C2). Swaggerers and soldiers are at least in the theoretical neighborhood of Romeo's Verona, but of what possible relevance are an alderman, or courtiers, or lawyers, or, especially in a play that gives such weight to Friar Lawrence and Friar John, a distinctly unItalian and unRoman parson complete with (save us!) tithe-pig and benefice. Moreover, neither Mercutio nor his hearers, nor anyone else ever refers back to the Queen Mab speech. As far as its subject matter is concerned, the play simply moves along exactly as though Mercutio had never spoken. Queen Mab is hermetically sealed off from the body of *Romeo and Juliet;* nothing from the remainder of the play diffuses into the speech, and nothing from the speech diffuses into the play.

Irrelevant in content, the speech is inessential to plot. Mercutio's role in the action is to provoke the fatal quarrel with Tybalt. His death at Tybalt's hands arouses Romeo and goads him to the revenge that precipitates the banishment, tears, potion, and suicides. Shakespeare was therefore required to present Mercutio as a friend and ally of Romeo who was short-tempered and martial in character. In order to add heft to this minimal demand, Shakespeare also made Mercutio stand as the exemplar of a cadre of youth who are hostile to poetry and love, who place a high value on loyalty to their fellowship, and who indulge in a sharp bawdy wit that converts rapidly to real violence. When, against his better judgment, Romeo assaults Tybalt, he not only kills his man but temporarily surrenders himself to the violent and alien world exemplified by Mercutio. What is the purpose of the Queen Mab speech in this context? As far as the friendship between Mercutio and Romeo is concerned, it neither subtracts nor adds, only distracts. But if Mercutio's materialism and hostility and violence are functional, his fantastical and poetical outpourings are counterproductive, because they undermine what Shakespeare has otherwise taken care to create. To turn Mercutio into a satirist and a scourger of dreams is decorative, inessential, and misleading.

Unrelated to content or to plot, the Queen Mab excursus also distorts the character of its speaker. Except for this one speech, Mercutio's progress is all of a piece and his character is always subordinate to the needs of the fable. Mercutio begins as a scoffer at Romeo's Petrarchan obsessions: "You are a Louer, borrow *Cupids* wings, / And sore with them aboue a common bound" (1.4.17–18; sig. C1v). In the handful of lines Mercutio speaks before he launches Queen Mab, his speech is already saturated with sexual—"prick loue for pricking" (28)—and scatological—"the mire / Or saue you reuerence (i.e. sirreverence) loue" (41–42)—references. Shakespeare amplifies these hints in the scene in which Mercutio tries to intercept Romeo as he makes his way from the masque to the orchard. Now Mercutio creates a devilish alternative to Romeo's religion of love by compiling a subversive anti-Petrarchan counterblazon:

> I coniure thee by *Rosalines* bright eyes,
> By her high forehead, and her Scarlet lip,
> By her fine foot, straight leg, and quiuering thigh,
> And the demeanes, that there adiacent lie.
>
> (2.1.16–19; sig. D1v)

To prepare for the culminating swordplay, Shakespeare joins pride and a violent temperament to Mercutio's catalogue of traits. When Mercutio criticizes Romeo's sexual longings, he does so in terms infiltrated with violent imagery: "Alas poore *Romeo,* he is alreadie dead, stabd with a white wenches blacke eye, runne through the eare with a loue song. . . ." (2.4.13–14; sig. E2). Mercutio becomes, for the first time, a prose speaker in whose angry wit a hostility to love hypostatizes into a hostility to women (as in his superfluous and almost inexplicable antagonism to the Nurse—the go-between whom he insists on describing as a bawd). It is only at this point that Shakespeare invents Mercutio's interest in duelling. Mercutio's attachment to Romeo now becomes a mad possessive jealousy; he urges Romeo to repudiate love, romance, and womanhood in terms that are both mean and brutish:

> Why is not this better now then groning for loue, now art thou sociable, now art thou *Romeo:* now art thou what thou art, by art as well as by nature, for this driueling loue is like a great natural that runs lolling vp and downe to hide his bable in a hole.
>
> (88–93; sig. E3)

In contriving Mercutio, Shakespeare is on the whole utilitarian, bringing to the fore characteristics that are colorful and vibrant but also essential to the role that Mercutio plays in the larger scheme of the play. Mercutio sneers at love while Romeo indulges his private infatuations; he brandishes his machismo to contrast with Romeo's more irenic masculinity; he is coarse because Romeo is ethereal and he is ironic because Romeo is too fond to appreciate the complexity of things. But when Mercutio sails off into a flight of fancy about the "fairies midwife" driving an "emptie Hasel nut" chariot "ore Lawyers fingers," he acquires traits that are purposeless in the larger scheme of the play and that are in flat contradiction to the vectors of character that are otherwise carefully established. His fanciful poesy consorts ill with a personage who moves from verse to prose, from genial mockery to crude attack, and from dissent to ungovernable violence. Mercutio is by turns a scoffer at love, a nasty boy, a roisterer, a duellist, a jealous buddy; the Queen

Mab speech is at odds with every single one of his manifestations. Without the Queen Mab speech, Mercutio is consistent and coherent; once the speech is added, his character is incoherent on the page and must be reinvented by the collaboration of performer and audience or by the ingenuity and faith of stage-literate readers.

Mercutio's famous speech seems, then, to be detached in content, extraneous to plot, and retrograde to the character of its speaker. But what does the speech actually say? Romeo indifferently asserts the claim that dreamers "dream things true" (1.4.52). Mercutio does not specifically contravert Romeo but instead catapults into a discussion of the cause and origin of dreams. Queen Mab, he says, is the agent who provokes people to dream dreams that are appropriate to their rank and nature. Mercutio also asserts that Mab is to blame for such frolics as tangling horses' manes. He proclaims the folklore of dreams so elaborately and in such profuse detail that he must be regarded as a proponent of dream and by extension a partisan of the world of the imagination. Yet when he is challenged by Romeo, he quits his position and concedes that he has been giving voice only to the "children of an idle braine" (97, sig. C2v). His celebration of Queen Mab is framed by a confusing skepticism and embedded in a context of disbelief, for while Mercutio asserts that dreamers often lie, his fabrication of Queen Mab pranked up for her nightly voyage unquestionably embraces and lends credence to the romance of dream. Mercutio's surface cynicism is overwhelmed by the enthusiasm of his presentation. Mercutio subscribes to agnostic commonplaces but, at least while he speaks the speech, lives in the imagination; in his every other appearance, he lives in a materialistic world from which poetry, dreams, and imagination have been expelled.[21]

There are also bibliographical reasons for regarding the speech as an afterthought or interpolation. The transition between the body of the play and Mercutio's excursus is ungainly. While waiting for the masking to begin, Romeo simply announces that "I dreampt a dreame to nighte"; at this hint, Mercutio speaks. Romeo's dream, which Shakespeare does not bother to supply, is transparently an expedient to carve out a space for Mercutio's address.

Shakespeare may have originally planned to bring the scene to conclusion with a compressed couplet of Mercutio's that had appeared a few lines before the eruption of Queen Mab: "Take our good meanings, for our iudgements sits, / Fiue times in that, ere once in our fine[22] wits." Mercutio's wordplay depends on a distinction between judgment and wit; he claims that Romeo should take seriously his "good meanings," that is, the better purposes of his judgment rather than the swits and spurs of his "fine (or refined) wit." If the long section that begins on line 48 and ends with line 106 had not been inserted, Romeo's response would have joined two half-lines that are now separated:

> And we mean well in going to this Maske,
> But tis no wit to go, for my mind misgiues,
> Some consequence yet hanging in the starres.
>
> (1.5.47–48; 106–07)

Wit presses him to the masque, mind would keep him from it. The distinction between the play of wit and the better judgment of mind is maintained by both parties to the exchange—but it is only when the separated passages are brought together that the continuity of the conversation may be appreciated.

Still another reason to think the Queen Mab speech to be an addition is drawn from the manner in which it is printed. In Q2, the bulk of the speech, beginning with "She is the Fairies midwife," and continuing to "which once vntangled, much misfortune bodes" (54–91; sig. C2) is set not as verse (although it is obviously iambic pentameter) but as prose. It is clear not only from the prose setting, but also from the compression of type, that the compositor attempted to save as much space as possible. The passage has been extensively analyzed by bibliographers[23] who are at odds about minor points but in agreement that the compositor erred when he estimated the length of the manuscript and that he attempted to compensate by setting the passage densely, preferring rather to sacrifice the verse format than to eliminate whole lines. The text is confusing in other ways. There is a widely-held conviction that Q2 prints the lines in a mistaken order. The three-line passage beginning "Her Charriot is an emptie Hasel nut" (59–61) appears eight lines too late; most editors re-insert it after "ouer mens noses as they lie asleep" (60) on the grounds that Mab's chariot should not be itemized in detail before being described in general. In addition to mislineation, the passage seems to contain anomalies that are characteristic of Shakespeare at work (revisions within revision, as it were). The single line "On [Q1 O're] Courtiers knees, that dreame on Cursies straight" (72) is separated from an amplification that sharpens its satirical edge: "Sometime she gallops ore a Courtiers nose, / and then dreames he of smelling out a sute" (77–78). Similarly, the slack and redundant "Through louers brains, and then they dreame of loue" (71) is separated by two lines from its much more picturesque three-line expansion ("ore Ladies lips who strait one kisses dream, / which oft the angrie Mab with blisters plagues, / because their breath with sweete meates tainted are" (74–76). It appears that the Queen Mab speech came disorderly to the printer's hands, possibly on a sheet that was of separate origin and that was burdened with marginal insertions or pasted slips. Such addenda made the length of the speech difficult to estimate, perhaps, and caused the compositor to cast off inaccurately. The inference that Mercutio's speech is different in content is strengthened by the knowledge that it was also distinct in kind.

Mercutio's speech does not draw its subject matter from the play in which it is embedded, contradicts the psychological development of its speaker, is inessential to plot, barely tangential to theme and ideas, and bears the typographical signature of separate creation. Its dreams, miniature fairies, fantastical lovers, and satiric tone are native to the world of Theseus and Hippolyta but are recent migrants to sultry feuding Verona. Is it possible that the speech was originally written for an Ur-version of *A Midsummer Night's Dream?* or for some other play begun but not completed? or from a poem similar to Michael Drayton's mock epyllion *Nimphidia,* in which Mab is Oberon's "merry Queene by night" who "Bestrids young Folks that lye upright"?[24]; or for a performance such as Ben Jonson's *Entertainment at Althrope,* in which Queen Mab is "the mistris-Faeirie / That doth nightly rob the dayrie" (53–54), and who

> empties cradles,
> Takes out children, puts in ladles:
> Traynes forth mid-wiues in their slumber,
> With a siue the holes to number.
> . . . .
> Feed[s] them with a promise'd sight,
> Some of husbands, some of louers,
> Which an emptie dreame discouers?[25]
>   (66–68; 75–77)

If the Queen Mab speech was not part of Shakespeare's original conception, but was written for another purpose and rescued from oblivion by its insertion into *Romeo and Juliet,* then its inclusion is similar to Kemp's scene in that it toys with the balance of the play. But the jesting about music's silver sound depends almost entirely on the artistry of the comedian for whom it was written. Queen Mab may be equally occasional in origin but its effect has been quite different, for it overpowers the moment with its vision and poetry. It is so vigorous an irrelevance that it creates its own context. For a splendid moment, the playwright suspends the rules of rationality and coherence. He transforms Mercutio from a scoffer into an enthusiast, a madman, a *vates,* a *daimon,* a seer, who repudiates his own character as he defies down-to-earth Verona. Superfluous and irrelevant by the yardsticks of decorum and convention, Mercutio's excursus is nevertheless an unequivocal triumph of dramatic art. It is so attractive a digression that it tugs the play into its own eccentric orbit.

When Shakespeare inserted Queen Mab into Mercutio's part, he sacrificed coherence, narrowly defined, for gains in suggestiveness, in dimension, in illusion; he transformed his play from a mirror of Verona to a mirror of mystery. Yet it is all an illusion; there is no mystery aside from the perpetual enigma of artistic creation. Shakespeare was willing to compromise the structure and design of his play because he knew the speech was a good one and deserved a place; it was his privilege as it was his play. And if the traditional idea that as he matured as a playwright Shakespeare gradually learned to subordinate verbal ingenuity and exuberance to larger psychological and thematic purposes is still to be given credence, then the intrusion of the Queen Mab speech into *Romeo and Juliet* is retrogressive in all the easy ways and only progressive in that it transcends conventional conceptions of dramatic ends. It is difficult to decide whether the genius of Queen Mab should be assigned to expediency or effrontery.

VI

It appears, then, that *Romeo and Juliet* was open not only to verbal tinkering but also to major structural reform. Of course it is impossible to know when or in what order Shakespeare made these various changes. Yet if Shakespeare did write his plays consecutively from beginning to end, it is surely of interest that even as he brought *Romeo and Juliet* to conclusion, he was still pushing against the limits. The conclusion of Romeo's very last speech survives in Q2 in a form in which a first brief attempt is succeeded by a longer re-writing. It would appear that Shakespeare originally wrote:

> I will beleeue
> Shall I beleeue that vnsubstantiall death is amorous,
> And that the leane abhorred monster keepes
> Thee here in darke to be his parramour?
> For feare of that I still will staie with thee,
> And neuer from this pallat [Q3 palace] of dym night.
> Depart againe, come lye thou in my arme,
> Heer's to thy health, where ere thou tumblest in.
> O true Appothecarie!
> Thy drugs are quicke. Thus with a kisse I die.
>
> (5.3.102ff; sig. L3)

Once again Shakespeare returned to the love-death trope, this time inventing a figure of amorous death who takes Juliet as his "parramour." But the speech did not go right. "For feare of that I still will staie with thee" are ten low words that creep in a particularly dull line. Romeo's toast to Juliet is inappropriately sardonic, and the interrupted phrase "where ere thou tumblest in" is inexplicable as it stands (although it anticipates the sea imagery that will condense in the revision). Shakespeare seems to have broken off at this point and taken a step backward, for the speech returns to "Depart again," deletes "come lie thou in my arms," replaces it with the macabre "here, here will I remaine / With wormes that are thy Chamber-maides," and then sets out in an entirely new direction.

> O here
> Will I set vp my euerlasting rest:
> And shake the yoke of inauspicious starres,
> From this world wearied flesh.

Shakespeare charts new territory when he introduces a note of eternity into these penultimate moments. Romeo becomes for just an instant a tragic figure who searches for relief from the weariness of life through the shackling of accidents. The moment passes quickly, alas, and Romeo returns to the high-risk rhetoric that marked his discourse earlier in the play (the perpetuation of which, incidentally, contradicts the commonplace of criticism that the mature Romeo of the last act abandons studied conceits for a more naturalistic and authentic language):

> eyes looke your last:
> Armes take your last embrace: And lips, O you
> The doores of breath, seale with a righteous kisse
> A datelesse bargaine to ingrossing death:
> Come bitter conduct, come vnsauoury guide,
> Thou desperate Pilot, now at once run on
> The dashing Rocks, thy seasick weary barke:
> Heeres to my Loue, O true Appothecary:
> Thy drugs are quicke. Thus with a kisse I die.
>
> (112–20)

In these last lines, Romeo transforms and reinvigorates traditional conceits in order to give voice to the vulnerability of love. Instead of the ironic "Here's to thy health," Romeo embraces death forthrightly. The physicality of "bitter" and "unsavoury" recall the previous emphasis on the macabre while a series of submerged oxymora, especially "desperate Pilot," recall less pliable uses of the same trope. At the same time, Shakespeare expands on "tumblest" and resurrects the Petrarchan commonplace of the lover as a storm-tossed ship, except that while Romeo had once declared "I am no Pylat" (2.2.82; sig. D3), he now finds a pilot in the poison that wrecks his "seasick weary barke."[26] The impetuous anaphora "Come bitter conduct, come vnsauoury guide" directly echoes Juliet's earlier "Come night, come *Romeo*" (sig. G1v; 3.2.17) and therefore effects an inspired rather than merely mechanical linking of love and death. Shakespeare rescues and retains the pointed irony of "true Appothecary," with its suggestion that Romeo has been betrayed by everyone but the honest man who has provided him with effective poison. Like Mercutio, Romeo dies quibbling: "quick" is both "rapid" and "alive." In this passage, Shakespeare scores some brilliant hits but also produces a moment or two that he himself would soon repudiate. Romeo's apostrophe to his own parts—"Eyes look your last," etc.—will very shortly be directly parodied by Bottom/Pyramus ("Eyes, do you see?" "Tongue, lose thy light" (5.1.268, 293).

Romeo's last speech is marked by the same restless quest that characterizes *Romeo and Juliet* in its entirety. The playwright who was as hospitable to Kemp's fooleries as to Mercutio's fairies once again balances tradition with novelty, conservation with innovation, verbal precision with experimentation. In rewriting this speech, just as in other acts of revision, Shakespeare continually extended the emotional range of the play. In the course of composition, *Romeo and Juliet* became more rhetorically complex, more emotional, more unpredictable. It is a part of its magic that it became more trivial and yet more grave, more sordid and brutal and yet more ethereal and fanciful. In writing *Romeo and Juliet,* Shakespeare gambled again and again for extremely high stakes; his occasional losses were more than offset by great victories.[27]

Notes

1. Stanley Wells, *Re-editing Shakespeare for the Modern Reader* (Oxford, 1984), p. 89; Eugene M. Waith, "Appendix E: The False Start in 4.4" in *Titus Andronicus* (Oxford, 1984), p. 211–12; Waith, *Titus Andronicus,* p. 40–41. Except for *Romeo and Juliet,* citations are to *William Shakespeare, The Complete Works,* ed. Alfred Harbage (Baltimore, 1969).

2. Persuasively argued by Clifford Leech in the New Arden *The Two Gentlemen of Verona* (London, 1969), pp. xiii–xxi.

3. A. S. Cairncross, "Appendix III: Alternative Q Passage to ii.iii.15–22" in the New Arden *The Third Part of King Henry the Sixth* (London, 1964), p. 180; Stanley Wells and Gary Taylor, with John Jowett and William Montgomery, *William Shakespeare, A Textual Companion* (Oxford, 1987) (henceforth *Tex Ox*), pp. 179–208.

4. The redesign of Berowne's speech is sensitively analyzed by G. R. Hibbard, *The Making of Shakespeare's Dramatic Poetry* (Toronto, 1981), pp. 20–24. It has also been suggested that the Folio text of *The Taming of the Shrew* reveals evidence of revision. For a recent discussion, see Stanley Wells and Gary Taylor, "No Shrew, A Shrew, and The Shrew: Internal Revision in *The Taming of the Shrew,*" in *Shakespeare: Text, Language, Criticism, Studies in Honor of Marvin Spevack,* ed. Bernhard Fabian and Kurt Tetzeli von Rosador (Hildesheim, 1987), pp. 351–71.

5. A summary of textual scholarship on *Romeo and Juliet* is presented in *Tex Ox,* 288–90. Editions of *Romeo and Juliet* by Richard Hosley (New Haven, 1954), J. D. Wilson and G. I. Duthie (Cambridge, Eng., 1955), Brian Gibbons (London, 1980), G. Blakemore Evans (Cambridge, 1984) have all been drawn upon in this essay. Also invaluable are Harry R. Hoppe, *The Bad Quarto of "Romeo and Juliet"* (Ithaca, 1943) and G. W. Williams, *The Most Excellent and Lamentable Tragedie of Romeo and Juliet, A Critical Edition,* (Durham, 1964). To *Tex Ox*'s comprehensive bibliography of textual studies of *Romeo and Juliet* should be appended Michael Mooney's "Text and Performance in *Romeo and Juliet,* Quartos 1 and 2," (*Colby Quarterly* 26 [1990], 122–32). See also R. Cloud, "The Marriage of Good and Bad Quartos," *Shakespeare Quarterly* 33 (1982), 421–31.

6. Citations from both Q1 and Q2 *Romeo and Juliet* are drawn from *Shakespeare's Plays in Quarto,* ed. Kenneth Muir and Michael J. B. Allen (Berkeley, 1981), and are identified both by signature and by the line numbers in Gibbons' Arden edition. A complete list of "false starts" is provided by Evans, p. 208.

7. But see Williams, 104–05; Gibbons 1.2.14–15n.; Evans, 1.2.14 *supp. note.*

8. *The Two Gentlemen of Verona,* 2.3.7.

9. Textual questions raised by this passage are elucidated by E. A. J. Honigmann, *The Stability of Shakespeare's Text* (London, 1965), pp. 130–32. See also Richard Hosley ("The Corrupting Influence of the Bad Quarto on the Received Text of *Romeo and Juliet," Shakespeare Quarterly* 4 [1953], 11–33) and Williams, 128–29. Perhaps this passage is one of those that provoked Richard Fly's complaint that *Romeo and Juliet* "is frequently impeded by verbiage and clotted by rhetoric" (*Shakespeare's Mediated World* [Amherst, 1976], p. 6).

10. And why is it that when the compilers of the Folio came to print *Romeo and Juliet* (which they did from quarto copy), they omitted the *Prologue* and simply began with *"Actus Primus, Scoena Prima"* (see *The First Folio of Shakespeare,* ed. Charlton Hinman [New York, 1964])? The Folio text—it is believed—was set by the apprentice compositor E. He followed "an editor who worked through Q3's text with (for his day) considerable care, annotating the printer's copy where it struck him as deficient and relying mainly on the context to do so, though perhaps occasionally—and certainly not often enough—consulting a playhouse manuscript" (so S. W. Reid, "The Editing of Folio *Romeo and Juliet," Studies in Bibliography* 25 [1982], 66.) Reid does not consider the omission of the *Prologue. Tex Ox* attributes its absence to an error in casting off copy.

The Folio retains the chorus which appears at the conclusion of the masquing scene.

11. *A New Variorum Edition of Romeo and Juliet,* ed. H. H. Furness (Philadelphia, 1871), 1.5.143n.

12. *Works of Thomas Kyd,* ed. Frederick S. Boas (Oxford, 1901); Robert Yarington, *Two Lamentable Tragedies* (Amersham, 1913); Christopher Marlowe, *Complete Plays and Poems,* ed. E. D. Pendry (Totowa, N.J., 1976); Robert Greene, *Alphonsus King of Aragon,* ed. W. W. Greg (Oxford, 1926); *The Tragedy of Locrine,* ed. R. B. McKerrow (Oxford, 1908); *The Tragedy of Master Arden of Feversham,* ed. Martin White (New York, 1908).

13. "The Argument" ll. 1–3 and 13–14 in Arthur Brooke, *The Tragicall Historye of Romeus and Juliet* (1562), in *Narrative and Dramatic Sources of Shakespeare,* ed. Geoffrey Bullough. 8 vols. (New York, 1961–1975), vol. 1, pp. 284–363. Shakespeare's fidelity to his source is discussed in E. Pearlman, "Staging *Romeo and Juliet:* Evidence from Brooke's *Romeus," Theatre Survey* 34 (1993), 22–32.

14. John Downes, *Roscius Anglicanus* (London, 1708), p. 22. The comic devices in *Romeo and Juliet* have been catalogued and carefully explicated by Susan Snyder (*The Comic Matrix of Shakespeare's Tragedies* [Princeton, 1979], pp. 56–70).

15. "Either Shakespeare intended it to strike an almost unbearably false note or else he mismanaged it to an astonishing degree" (Derick R. C. Marsh, *Passion Lends them Power* [Manchester, 1976], p. 80). See also Charles B. Lower, "*Romeo and Juliet,* IV, v: A Stage Direction and Purposeful Comedy," *Shakespeare Studies* 8 (1975), 177–94; Thomas Moisan, "Rhetoric and the Rehearsal of Death: the 'Lamentations' Scene in *Romeo and Juliet," Shakespeare Quarterly* 34 (1983), 389–404; Ann Pasternak Slater, "Petrarchanism Come True in *Romeo and Juliet"* in *Images of Shakespeare,* ed. Werner Habicht et. al., (Newark, Delaware, 1988), pp. 136, 144.

16. Q1 clarifies exits and entrances. At the end of the lament comes the instruction *"They all but the Nurse goe foorth, casting Rosemary on her and shutting the Curtens. Enter Musitions."* After a couple of lines of dialogue, the Nurse exits; then comes the unambiguous *Enter Servingman.*

17. Proposed by Wilson and Duthie, p. 209, whose suggestion has been frequently repeated: Williams, p. 136; Gibbons 4.5.99n; Evans 4.5.99n; *Tex Ox:* "the following episode could have been added as an afterthought in Shakespeare's manuscript" (p. 300). Giorgio Melchiori ("Peter, Balthasar, and Shakespeare's Art of Doubling," *Modern Language Review* 78 [1983]) thinks that it "is likely" (780) that the episode was added. Melchiori also speculates that the passage might be written by Kemp himself (782). Kemp's part in *Romeo and Juliet* is discussed by David Wiles in *Shakespeare's Clown, Actor and Text in the Elizabethan Theatre* (Cam-

bridge, Eng., pp. 83–93. Joan Hartwig (*Shakespeare's Analogical Scene* [Lincoln, 1983]) argues that both the lament and the clown function as "preparative parody" and are designed to contrast with Romeo's melancholy and suicide.

The printing of this scene requires comment. Paul L. Cantrell and George Walton Williams ("The Printing of the Second Quarto of *Romeo and Juliet* (1599)," *Studies in Bibliography* 9 [1957], 107–28) argue that Q2 was set by two compositors: A, who set everything from the beginning to sig. L2v (5.3.86) with the exception of the single page sig. K3v, and B, who set sig. K3v and sig. L3 to the end. If Cantrell and Williams are correct, sig. K3v is anomalous in that in this instance alone B's work appears within a block otherwise entirely assignable to A. Sig. K3v is the page on which all but the last three lines of Kemp's scene are printed, i.e. from "*Enter Will Kemp*" to "Then Musique with her siluer sound with speedy help doth lend redresse. *Exit*" (99 s.d.–135). Cantrell and Williams' compositor attributions are derived from typographical idiosyncrasies in the setting of stage directions, speech prefixes, catchwords and orthographical preferences. Their argument, which is far too involuted to be briefly recapitulated, is engaging but indecisive. The unique sig. K3v is inconvenient to Cantrell and Williams, who are forced into an elaborate argument about printing-house practice, the work schedules of compositors A and B and the printing of sheets K, L, and M. "Perhaps," they concede about one facet of their complex exposition, "this hypothesis is too nice" (115). It may be simpler to concede that sig. K3v is simply unlike any other page. It contains a number of unique spellings: "dry" (in seven other uses in Q2 always spelled "drie"); "cry" (three other appearances as "crie"); "music" appears four times on sig. K3v spelled "musique" and occurs six times elsewhere, always spelled "musick(e); "yron" appears twice on sig. K3v and is in two other cases spelled "iron"); sig. K3v gives "mary" which turns up ten other times as "marrie." Sig. K3v is the only page in which a prefix ("*Minst.*") is used as a catchword; it is the only page in which there is a blank above the catchword. In short, the evidence, which falls far short of statistical proof, opens the real possibility that sig. K3v is not the work of the hypothetical compositor B but is simply different from all other pages. While it is not impossible that its uniqueness may be accounted for by printing-house practice, simpler hypotheses may also be entertained. Copy may have come to the hands of the compositor in a different form than the rest of the manuscript—either in Shakespeare's hand but written at another time (in consultation with Kemp?), or in another hand (Kemp's?), or in some other form easy to imagine but impossible to prove. Even the most agnostic review of the evidence must acknowledge that, just as Kemp's jibes are different, so sig. K3v is different.

18.   Ed. G. R. Proudfoot, Oxford, 1964.

19.   The improvisational practices of clowns have been most recently elucidated by Eric Rasmussen ("Setting Down what the Clown Spoke: Improvisation, Hand B, and *The Book of Sir Thomas More*," *The Library* 13 [1991], 126–36).

20.   The discords created by the Queen Mab speech have not dulled admiration. Levin L. Schucking thought that "the wonderful passage resembles an operatic air, inserted for the sake of the music without regard for the characterization" (*Character Problems in Shakespeare's Plays* [London, 1922], p. 99). H. R. Granville-Barker took the same position: the speech "is as much and as little to be justified as a song in an opera is" (*Prefaces to Shakespeare* [Princeton, 1947], vol. 2, p. 305). Arguments that the speech is relevant are more difficult to sustain. The most determined case was made by Robert O. Evans in *The Osier Cage* (Lexington, 1966), pp. 69–86. Evans confronted the question directly: "Did Shakespeare just dig it out of his notebook or his brain and find that he could not resist setting it? Or did he have a dramatic reason?" (Evans does not consider the possibility that its inclusion is appropriate in ways that transcend the conventional laws of play-making.) He proposes that it is relevant because "Mercutio considers . . . money, place and love to be madnesses" (p. 79), but he then immediately retreats to acknowledge that "actually neither money nor place . . . have anything to do with the major action of the play. . . . Money is never even mentioned" (p. 79). Evans also argues that both the Queen Mab speech and the play as a whole correspond because both are replete with rhetorical

figures. This is an argument that would satisfy those who trust that rivers in Macedon and rivers in Monmouth are identical because "there is salmons in both." Evans' principal argument is both circular and idolatrous: if *Romeo and Juliet* is "a mass of disparate elements, which it certainly is not, [then] Shakespeare is a weaver of rag-mats, which he certainly was not" (86). Elton F. Henley ("Relevance of Queen Mab's Speech in *Romeo and Juliet* I.iv.53–94" [*Language Quarterly* (Tampa)] 4 [1965], 29–32), concedes that "the speech is couched in language not typical of Mercutio," and argues the paradox that "its relevance to the play as a whole is this inconsistency, for the play itself is a study of inconsistency at all levels" (p. 30). Both Joseph S. M. J. Chang ("The Language of Paradox in *Romeo and Juliet*" [*Shakespeare Studies* 3 (1967)], pp. 35–36) and Nicholas Brooke (*Shakespeare's Early Tragedies* [London, 1968]) make much of a tangential association of Mercutio's speech and Juliet's epithalamium—"Phaeton's coach of day is driven into the night of Juliet's desire; Queen Mab's coach is driven through the night of dreams to fulfill the real ambitions of men and women, greed and lust" (Brooke, p. 85). Marjorie B. Garber advances the unfalsifiable proposition that the Queen Mab speech "is Mercutio speaking in an assumed voice, the voice of the romantic daydreamer and fabulist" (*Dream in Shakespeare* [New Haven, 1974], p. 39). Clifford Leech ("The Moral Tragedy of *Romeo and Juliet*," *English Renaissance Drama: Essays in Honor of Madeleine Doran and Mark Eccles,* ed. Standish Henning et. al. [Carbondale and Edwardsville, Ill., 1976]) proposes that "what is most important is that the speech puts Mercutio outside the general Christian framework of the play." "He is surely a pure pagan: his last call is for a surgeon, not a priest" (p. 74). Once again Mercutio's difference becomes his pertinence.

The case for the speech's success on stage is cogently made by Kent Cartwright, *Shakespearean Tragedy and its Double: The Rhythms of Audience Response* (University Park, 1991), pp. 53–55.

21.   "Mercutio professes a robust disbelief in [the truth of dreams], yet the racing uncontrolledness of this speech . . . undermines his claims." "We have lost sight of the supposed argument, that men's dreams are merely the twitches of habitual thoughts during sleep" (T. J. Cribb, "The Unity of *Romeo and Juliet*," *Shakespeare Survey* 34 [1981], 103, 102).

22.   Often but perhaps erroneously emended to "five"—the n in fine interpreted as a turned u. Q1 gives "right wits" (sig. C1v).

23.   Bibliographical problems presented by proper ordering of the Queen Mab speech are discussed by Hosley, 1.4.56n., Wilson and Duthie, pp. 140–42; Williams, 1.4.70n., Sidney Thomas, "The Queen Mab Speech in *Romeo and Juliet*," *Shakespeare Survey* 25 (1972), 73–80; Evans, pp. 209–10; *Tex Ox,* pp. 292–93.

24.   *Nimphidia, The Courte of Fayrie,* ll. 53–54, in *The Works of Michael Drayton,* ed. J. William Hebel. 5 vols. (Oxford, 1931–1941), vol. 3, pp. 125–46.

25.   *The Entertainment at Althrope* (1604), in *Ben Jonson,* ed. C. H. Herford and P. and E. Simpson. 11 vols. (Oxford, 1927–1952), vol. 7, pp. 119–31.

26.   Jill L. Levenson gathers and elucidates Petrarchan transformations in this speech ("The Definition of Love: Shakespeare's Phrasing in *Romeo and Juliet*," *Shakespeare Studies* 15 [1982], 33).

27.   The contention that Elizabethan authors revised by tinkering with words and phrases, but not with longer units, scrupulously advanced by John Kerrigan ("Revision, Adaptation, and the Fool in *King Lear*," in *The Division of the Kingdoms,* ed. Gary Taylor and Michael Warren. [Oxford, 1983], pp. 195–242) does not apply to *Romeo and Juliet,* a work-in-progress in which Shakespeare both tinkers and inserts. The subject of Shakespeare at work has been recently surveyed by Grace Ioppolo (*Revising Shakespeare* [Cambridge, 1991]). For *Romeo and Juliet* see pp. 89–93 and *passim.*

The Webbing of *Romeo and Juliet*

Donald W. Foster

Electronic technology has opened the door to a new world of computer-assisted textual analysis. Interested literary scholars (rightly cautious when it comes to such matters as new-fangled technology mixed with old-fashioned mathematics) have faced this bright vista with ambivalence, not unlike the dairy cow who stands before a new barn door, wondering if it's safe to pass through. Old ways are often the best ways. In the view of many seasoned academics, a machine can teach us nothing about such complex matters as influence, attribution, dating, or textual authority. And indeed, the landscape of computer-assisted research may be as fraught with peril as work conducted on more familiar soil. Pratfalls are likely, perhaps inevitable. But electronic scholarship is the way of the future, the potential for which may be limited only by our own imagination and yesterday's technology.

Among the many resources being developed for twenty-first-century literary studies none has been more widely publicized than Shaxicon—to speak of which begs some modesty on my part since it is a database of my own making (though the publicity was not).[1] Shaxicon began long ago as a simple handlist of rare words in Shakespeare. Ten years in development, having outgrown a succession of personal computers, Shaxicon is almost ready to make its public debut. Portions of "The Shaxicon Notebook" have already been mounted on the World Wide Web, with more to follow soon, play by play.[2]

To understand Shaxicon, it will help to think of the Shakespeare corpus as a verbal tapestry extending from about 1591 at the bottom end, to the last draft of the poet's will in 1616 at the top. The more-or-less vertical fibers are those words, mannerisms, grammatical habits, that reappear throughout Shakespeare's career, even if they are not visible in every work. The more-or-less horizontal threads are such stuff as one finds at a particular stage in his career, or in a specific text. Each vertical thread was first quilled into the larger web at a particular moment in time, often with thread borrowed from someone else's store of material. Many verbal threads in the Shakespearean tapestry are unique. Most are not. There are other texts in the same hall—the canvases of Spenser, Marlowe, Nash, Jonson, Webster, Ford, and hundreds of others—that contain much of the same material, though arranged in a fundamentally different structure.

Ignoring the beauty of the larger image, Shaxicon traces the internal structure of the web. By considering millions of bits of information (words appearing or not appearing in Shakespeare; words found or not found elsewhere in early modern English), Shaxicon does a reasonably good job of charting Shakespeare's protean vocabulary as it developed throughout his career. Common words are disregarded. Shaxicon considers only the most distinctive verbal fibers—words appearing least often—and follows those threads as they enter the tapestry, cross other threads, and finally vanish from sight. By further locating all of those same threads—as many as can be found—in the work of other writers, scholars can now construct a virtual model of Shakespeare's linguistic development, and of other authors whose work Shakespeare either borrowed from, or influenced.

When speaking of "influence," I intend only the quantifiable flow of new or rare diction from one text to another, directly or indirectly, without regard to conscious borrowing, or to Bloomian precursors, or to fruitless debates over verbal parallels. The traditional metaphors of indebtedness, borrowing, and theft are unavoidable but misleading in their notion of language as personal property. We do not talk of a child's indebtedness in reproducing the speech of significant others, but of acquisition and development. I subscribe to the developmental model even while invoking familiar metaphors of indebtedness. Most of the new words that Shakespeare acquired from 1591 to 1613 were not "stolen," or "borrowed," or even "chosen." Words are like burrs: they stick.

Imagine a text written in 1997 by the good citizen John Doe (a screenplay, perhaps) whose rare words include *anomies, collectivistic, darkies, irrationalism, isopropyltrimethylmethane, leftish, nonattainment, oversocialization, superhumanly, technologization, technophile,* and *transex.* An electronic search that takes the World Wide Web as its lexical field would reveal that these words first appeared together in "Industrial Society and Its Future," the Unabom manifesto, first published on the Web by the FBI in May 1995.[3] Mr. Doe, in a word, has been *influenced* by that text—which is not to say that he shares the Unabomber's ideals or particular artistic skills. Shakespeare was similarly influenced, in everything that he wrote, by what he read, and his own writing influenced other readers. By considering only words themselves, not "verbal echoes," scholars can now trace the word-spinners' web of Elizabethan literature in which Shakespeare's language is itself reticulated. It takes some mental stretching to wrap one's brain around this concept; but once the phenomenon has been assimilated, Shaxicon has been understood.

Some influence is quite specific. The books to which Shakespeare turned for his narrative material had, typically, a sudden and profound effect on his vocabulary. So, too, for theatrical study. When reading a book of particular interest, or rehearsing a theatrical role, Shakespeare acquired new words by the bucketful, many of which entered his written work. The same thing happened when other poets and playwrights engaged Shakespearean texts. Taking the Shakespeare corpus as its point of focus, and early modern English as its lexical field, Shaxicon measures the relative strength of textual interrelatedness, enabling scholars to arrange texts in the very order in which they were written and read; if there has been borrowing (direct or indirect) by one author from another, Shaxicon can usually identify which text is the source and which is the receptacle for the transmitted material. It needn't be supposed that Shakespeare actually sat down and read every text identified by Shaxicon as having influenced his work; some new words were simply in the air, in the pulpit or court or theater, in London or Oxford or Warwickshire; those words, too, can be charted.[4] Literary influence, in the sense that will be operative here, is a network of spoken and written language, not a unilinear chain of causality.

Because these structural forces in the poet's writing derive from his reading and theatrical study, they may have some value as biography, but they are principally useful in textual scholarship. Any Shakespearean text (or fragment thereof) can be dated relative to other Shakespearean texts, early and late. Each can be independently tested for evidence of Shakespeare's theatrical study, which in turn may have a bearing on matters of dating and attribution. For example, canonical texts later than *Romeo and Juliet* employ a disproportionate number of rare words from the Friar Lawrence role (relative to the Friar's share of all rare words in the play). The same phenomenon is true of Adam in *As You Like It*. After 1599 Adam's rare words are recalled in Shakespeare's new writing while the rare diction of most other characters is forgotten (except Corin, who with Adam influences the poet's later writing). Shakespearean texts written after *Romeo and Juliet* but before *As You Like It* register the influence of the Friar's words, but not of Adam's. Shaxicon further reveals something about "the memorial reconstructor" of the "bad" Quartos—that mysterious interlocutor who remembers just one or two roles while substantially changing everything else in Shakespeare's script. This ghost has haunted study of the multiple-text plays since 1902, when first conjured by W. W. Greg from Q1 *Merry Wives*. Shaxicon reveals that the actor who usually altered Shakespeare's texts (but from usually first to second quartos, not vice versa) was Shakespeare himself.

When linked to the electronic *OED* or a comprehensive text archive for the early modern period, Shaxicon enables the scholar to consider a broader context and to locate those texts from which Shakespeare acquired his new words. For example, in the latter months of 1592, beginning with *3 Henry VI,* Shakespeare imports new words in a big way from Arthur Brooke's *Romeus and Juliet,* whose influence on the poet's vocabulary suddenly swells in 1593, not fully dissipating until 1596. It is also in 1592–1593 that Shakespeare first plucks whole clusters of rare words from Thomas Nash's *Pierce Penilesse* and *Summers Last Will,* from John Eliot's *Ortho-epia Gallica,* Barnabe Barnes's *Parthenophil and Parthenophe,* and from Samuel Daniel's 1593 edition of *Delia.* Each of these works alters Shakespeare's vocabulary, beginning typically with a large infusion of new words, followed by a gradual tapering off in his later writing. Some of the newly imported words are soon forgotten; others become part of the poet's "common" vocabulary. (When a word exceeds 12 occurrences in the canonical plays, it falls out of Shaxicon's purview.)

Shaxicon traces a gradual rollover in the relative pressure exerted by these and other texts on Shakespeare's writing: Eliot and Nash condition *Romeo and Juliet* and *The Rape of Lucrece,* but not *Venus and Adonis.* Marlowe's "Hero and Leander" influences all three. *The Jew of Malta* contributes significantly to *Romeo and Juliet* and *The Merchant of Venice* but not to *The Comedy of Errors.* This matrix of reading and writing invites collation, which is a fairly simple task and one that can be accomplished without obvious self-contradiction. The sticking points are precisely those that invite closer scrutiny. The 1593 edition of Daniel's *Delia* (containing both "Rosamond" and "Cleopatra") influences Shakespeare's poetry from *The Rape of Lucrece* through "A Lover's Complaint" (1593/4–1608), and his plays from *Romeo and Juliet* through *The Winter's Tale* (1593/4–1610). But as measured by Shaxicon, Daniel's text shapes only the Q2 *Romeo* variants, not the Q1 variants or the material shared by Q1 and Q2.

Nothing can be inferred concerning the date or relative textual authority of the Q1 and Q2 variants without first isolating the material that is unique to Q1 and to Q2. The catalogue of *Romeo*'s rarest words must be considered in three mutually exclusive parcels: words appearing in both quarto versions, those found only in Q1, and those only in Q2. These three classes of lexical material in Shaxicon-assisted study are denoted "ROM Qq," "ROM q1," and "ROM q2" (thereby to distinguish the text proper from the rare words that appear in it). With only a few keystrokes, Shaxicon can supply a catalogue of the "rare" words in *Romeo and Juliet*—words that appear elsewhere in Shakespeare's plays, or poems, or both, no more than 12 times (or 10, or 7, or 2). One may then search for these words elsewhere—in the electronic *OED* or in a comprehensive text archive—to see where they came from and to follow their transmission to the work of other writers.

The results of that labor, already performed, are posted on the World Wide Web in some detail.[5] Perhaps the most controversial (but I think inescapable) conclusions to be drawn from Shaxicon's evidence are that Q1 precedes Q2 in point of date, and that both are principally or entirely Shakespeare's own work. When mapped against the Shakespeare canon generally, the Qq and q1 samples come before *The Rape of Lucrece,* and q2 afterward. When charted against non-Shakespearean citations in the *OED,* the Qq and q1 samples draw chiefly on texts published in 1592–1593, and on a few earlier texts such as Holinshed's *Chronicles* (1587 ed.) and Spenser's *Faerie Queene,* books I–III (1590) that we know Shakespeare read. ROM q2 shares comparatively more rare diction with the *OED*'s 1594–1597 texts, and far less with its 1590–1593 sources. As measured by its diction, Q1 is all of a piece; Q2's difference represents a later refinement. Shakespeare did not borrow each one of his new words from each one of the *OED* texts cited; rather, the *OED* citations collectively indicate that the rare diction of Q1 was generally available to Shakespeare as linguistic bricoleur from 1590 to 1593.

The three ROM samples have also been mapped in great detail against the Vassar Electronic Text Archive (VETA), with results that confirm both the internal evidence of the Shakespeare canon and the intertextual evidence supplied by the *OED*.[6] The Q1 variants (represented by ROM q1) are drawn from the same non-Shakespearean lexicons as the rare words of the "core" text (Qq), and both can be firmly dated 1593. The q2 sample draws on other lexicons, extending to 1594 and perhaps beyond. The VETA 1996 contains 172 STC I files that are earlier than 1594. Of these, only seven register a strong and significant affinity with ROM Qq: Marlowe's *Tamburlaine* (pub. 1592) and nondramatic canon (complete by 1593, pub. 1598–1600); *Edmond Ironside* (a manuscript play by Robert Green, ca. 1589–1590, n.p.); Nash's *Summers Last Will* (performed in 1592, pub. 1600); John Eliot, *Ortho-epia Gallica* (1593), Barnabe Barnes's *Parthenophil* (1593); and Arthur Brooke's *Romeus and Juliet* (1562, repr. 1587). That Shakespeare knew these texts by 1594 is already a matter of record. All were identified by Shaxicon as likely sources for *Romeo and Juliet* without recourse to that scholarship, including Brooke's poem, which is universally acknowledged to be the play's principal source. But Brooke's influence is felt only on Q1, not on Q2, as if Brooke's influence has already begun to dissipate since the poet's first acquaintance with the text in 1592. Among the seven texts most strongly influencing the ROM q2 sample, three were published in 1594, one in 1595—with Thomas Heywood's *Oenone and Paris* (1594) heading the list.[7]

The lexical distributions for *Romeo and Juliet* and *A Midsummer Night's Dream* indicate that both quartos of the tragedy are earlier than the comedy. But from 1595 onward, the two plays track together in their rise and fall of influence on Shakespeare's new writing, having nearly identical distributions, as if they were staged as companion plays repeatedly from 1595 to 1613: no other play or poem but *A Midsummer Night's Dream* closely matches *Romeo and Juliet*'s distribution of influence during those years.[8] Shaxicon intimates that Shakespeare most likely performed the Friar role in both quarto versions (this is, at least, the only role besides the Chorus whose rare words he insistently recalls in later writing), but the influence of the Q1 Friar is registered before that of the Q2 Friar, with *A Midsummer Night's Dream* providing the pivotal moment at which Q2 Friar's influence first surpasses that of his Q1 predecessor. Both scripts appear to have been altered later than 1593/4, with the Q1 changes consisting primarily of cuts. Q2 may have been augmented slightly just before publication or may contain material that was not always acted.

Some of these hypotheses fly in the face of conventional wisdom. In an attempt to account for the anomalies, I will turn next to traditional scholarship, to see whether its methods and conclusions may be reconciled with those of Shaxicon. There is a strong suspicion in some quarters that textual scholarship and computers don't mix. This thinking was confirmed when the news was bruited abroad in January 1996 that Shaxicon (not by design, but as a windfall) had confirmed Shakespeare's authorship of *A Funeral Elegy*. The evidence was not directly challenged but "the Computer" nevertheless got roasted in the English press for weeks on end (and me along with it).[9] Peter Levi announced that "Such analysis is almost always rubbish."[10] Katherine Duncan-Jones cited the elegy attribution as a prime example of all that has gone wrong with America's politically correct universities and "irresponsible" professoriate.[11] Stanley Wells in a television interview said his "gut feeling is that the computer and the methodology that has been used to operate it, are wrong."[12] And for Brian Vickers I represented "that recently emergent type of scholar who performs elaborate analyses of poetic language by using concordances and other electronic resources rather than by reading poems. But what," asks Vickers, "do machines know about literary conventions, genre, rhetoric, or figurative language?"[13]

In such a climate it cannot accomplish much simply to report what Shaxicon has to say about the authority and textual transmission of the multiple-text Shakespeare plays. First it must be understood that the patterns of language traced by Shaxicon are found in the literature itself, not in a computer program. I will therefore explore the problems of Q1 and Q2 *Romeo and Juliet* without further help from Shaxicon, using only the methods of traditional textual scholarship; but my analysis depends on Shaxicon's model of literature as a network, a linguistic system in which the texts of a particular cultural moment, or author or genre, mutually inform one another.

II

Two households, both alike in dignity . . .
—the Chorus (Pro. I.i.)

A plague a' both your houses!
—Mercutio (III.i.100)

The Most Excellent and Lamentable Tragedy of Romeo and Juliet was published in two quartos (1597, 1599). According to a long-established scholarly consensus, the second is most excellent, and the first, lamentable. But the methods of traditional scholarship have failed to untangle *Romeo and Juliet*'s complex textual development. With capable scholars tugging in opposite directions, the knots seem only to have grown tighter. Brian Gibbons states as an established fact that Q1 is a memorial reconstruction, "piratical and dependent on an especially unreliable means of transmission for the text." Gibbons identifies speeches, lines, and even particular phrases that, because of their perceived badness, could not have been written by Shakespeare. Taking for granted the priority of Q2, Gibbons concludes that "Q1 is by contrast dramatically, not simply verbally, shoddy."[14] That Q1 is "bad" and therefore a rogue actor's faulty reconstruction of Q2 has looked to other scholars like a circular argument. There has been a tendency in the most recent studies to vindicate Q1, or at least to hedge one's bets. The first quarto has been variously defended as Shakespeare's rough draft, or as the original stage version, or as the company's authorized (if inept) adaptation for performance with a reduced cast. In Jay Halio's view, Q1 is Shakespeare's own theatrical redaction of an antecedent Q2, shortened for performance and a better play all around than the more literary Q2 script.[15] No consensus has yet been reached concerning these theories.

Dates of composition for Q1 and Q2 have ranged from 1591 to 1596. The *OED* usually dates the "good" script in 1592 (1591 for some citations), and Q1 in 1597. Most scholars now agree that the play cannot have been completed (in its printed forms) earlier than 1593, given obvious and shared borrowings from Samuel Daniel's "Complaint of Rosamond" and John Eliot's *Ortho-epia Gallica.* Recent editors have tended to date *Romeo and Juliet* in 1596. The late dating receives support from Joan Ozark Holmer, who argues that Shakespeare borrows directly from the fencing manual of Vincentio Saviolo—*Saviolo his Practice*—which in Holmer's view establishes "a terminus *a quo* of 1595 for *Romeo and Juliet.*"[16] In a follow-up study, Holmer finds Shakespeare borrowing from a variety of texts by Thomas Nash, principally *Terrors of the Night* (1594) and *Have With You to Saffron-Walden* (1596).[17] Holmer also notes Edward White's 1596 publication of an anonymous "new ballad of ROMEO AND JULIET" (ent. 5 August; not extant). Finding that Shakespeare's play takes its inspiration from the ballad, Nash, and Saviolo, rather than vice versa, she concludes that the original composition of *Romeo and Juliet* must date from the autumn of 1596.[18] J. J. M. Tobin, who has done extensive work on the artistic relationship between Shakespeare and Thomas Nash, agrees. He was the first to note the affinity between *Romeo and Juliet* and Nash's *Saffron-Walden* (1596).[19] On the not unreasonable assumption that the first-published text was the source, Tobin concludes that Shakespeare must have borrowed from Nash. Persuaded by Tobin's argument that Shakespeare is the debtor in this exchange, G. Blakemore Evans dates Q2 *Romeo and Juliet* in the spring of 1596.[20] The scholarship seems thus to be moving toward consensus.

The dates that we assign to Q1 and Q2 are not unrelated to the problem of textual authority. Though most editors tend to speak of *Romeo and Juliet*'s "date," no one can assume that Q1 and Q2 were composed simultaneously, or that either version was completed at a single sitting by a single author. If it could be shown, for example, that Q1 or Q2 borrows more directly than the other from Shakespeare's narrative sources, that would go far toward establishing chronological priority and perhaps shed light on matters of textual authority as well. If it were discovered that Q1 but not Q2 is indebted to a text published in 1595, that might confirm the advertisement of Q1's title page that the text represents the script as it was performed in 1596–1597 by "the L. of *Hunsdon* his Servants," and so on. But the available evidence has proved so equivocal that the methods of traditional scholarship have produced only conflicting results, with no firm date for either quarto; and there remains a general consensus that Q1 is "bad" but no agreement on how it came to be that way.

Everyone agrees that Arthur Brooke's *Romeus and Juliet* is Shakespeare's main narrative source, but its dates of publication (1562, repr. 1567, 1587) are not helpful in establishing either a terminus *a quo* or *ad quem* for Shakespeare's *Romeo and Juliet.* Holmer has provided more promising candidates in Saviolo's *Practice* (1595) and Nash's *Terrors of the Night* (1594). Nash's *Saffron-Walden* (1596) can provide a third test case, and John Eliot's *Ortho-epia Gallica* (1593) a fourth.

Joan Holmer's evidence that Shakespeare knew Saviolo's *Practice* lies principally in Mercutio's familiarity with things Italian, including the rapier and the new style of Italian fencing (new to the English) that Saviolo brought with him to London about 1590; and her case is plausibly argued: Saviolo, who taught in the fencing school of Rocco Bonetti, became quickly famous for his skill with the rapier, so that the new "Spanish blade" soon threatened to displace the English sword as a gentleman's weapon of choice. There can be no doubt that Shakespeare's play glances quite directly at Saviolo's Italian practice, which was the talk of hot-blooded London youths in the early 1590s, and the object of Mercutio's rapier-like wit. But if Shakespeare ever read Saviolo's *Practice,* it is not clear that Mercutio has done so. Mercutio has heard of the new style, but he disdains Saviolo's practice together with the Italian fashion of dress, manners, and speech that came to England in the same continental package. The Italian Mercutio sounds, in fact, like a closet Englishman. He ridicules the new form, though he still knows very little about it.

In the first of his jibes at Italian fencing, Mercutio mocks the "immortall Passado, the Punto reuerso, the Hay" (Q1, E2v).

"The what?" asks Benvolio.

Benvolio is still unfamiliar with these fire-new words, and even Mercutio gets them wrong. Mercutio supposes a *hay* to belong with the *passado* and *punto* in a manual of new-fangled Italian snicker-snack, but he is mistaken. The *hay* is not a fencing thrust. Nor does the word ever appear in Saviolo's lengthy discourse on fencing in 1595. When the English (and anglicized Danes) scored a touch, the cry was a good round Anglo-Saxon "*Hit!*" ("a very palpable hit!"). With the Italian fencing masters, the cry was always "Hai!" (Lacking a precedent for Shakespeare's odd usage, the *OED* guesses that Mercutio thinks the *hay* to be "a home thrust" [vb.4.B]).

It was not the *passado* or *punta riversa,* nor crying "Hai!" but the *stoccata* for which Vincentio Saviolo was best known. According to Saviolo's instruction, the *stoccata* was "the chiefest matter of all . . . the skil of this arte in effect, is nothing but a stoccata."[21] This was his most prized contribution to the art of fencing. But the *stoccata* is another Italian term that confuses Mercutio. He doesn't mention the *stoccata* when first railing against Italianate fencing, and when he comes to it a few scenes later, he gets it wrong:

> O dishonorable vile submission. *Allastockado* caries it away.
> You Ratcatcher, come backe, come backe.
>
> (Q1, F1[III.i])

"*Allo stoccata*" was not the name of a new fencing thrust. This was the instruction (imperative mood) of an Italian fencing coach, meaning, roughly, "Now go for the stoccata!" It is odd that Mercutio misunderstands the Italian *allo* because he is, after all, *Italian.* He seems, in short, to have picked up his fencing lore not from a book (the phrase appears nowhere in Saviolo's *Practice*) but from having overheard the jargon as an Italian master instructed English players (or other would-be duelists) in rapier work: "Passado! punta riversa! allo stoccata! Hai!"

It is no surprise that Italian fencing terms appear in *Romeo and Juliet:* it is an Italian play, with Italian characters who—if they were to fight like Italians—needed to know something of the fencing craze that had inspired the likes of Tybalt. It seems odd only that Mercutio and Benvolio should know so little about the Italian style when it had been topical since 1590.[22]

Saviolo his Practice adds nothing to *Romeo and Juliet* that was not in print from 1591. John Florio's *Second Frutes* (1591) is a book that Shakespeare certainly knew and often consulted, not only as a guide to the Italian language but also as a source for theatrical dialogue. Florio's Italian primer inspires Shakespearean dialogue in plays as early as *The Taming of the Shrew* and as late as *Hamlet.* And though Mercutio registers no acquaintance with *Saviolo his Practice,* he is familiar enough with Florio's account of Saviolo in the *Second Frutes,* published four years earlier. In his description of "these new tuners of accent . . . these fashionmongers, these pardonmees," Mercutio describes Florio and Saviolo down to the silk buttons on their Italian doublets. There are two pages in particular from the *Second Frutes* that Mercutio seems to recall. In a conversation beginning directly with one of his habitually courteous *pardon mes,* Florio compliments "master V[incent] S[aviolo]," "that Italian that lookes like Mars himselfe." A marvelous tuner of new accents, Florio's V.S. "differs verie much from other fencers": V.S. is "a good dancer, hee danceth verie well, . . . hee vaultes most nimblie, and capers verie loftilie." He is also a master duellist who—with the "punta, o di stoccata, . . . o di riuerso"—"will hit any man, bee it with a thrust or stoccada . . . with a right or reuerse

blowe, . . . euen as it liketh him." He is "valiant, and a talle man of his
hands," "more valiant than a sword it selfe," "a notable talle man" who with
"true and right gentleman-like weapons . . . teacheth verie well, and very
quicklie" (Q3–4). Mercutio's Tybalt is "By Iesu a very good blade, a very tall
man, a very good whoore . . . a Duellist, a gentleman of the very first house of
the first and second cause, ah the immortall Passado, the Punto reuerso . . . "
(Q1 Rom., E1v [II.iv]). As "the couragious captaine of complements, Catso,"
Tybalt seems to rival both Saviolo and Florio. Florio's skill in the art of compliment is what the Second Frutes is really all about. And it is Florio's Saviolo,
not Saviolo his Practice, that is the object of laughter in Shakespeare's Romeo
and Juliet. Mercutio turns Florio's courtly art of compliment into a joke and
makes Saviolo the butt of English satire.

On the subjective level of close reading I can find no evidence that
Shakespeare ever read Saviolo his Practice.[23] Holmer acknowledges the emphasis placed by Saviolo on the stoccata, his favorite thrust ("a crucial term for
Saviolo" [168]), which he describes in great detail. Saviolo also explains the
imbroccata, incartata, mandritta, passado, punta riversa, and punto with complete
clarity. Shakespeare tries out three of these terms, gets the main one wrong,
and adds a fourth that does not belong in the catalog. Holmer remarks in
passing that "Romeo and Juliet is filled with duello language found in Saviolo's
text" (174), but her close survey yields no obvious parallels of phrasing or
imagery with Shakespeare's play apart from the fencing terms—to which she
adds an original and useful observation concerning Saviolo's preoccupation
with "worm's meat." Displayed quite prominently in both parts of Saviolo his
Practice is a woodcut with the legend: "O WORMES MEATE: O FROATH:
O VANITIE: WHY ART THOV SO INSOLENT." As noted by Holmer, the
woodcut "appears in Book 1 as the only nontechnical illustration (K3) and as
the only pictorial ornament in Book 2 (Gg6v)" (174).

Attributional and source study has often been a subjective contest
whereby one scholar advances verbal parallels without proof of their distinction only to have other scholars dismiss those parallels as worthless without
showing them to be commonplace. Skeptics might be inclined to dismiss the
"worm's meat" of Mercutio and Saviolo as ordinary—but they would be mistaken. That the human body is food for worms is indeed a familiar sentiment,
and has been since time out of mind. The epithet, "worm's meat," is not. But
Holmer misses its significance for Saviolo, why Saviolo chooses this motto for
both volumes of the Practice.

By the time Saviolo's two-volume Practice hit the bookstands, Romeo and
Juliet may have been known to London audiences for at least a year, maybe
two. In every performance of the play, an English mocker ridiculed Saviolo's
Italian style, bringing down hoots of laughter on Italian fashionmongers,
Spanish blades, and would-be butchers of a silk button. In each performance
Mercutio taunted Tybalt as a Saviolo wanna-be. But the sarcasm always ended
when Tybalt's rapier turned the insolent Englishman into food for worms:

> *Mer.*   I am sped yfaith, he hath made wormes meate of me.
> (Q1 F1v [III.i])

Savoring Mercutio's last words, Saviolo makes them an emblem of vindication:

> Saviolo: "O wormes meate: o froath: o vanitie: why art thou so insolent?"

As Saviolo makes clear throughout the *Practice,* he cannot endure for his Italian manhood and *stoccata* to be mocked. In the *Practice* it is Vincentio Saviolo, not Shakespeare's Mercutio, who has the last laugh.[24]

Linear models of literary influence often fail because two related texts are mutually conditioned by a third, antecedent text. In "No 'Vain Fantasy' " (1995), Holmer argues that *Romeo and Juliet* is indebted chiefly to Nash's *Terrors of the Night,* which she takes, not implausibly, to be a source for Shakespeare's fairy lore: "Shakespeare breaks new dramatic ground in *A Midsummer Night's Dream* and *Romeo and Juliet*" by associating "the subject of mortals' dreams with . . . very diminutive fairies" (59), having obtained this otherwise original notion from Nash's *Terrors,* which registers "the first literary association of extremely dimunitive spirits and their causative roles in the dreams we mortals have" (50). But a quick computer scan of an electronic text archive indicates that the collocation of dreams and tiny sprites is indeed found elsewhere, including at least one text that Shakespeare read long before 1596. Consider Book I of the *Faerie Queene* (1590): in the opening canto, Archimago calls forth "Legions of Sprights, the which like little flyes / Fluttring about his euer damned hed, / A-waite whereto their seruice he applyes" (I.i.38.2–4). Choosing two fairies, Archimago sends one to the house of Orpheus, to collect "A fit false dreame, that can delude the sleepers sent" (I.i.43.9). "[O]n his litle winges" the sprite delivers the dream to Archimago, "Who all this while with charmes and hidden artes, / Had made a Lady of that other Spright" (I.i.44.8, 45.1–2), a figure not unlike Mercutio's Queen Mab. The two fairies then dance on the head of Archimago's noble guest, and "made him dreame of loues and lustfull play, / That nigh his manly hart did melt away" (I.i.47.2–5).[25]
    Later in Book I, Spenser introduces a "Queene of Faeries" who visits Arthur with dreams not unlike those of Bottom the weaver (I.ix.13–16). The association of "Infernall Hags," "flyes" ("those were idle thoughts and fantasies, / Deuices, dreames") returns in Book II, with a Mercutio-like Phantastes, that "full of melancholy did shew," with "beetle browes" (II.ix.50–52). Spenser's diminutive sprites and fly-sized fairies are again found busy at their dreamwork in Book III. What Holmer takes to be "markedly original" (50) is in fact the product of antecedent Spenserian influence on both poets.
    Shakespeare may have yet read *The Terrors of the Night,* but not in 1595. Holmer mistakes in supposing *Terrors* to be later than *Christs Teares* (64). The latter text was entered in the Stationers' Register on 8 September 1593

and published in that year, probably within four months of its registration, before or after. Nash's *Terrors* was first entered more than two months earlier, on 30 June 1593, and again on 25 October 1594 (both times to John Danter, the stationer who acquired the first [Q1] copyright to Shakespeare's *Romeo and Juliet*). Why the printing of Nash's *Terrors* was deferred for so long, and where the manuscript lay in the interim, may be anybody's guess. If Holmer is right that Shakespeare borrowed from the *Terrors* (and I think she is), then perhaps the manuscript was in Shakespeare's hands during this interval. But Nash's *Terrors* offers no evidence that *Romeo and Juliet* can be dated later than 1593.

Nevertheless, if *Romeo and Juliet* is indebted to Nash's *Have With You to Saffron-Walden,* then the play cannot have been written much earlier than 1596. In exploring this textual relationship, J. J. M. Tobin quotes the Q2 version of *Romeo,* ignoring Q1 except to observe that Q2 "phantacies" may be a misprint for "fantasticoes" (as in Q1): Nash's text has "fantasticos." But Tobin introduces several orthographical errors when comparing Q2 and Nash's *Saffron,* errors that produce a false match between Nash and Q2.[26] I have corrected Tobin's list directly from Q2, and have augmented his list of parallels with the corresponding phrases in Q1:

Q1 *Romeo and Juliet* (pub. 1597)	*Saffron-Walden* (pub. 1596)	Q2 *Romeo and Juliet* (pub. 1599)
take the wall (A4 [I.i])	take the wall (76)	take the wall (A3 [I.i])
prince of cattes (E1 [II.iv])	Prince of Cattes (51)	Prince of Cats (E2 [II.iv])
fantasticoes (E1 [II.iv])	fantasticos (31)	phantacies (E2v [II.iv])
single soald (E2 [II.iv])	single-soald (38)	single-solde (E3 [II.iv])
omitted [E3]	with an R. (58)	with an *R.* (E4v [II.iv])
Flower of curtesie (E3v [II.v])	floure of curtesie (49)	flower of curtesie (F1 [II.v])
Ratcatcher (F1 [III.i])	Rat-catcher (76)	ratcatcher (F3v [III.i])
King of Cates (F1v [III.i])	—	King of Cats (F3v [III.i])
Huntsvp (G3v [III.v])	Hunt is vp (t.p.)	Huntsup (H3 [III.v])
set vp his rest (Il [IV.v])	set vp his rest (101)	set vp his rest (K2 [IV.v])
Aligarta (I3v [V.i])	alligatur (67)	allegater (K4v [V.i])

That Nash's text is generally closer to Q1 than to Q2 will be obvious without further commentary, except in two instances. Nash's "alligatur" may be thought to approximate Q2's "allegater" more closely than Q1's "aligarta." But the *OED* has tracked this Promethean reptile, noting that it entered the English language about 1568 as *largarto;* but in England "soon became *allagarto,* . . . *alegarto, alligarta,* whence by pop[ular] corruption to *alligarter, allegator, alligator.* Q1's "aligarta" preserves an earlier form of the word than Q2's "allegater." And Shakespeare's aligarta is stuffed, hanging in an apothecary's shop: apothecaries proverbially displayed such curios so that distracted customers would not notice while being cheated on the scales.[27] Shakespeare takes his apothecary not from Nash but from Brooke (whose text hangs the apothecary instead of the alligator). The alligator followed as a matter of course from Brooke's apothecary's shop, and both apothecary and alligator passed on to Nash's *Saffron*.

On this evidence, it appears that the manuscripts underlying these texts were copied out in the order MS_1 [Q1 *Rom.*] > MS_2 [*Saffron-Walden*] and MS_3 [Q2 *Rom.*]. It is hardly possible to suppose that Shakespeare used Nash's text in 1596 as a source for *Romeo and Juliet* only to have a memorial reconstructor come even closer to Nash's orthography, or to suppose that the Q1 compositor consulted Nash. Then, too, Tobin neglects to mention that *Saffron*'s "Prince of Cattes" is named "Tibault" (51), a figure by which Nash satirizes Gabriel Harvey and his Italianiate fashionmongering. Shakespeare cannot have taken the name "Tybalt" from Nash, for the name is supplied by Brooke's *Romeus and Juliet*. Nor is a third source likely for the collocation: Tybalt was a traditional name for a cat, but the collocation of "Tybalt" and "prince of cats" is recorded only in *Romeo and Juliet* and in Nash's *Saffron*.[28] Nor is there recorded any English instance of *fantastico* prior to Nash and Q1 *Romeo*. The most economical explanation is that the underlying manuscript for Q1 precedes Nash's text in point of date. Perhaps his intent to lampoon Harvey in the figure of Shakespeare's Tybalt supplied Nash with the motivation to consult Shakespeare's own, or a stagehouse, copy; or perhaps he had access in 1596 to a copy in John Danter's bookshop (Danter undertook to print Nash's text before Shakespeare's, but he entered neither one in the Register; it's impossible to say in which order the two manuscripts were given to him). But however Nash came by a copy of the text, his satire on Gabriel Harvey gains capital from Shakespeare's Tybalt (that Italian dandy of recent stage memory), not the other way around. Far from providing a terminus *a quo* for Shakespeare's *Romeo and Juliet*, Saviolo's *Practice* and Nash's *Have With You to Saffron-Walden* indicate that Shakespeare's play was complete (in one form or another) and acted on the English stage no later than 1595, and probably no later than 19 November 1594, the date on which Book 2 of Saviolo's *Practice* was first entered for publication.[29]

John Eliot's *Ortho-epia Gallica* (1593) is a French primer closely modeled on John Florio's Italian primer, *Second Frutes* (1591), but with English humor taking the place of Florio's ponderous and sometimes almost comical excess with respect to the art of compliment. Shakespeare's debt to Eliot is apparent in *King John, Romeo and Juliet, 2 Henry IV, Henry V, King Lear, The Winter's Tale,* and possibly *Richard II*.* Eliot's book is in three parts. The first is a discussion

---

*Indeed Eliot's manual resolves the most famous crux in English literature, for it justifies Theobald's emendation, "'a babbled of green fields," in Mrs. Quickly's account of Falstaff's death in *Henry V*. See Joseph A. Porter, "More Echoes from Eliot's *Ortho-epia Gallica,* in *King Lear* and *Henry V*," *Shakespeare Quarterly* 37 (1986), 486–88—Ed.

of pedagogy in which Shakespeare registers little interest. Parts 2 and 3 are a series of dialogues called "The Parlement of Pratlers," with adjoining French translations. Eliot's "Parlement" supplies Shakespeare with rare words, jests, quibbles, and the substance of whole conversations. And this triangular textual relation between Eliot, Florio, and Shakespeare presents an interesting exhibit of what is meant throughout this essay by intertextual influence.

Eliot's book was printed at about the same time as *Venus and Adonis.* Shakespeare's poem was entered in the London Stationers' Register on 18 April 1593. Ten days later, Eliot finished the front matter for *Ortho-epia Gallica,* dating his preface 28 April—at which time his book may already have been in press, since it was registered for publication four months earlier (on 18 December 1592). By May, Eliot's *Ortho-epia* was probably available for sale in John Wolfe's bookshop. According to Shaxicon's dating, Shakespeare at this time was still tinkering with *3 Henry VI* (begun earlier), after which he turned to a first draft of *Romeo and Juliet* and *The Merchant of Venice,* then to a publishable version of *Titus Andronicus* and *The Rape of Lucrece.* But if 1593 was an unusually productive year for Shakespeare, he nevertheless found time for reading, and Eliot's "Parlement of Pratlers" is a text that he studied closely.

The first thing worth mentioning about the "Parlement" is that it further contextualizes the relationship between Shakespeare and Nash. By neglecting to consider Q1, Tobin's study of *Saffron* catches only the verbal parallels between *Saffron* and Q2 *Romeo and Juliet.* (The Q1 variants contain many others that he overlooks.) By neglecting to consider Brooke's *Romeus,* Tobin misses further evidence of Q1's priority (in the apothecary's alligator and in Nash's Tibault). By neglecting to consider Eliot, Tobin misses a few more items of interest. In his brief but instructive list of verbal parallels between *Saffron* and *Romeo and Juliet,* most of what cannot be found in Brooke can be found in Eliot. Tobin compares *Saffron*'s "single-soald" with Q2 "single-solde" (Q1, "single soald"): Eliot speaks repeatedly of single-soled (and double-and triple-soled) shoes and pumps (C1, M3–M4).[30] All three instances of "huntsup" are similarly derived from Eliot.[31] And Tobin's list is easily augmented with material that passes from Eliot to Q1 *Romeo and Juliet* to Nash, or from Eliot through Shakespeare to other writers, such as Jonson, Marston, Porter, Dekker, and Webster. For example, Mercutio addresses Tybalt not only as the prince of cats, but also as "Catso" (i.e., "Italian penis," with another feline pun on Tybalt's name). But "Catso" appears only in Q1, not in Q2. Shakespeare found the word in Eliot's "Parlement"—"Caetzo great Divel of hell" (52)—which is one of the few instances in English literature where a catso may be found, and the only other instance, I believe, of its use as a "proper" name. Shakespeare's "Catso" was transmitted thence, directly or indirectly, to Jonson, Marston, Middleton, and Dekker as a common noun.

Shakespeare borrowings from the "Parlement" are obvious and persistent, as in the dueling scene, which has three notable sources, Brooke's *Romeus,* Florio's *Second Frutes,* and Eliot's dialogues called the "The Slasher"

(Q3–R4) and "The Bragger" (R4–T1).[32] Material from these two dialogues may illuminate *Romeo and Juliet*'s complex textual history:

> [*Vesp:*]   And if thou wouldest consort with me, we would plaie the Diuels.
> [*Val:*]   No, no, by Saint Andauras, for thou shalt be hanged . . . By Gogs nownes . . .
> [*Val:*]   Go thou art a villaine . . .
>
> (Q4–R1)

> *Tyb:*   *Mercutio* thou consorts with *Romeo?* . . .
> *Mer:*   Consort Zwounes consort? . . . If you doe sirra, . . . Ile be hanged, sir, . . .
> *Tyb:*   *Romeo* . . . thou art a villaine. . . .
>
> (Q1, F1 [III.i])

> [*Vesp:*]   Draw, I will break thy head in nine places. . . . Come rogue, come, . . . I . . . gaue him the fig vnder his cappuche brauely, . . . stoccado thorow his right arme, . . . and had almost slaine him outright. I did it by God in your quarrell, and for the loue of you, . . .
>
> (R1–R3)

> *Mer:*   You Ratcatcher, come backe, come back.
> *Tyb:*   What wouldest with me?
> *Mer:*   Nothing King of Cates, but borrow one of your nine liues, therefore come drawe. . . .
> *Mer:*   What meant you to come betweene vs? I was hurt vnder your arme.
> *Rom:*   I did all for the best.
>
> (Q1, F1–F1v, [III.i])

In the next dialogue (which contributes also to *2 Henry IV*), "The Bragger" Crocodill anticipates the death of Mercutio:

> [*Crocodill:*]   Ho death of a louse, blood of a bat, . . . It is inough
>
> (S3–S4)

> *Mer.*   tis inough, twill serue . . . sounds a dog, a rat, a mouse, a cat, to scratch a man to death: a braggart . . .
>
> (Q2, F3v [III.i])

But I have shifted from Q1 to Q2: The Bragger's meditation on death does not appear in the Q1 version. Q1 has only:

> *Mer.*   . . . but it will serue I warrant.
>
> (Q1 F1v)

This is just one of several points in the text where Q2 seems to preserve material that may have belonged at some point to an earlier version of Q1 that was much fuller than the abridged version published in 1597, even as Q1 has original material that has vanished from Q2. In other words, more than one "slasher" has come to play in the textual transmission of Shakespeare's *Romeo and Juliet*.

The dueling scene is further indebted to Florio's *Second Frutes* and contains similar evidence of different abridgements in Q1 and Q2. In Q2, Mercutio challenges Tybalt to duel with the remark, *"Tibalt,* you ratcatcher, will you walke? . . . Come sir, your Passado" (F3v [III.i]). In the ensuing fight, Mercutio "with one hand beates / Cold death aside, and with the other sends / It backe to *Tybalt,* whose dexteritie / Retorts it" (F4v [III.i]). This passage recalls the same passage in *Second Frutes* to which Q1 is indebted for the Saviolo material. Florio's V.S. can fight "left or right handed . . . no man that teacheth with more dexterity"; Florio then proceeds directly to a discussion of new fashion and "fine knacks," with the remark, "Pluck of[f] thy gloues, thou sillie fellowe, knowest thou not, that a gloued cat, dooth neuer catch good rat?" (Q4–R1). Q1 *Romeo* has "You ratcatcher," but omits the rest.

Then, too, Q1 lacks one item in Tobin's list—"with an *R*"—appearing in Q2 and in Nash's *Saffron.* Nash's text has *"Richard* with an R." Q2 *Romeo and Juliet* has "Rosemarie and *Romeo* . . . with an *R*." No corresponding line appears in Q1. This evidence might well be dismissed (there is, of course, no other letter with which Nash could have begun the name "Richard"). What makes the omission interesting is that the Q1 passage bears independent evidence of having been cut. (Q1 II.iv has often been cited in theories of memorial reconstruction for its sins of omission.) It is worth noting in this respect that Tobin's accounting of Nash's debt to *Romeo and Juliet* is not randomly distributed throughout Shakespeare's text as it is in Nash's. The shared material is drawn chiefly from scenes involving Tybalt. Six of Tobin's eleven parallels appear on signatures E1–F1v of the printed text (Q1)—and the seventh would have been "with an *R,*" but it has vanished from its expected position on E3, together with other probable cuts. Instead of a good quarto and a bad, we may have only two different scripts that have been cut, amended, augmented, miscopied, and badly printed. Evidence of this sort complicates past models of the play's textual development. If the old chicken-and-egg game of source study often ends in a messy scramble, the original texts are themselves partly to blame.

III

[W]e are such stuffe / As dreames are made on . . .
—Prospero (F1)

'Tis still a Dreame: or else such stuffe as Madmen / Tongue, . . .
—Posthumus (F1)

The source studies of Tobin and Holmer are neither better nor worse than most others that rely soley on the scholar's unaided eye. What is needed is an efficient means by which to trace intertextual relationships, and an objective standard by which to evaluate them. Shaxicon provides both. Editors and textual scholars have now an accurate, detailed, and stable grid from which to obtain a lexical sample that suits a variety of research needs—whether to explore a particular textual problem, or to chart the early stage history of Shakespare's plays, or simply to compare Shakespearean usage with that of other authors, whose texts belong to the same cultural and linguistic network.

My computer stuff, as it has often been called, cannot take the place of close reading and informed scholarly analysis, but it can provide a helpful check on the researcher's subjectivity, my own included. In the parlance of professional Shakespeare studies, Q2 *Romeo and Juliet* has always been a good play (maybe not as good as Q2 *Hamlet* or F1 *King Lear,* but middling good), while Q1 has always been just a bad quarto full of wretched stuff unworthy of the Bard, a "shoddy" performance, as bad, say, as *A Funeral Elegy* and worse than Q1 *Richard III* and *The Two Noble Kinsmen* (which used to be bad but are no longer), or *Edward III* (which is looking better all the time). The old paradigm of good Quartos and bad, of good Shakespeare and bad imitations, is an aesthetic that served a simpler age, when what was well liked was good, was *Shakespeare,* and what wasn't liked was something else. The obvious "un-Shakespearean" quality of Q1 is an impression caused partly by our unfamiliarity with what early Shakespeare looked like, and it wasn't all *good.* That true Shakespeare can be known by the scholar's "gut feeling" is a mode of scholarship with a long history but without much future to it.

Electronic textual analysis can provide a virtual interface between Shakespeare's language and modern scholarship, telling tell us things about Shakespeare's artistic development that he couldn't have known himself. John Eliot's "Grass-hopper" and his "spinner the spiders wife" who makes "thrids & cobwebs" for "flies . . . no bigger than a peaze" (V–V2) are again drawn "with a teeme of little Atomi" (Eliot, "Atomes," L1), to Q1 *Romeo* with its Midwife . . . no bigger than an Aggat stone," "spinners webs," "Grashoppers," and a "flie / Not halfe so big" (G1v). These lead to the "spinners legs," "traces of the smallest spider web," "lazy finger," and "foule sluttish haires" of Q2 (C2); which lead still inexorably onward to the "dead lazy march . . . / More sluttish farre then all the Spiders webs," in *The Devils Law-Case* of John Webster.[33] These few representative words and phrases from Eliot, Shakespeare, and Webster appear in a shared matrix of influence that extends through human time and around the globe, a web that cannot be fully accessed. But the linguistic system that constitutes early modern English can and will be navigated in the years ahead, and from our own keyboards. True, I talk of dreams. But Shakespeare's Mercutio and we mistake when we suppose that such dreams are begot of nothing but vain fantasy.

Notes

1.   It is to be lamented that press and television coverage—following the MLA Special Session on "Another Shakespeare" (Chicago, 30 December 1995)—gave Shaxicon its fifteen minutes of fame without providing substantive information about how it works. Shaxicon was even credited in press reports and Internet discussion with having helped me in February 1996 to identify Joe Klein as the "Anonymous" who wrote the best-selling novel *Primary Colors* (NY: Random House, 1996); and here Shaxicon's praises have exceeded its due.

2.   D. Foster, "Shaxicon Home Page," [on-line], World Wide Web, available at http://faculty.vassar.edu/~foster/shax.

3.   The document has since been republished on numerous World Wide Web sites.

4.   Examples include the fencing terms *staccata* and *hai,* discussed below.

5.   Foster, "Shaxicon Home Page."

6.   For a complete catalogue of the texts contained in VETA (1475–1700) on which these conclusions are based, see D. Foster, VETA [database on-line], World Wide Web; available at http://faculty.vassar.edu/~foster/veta. All major authors for the period are represented, together with several dozen lesser lights, a combined sample of thirteen million words.

7.   By tracking rare-word variants, Shaxicon further identifies which particular texts borrow from Q1 (Jonson's *EMHH,* Porter's *Two Angrie Women of Abington,* Ford's poetry and *Lovers Melancholy,* even Davenant's adaptation of *The Tempest*) and which borrow from Q2 (e.g., Middleton's *Black Book,* Webster's drama, and Milton's juvenilia). Surprisingly, Q1 had a more pronounced influence on Shakespeare's contemporaries than Q2, as is mutually registered by VETA and the *OED.*

8.   Q1 and Q2, however, may have been performed by turns even after Q2 was written. Shaxicon has uncovered a pattern whereby the staple plays tended to remain in repertory for two years, with one version being acted in the first year (not, of course, every week), and a revised version (or one augmented with a new scene) being acted in the next. *Romeo* fits the pattern quite perfectly, according to the statistical record, with Q1 being acted in 1594/5, Q2 in 1595/6; Q1 in 1598/9, Q2 1599/1600; Q2 in 1607/8, Q1 in 1608/9 (reversing the sequence); the F1 text appears to have been in acted 1612[-/13?] (or else Q2, but without the Chorus, which influences Shakespeare's writing only from 1599 to 1607/8); after 1613 Shaxicon provides no assistance for there is no new writing to use as a text sample.

9.   See, for example, Euan Ferguson, "Where there's a Will, there's a way to disagree." *London Observer* (14 January 1996): 14.

10.   Peter Levi, Quoted in Quentin Letts and Russell Jenkins, "Lost 'Sonnet' Starts a War of Words," *Times of London* (15 January 1996); quoted by Stanley Wells, "In Memory of Master William Peter," *TLS* 26 (26 January 1996): 28.

11.   Katherine Duncan-Jones, quoted in the *London Daily Telegraph* (28 May 1996).

12.   CBS Sunday Morning (17 March 1996).

13.   Brian Vickers, "The 'Funeral Elegy' for William Peter," *TLS* (12 April 1996): 17; for more in this vein, see Vickers, "Whose Thumbprints?" *TLS* (8 March 1996): 16–18.

14.   Brian Gibbons, ed., *Romeo and Juliet* (New York: Methuen, 1980), Introduction, 1, 9.

15.   Jay Halio, "Handy-Dandy: Q1/Q2 *Romeo and Juliet,*" *Shakespeare's* Romeo and Juliet, ed. Jay L. Halio (Newark: Univ. of Delaware Press, 1995), 123–50.

16.   Joan Ozark Holmer, " 'Draw, if you be men': Saviolo's Significance for *Romeo and Juliet,*" *Shakespeare Quarterly* 45 (1994): 163–89; p. 163.

17.   Joan Ozark Holmer, "No 'Vain Fantasy': Shakespeare's Refashioning of Nashe for Dreams and Queen Mab," *Shakespeare's* Romeo and Juliet, ed. Jay L. Halio (Newark: Univ. of Delaware Press, 1995), 49–82.

18.   Ibid., p. 72.

19.   J. J. M. Tobin, "Nashe and *Romeo and Juliet,*" *N&Q* (1980): 161–2.

20. G. Blakemore Evans, ed., *Romeo and Juliet* (Cambridge: Cambridge Univ. Press, 1984).

21. Vincentio Saviolo, *Vincentio Saviolo his Practice* (London, 1595), 239.

22. In Q2 (1599), Mercutio still gets it wrong: *"Allastockado"* becomes *"Alla stucatha,"* which would be a reasonably good phonological spelling for an Englishman who by 1599 had not recently seen the word in print, but it is another spelling without precedent.

23. Nor can Shaxicon; VETA contains the first 60,000 words of *Saviolo his Practice,* a text that strongly influences Ben Jonson, but not Shakespeare.

24. Well, not quite. In Q2, Mercutio's dying words are amended, as if by way of clarification: "a plague of both your houses, / *They* haue made wormes meate of me, . . ." (F4, my emphasis).

25. Edmund Spenser, *The Faerie Queene,* ed. Thomas P. Roche Jr. (London: Penguin, 1978).

26. Citations are to *The Works of Thomas Nashe . . . from the original texts,* ed. R. B. McKerrow, vol. 3 (Oxford, 1958). Tobin also supposes the Q2 spelling, "pallat" (L3 [V.iii]), to have been inspired by a "pallet" in Nash, but this is a stretch. Q2 "pallat" is an authorial or compositorial spelling for "palace" (Q3–4, F1, palace). Nash's "pallet" is a different word altogether, the head of an insect: "a moth's pallet" (Nash, 42; cf. *OED* pallet, *sb.*1²).

27. See, for example, John Webster, "A Purueior of Tobacco," in *Sir Thomas Overbuie His Wife . . . sixt impression,* ed. Webster (1616), M8.

28. The closest third instance appears to be Dekker's satirical reference to Ben Jonson as "Tyber the long-tail'd Prince of Rattes." *Satiromastix* (1602) V.ii.205, cited by McKerrow, ed. Nash (1958), 4.327.

29. Book 2 was evidently finished first and bears a 1594 title page; Book 1 of the *Practice* is dated 1595.

30. John Eliot, "The Parlement of Pratlers," in *Ortho-epia Gallica* (1593), C1–Y4.

31. Eliot has only "hunter," not "huntsup," but the contextual lines in *Romeo and Juliet*—Juliet's speech about the lark's sweet division ("hunting thee hence with hunt's up to the day")—are based on "The Conclusion" of Eliot's "Parlement" (T1–Y4), on which Shakespeare leans heavily; in fact, it is precisely this passage in Eliot that first drew scholarly attention to the "Parlement" as a source for *Romeo and Juliet.* For what it's worth, there is also a "Tibald" in the "Parlement": "MAN: Well said brother Tibald. What's price, how, and let us have but one word" (I3); cf. Shakespeare's Tybalt, "Gentlemen, good den, a word with one of you," and Mercutio's reply, "but one word?" (III.i.39–40). Eliot's text has no "prince of cats," only various cats and rats, a "prince of devils," and the "Caetzo, great devil of hell," discussed immediately below.

32. An aside: "The Slasher" begins with Valerian's greeting, "Let me giue you an accollado," which leads in just moments to Vespatian's boast, "I gaue him also a stoccado," either one of which may contribute to Mercutio's faulty construction *"allostoccado"* (Q3, R3, my emphasis).

33. John Webster, *The Devils Law-Case,* vol. 2, ed. F. L. Lucas, *The Complete Works* (New York: Gordian, 1966), 104–6. Among texts represented in VETA and the *OED,* the Webster corpus is the most persistent in registered borrowings from Q2 *Rom.*

Index

◆